SOUL WAZE

3 ESSENTIAL TOOLS TO UPGRADE YOUR LIFE'S JOURNEY

UNLOCKING THE TANYA FUNDAMENTALS OF

LOVE—אהבה | REVERENCE—יראה | COMPASSION—רחמים

Soulwaze Curriculum
Guidebook One

Copyright © 2018 Shimon Chyrek

All rights reserved. No part of this publication may be reproduced, stored in a retrieval system, or transmitted in any form or by any means, electronic, mechanical, photocopying, recording or otherwise, without prior written permission from the publisher.

* * *

Tanya and other texts of Chabad Chassidus are copyright of the Kehot Publication Society, a division of Merkos L'inyonei Chinuch Inc. and are reprinted here with permission.

This curriculum is designed to be learned together with the study of the original texts chapter by chapter in order.

Visit kehot.com to purchase the complete texts.

Cover design by Spotlight Design

INFORMATION & QUESTIONS
646-200-2801 • Rabbichyrek@gmail.com

CREDITS

Yehuda Altein	Leibel Krinsky
Mendy Browd	Shmuel Rabin
Shimon Chyrek	Avraham Raynitz
Yaakov Gershon	C L Witkes

לה"ו

This training guide belongs to:

_____

Learn it, Unlock it, Live it!

QUESTIONS BEFORE YOU START

1. What is the most important thing you want to achieve in your life?
_____
_____

2. What have you done so far to achieve this goal?
_____
_____

3. What steps are you taking to achieve this goal in the future?
_____
_____

4. How will you know you have achieved your goal?
_____
_____

5. How will you evaluate your progress?
_____
_____

6. What do you expect to gain from learning this guide book?
_____
_____

HOW TO USE THIS TRAINING GUIDE BOOK

With a pencil, make a dot next to anything practical or intersting that you read.

Notice the wide margins. Draw your own mind maps to help you remember key points.

BROWN title text and backgrounds throughout the book indicate **introductory** sections.

ORANGE title text and backgrounds are **guidance** and learning sections. **BLUE** titles are used as well.

PURPLE title text and backgrounds mark the **practice** and self-evaluation sections.

WHAT WILL YOU GET FROM SOULWAZE?

You will get the engine of Torah and Mitzvos.

An engine is something that moves a car to get to a certain destination. You can have nice seats, a nice music player, solid doors and windows; however, without the engine your car is missing life.

WHO IS SOULWAZE FOR?

Anyone that is Shomer Torah and Mitzvos will get results.

WHEN WILL SOULWAZE WORK?

Pause for a few minutes daily and do the three Soulwaze thinking strategies before Tefillah and you will get the intended results in about seven days.

HOW DOES SOULWAZE WORK?

Torah study and Tefillah are described as עסק התורה and עסק התפילה, which means the business of Torah and the business of Tefillah.

How does a business work? In a business you do certain activities that lead to predictable results. You then repeat these activities to multiply the predictable results. These activities are so clear that you can teach others to do the same activities and also get predictable results.

In Soulwaze, you will learn the fundamental activities that give you the engine of Torah and Mitzvos. They are clear and doable, they lead to predictable results, and they are upgradable.

You can do them yourself and teach them to others to do.

HOW TO TEACH SOULWAZE?

The difference between a business and our true responsibility to others is that in a business not everybody needs to be your customer, however in a military it is crucial that everybody understands how to do their job, and that no one is left behind. The Jewish people are described as צְבָאוֹת ה' (Shemos 12:41) which means the army of Hashem. This shows us how we have a responsibility to teach in a way that everyone understands how to do fundamentals and no one is left behind.

How does an army make sure everybody understands their job? Some armies organize their soldiers in small groups of four or five with their own commander. This way the commander is able to make sure that all his soldiers really understand their job.

Follow this battle-proven tactic and teach Soulwaze in small groups of **up to six students**, and everybody can take an active part in the discussion.

Different people grasp the same things in different ways. For this reason, Soulwaze sometimes repeats the same concept in various ways.

WHY IS 'PAUSE' IMPORTANT?

Shulchan Aruch (Orach Chaim 93) says, קודם שיתפלל צריך לשהות - pause before you pray. In Soulwaze you will learn exactly what to do when you pause.

HOW TO LEARN ANYTHING (SOULWAZE STUDY SKILLS)

There are three ways to learn something;

1. **Down River** (length - אורך) is a metaphor for being able to explain a core concept so well that a child can understand.

   When do you know you have grasped a concept? When you can explain it to a child.

   This is similar to taking a cargo boat and loading it with valuables and **delivering** them to a river port that did not have the valuables before.

   Down river is about delivery of a concept by connecting to a previous understanding.

   Benefits:
   - Simple ideas
   - Easy to remember
   - Easy to implement

   Down Side:
   - In a dynamic changing situation, you will not know how to apply it without the guidance of an expert

   How does something have **meaning**?

   When you use a **metaphor** to explain something new, the metaphor connects the new concept with something you already know from before and for this reason it's also easy to remember.

2. **Over River** (width - רוחב) is a metaphor for understanding the details of an idea, learning the same thing over and over in different

ways, and comparing and contrasting the details until you have an expert grasp of the core concept.

The benefit of width over length is that length is like delivering a fish and width is like getting a fishing rod.

Just like in length, you use metaphors. In width, however, you compare multiple metaphors.

Benefits:
- Understanding details leads to personal **impact**
- Able to apply your learning to a dynamic changing situation
- Become an expert
- Access the concept on a very deep **mature** level
- Being adaptable

Down Side:
- It takes time
- You have to do it yourself, a teacher can not do this for you.

3. Jump in (Experience - דעת) is experiencing the concept by taking some action that captures the idea through action, even though you do not understand and/or can not explain it yet.

Benefits:
- Immediate **implementation**
- When you do learn about it, your understanding will be deeper and you will explain it better
- **Apply** the idea to a dynamic situation more rapidly
- Become a real expert faster

Down Side:
- You do not know how to explain it yet
- You are not an expert yet
- Your experience is incomplete due to lack of understanding

In Soulwaze you will;

Learn simple ways to grasp and retain the ideas.

Learn details that will help you understand in a way that the concept will have greater impact on you. Details bring to impact.

Jump in.

Soulwaze will equip you with study skills that will transform how you learn and apply.

THE 12 FUNDAMENTALS OF THE ENGINE OF TORAH AND MITZVOS AT A GLANCE

Below is a chart listing the fundamental skills and where they are found within the Soulwaze manual. Six out of twelve skills are taught in this volume of Soulwaze. *B'ezras Hashem*, you will learn the other six fundamentals in a future volume of Soulwaze.

TOOLS	AHAVA	YIRAH	RACHAMIM	CHASSID/REBBE
Mental **THINK**	1. SOULWAZE 2	4. UNIT 2 PART 1	7. UNIT 3	10. SOULWAZE 2
Emotional **PREPARE**	2. SOULWAZE 2	5. UNIT 2 PART 2	8. SOULWAZE 2	11. SOULWAZE 2
Practical **DO**	3. UNIT 1 PART 1-3	6. UNIT 2 PART 3	9. SOULWAZE 2	12. UNIT 1 BONUS PART

FUNDAMENTALS AND STANDARD OPERATING PROCEDURES

Two students wanted to learn how to operate a business. The first student went to work in a store, learning through experience how to manage the store, and only then did he study business from textbooks. The second student studied business from books and only then went to the business world.

Which student, do you think, chose the more effective strategy to learn business? Why?

When the Jewish people accepted the Torah, they first said נַעֲשֶׂה וְנִשְׁמָע (Shemos 24:7) "We will do and we will listen." They committed to practice the Torah first and only afterwards to better understand what they practice. Can you understand why?

In this guide book, you will learn fundamental practices that belong to the core of Torah. The best way to grasp them is by first practicing them, even with minimal understanding, and adding more understanding as you learn more. You most probably practice them already in one form or another, however, you may have not yet created your own personal operating procedures to upgrade them.

Certain things that you were subconsciously aware of will now become part of your conscious awareness. In simple terms, this guide book will open your eyes.

IN ACTION

Here is an example how to design standard operating procedures in your daily life.

First, clarify the **goal** you are working to accomplish. Then, choose the **strategy** to accomplish your goal, and finally, think of **practical tactics**.

In the strategy stage, it is important to focus ahead to see how your strategy accomplishes your goal. In the tactical stage, it is best to focus no further than a drop ahead of the present task, focus on each step at a time. At this stage, focusing far ahead will take away from your attention from doing the task at hand in the best and most efficient way.

In the morning, when you *daven* and learn Torah, it is appropriate to think strategy and establish your direction for the entire day. Once your busy day starts, however, its best to focus fully on each task at hand and give it your best. At this stage, looking too far ahead could weaken your resolve and waste time.

HERE IS AN EXAMPLE OF A GOAL, STRATEGY, TACTIC CHART:

Goal	Achieve more every day, and specifically achieve _____ .	
Strategy	Wake up earlier, at _____ am.	
Tactics	Start your bedtime routine at _____ pm.	Set three alarm clocks far from your bed. (One electric, one mechanical, one battery operated.)

WHY THE NEED FOR STANDARD OPERATING PROCEDURES?

The fundamentals of Torah that you learn in this guide will become part of your standard daily operating procedures, and you will incorporate everything you learn in the future about these subjects into your standard daily personal operations.

In other words, everything you learn henceforth will enhance the basic fundamentals you will practice in this guide book.

Both amature and proffessional athletes practice warm ups and stretches before their workouts. The professional has most likely refined his warm ups to a high level, however, the warm ups he does now are based on the most basic warm ups he learned when he just started learning the sport.

WHY ESTABLISH STANDARD OPERATING PROCEDURES?

Discipline leads to more freedom. How is that possible? Aren't discipline and freedom opposites?

If you practice the discipline to get up early, you will find more time in the day to do more things. It turns out that discipline leads to more freedom. So when you create standard operating procedures for the things you do every day, like how you go to sleep and how you get up, you will do them faster, and this will help you to be more effective. Then you will have more time, more choices, and more control. Additionally, people will have more respect for you because you get things done, and therefore they will be motivated to help you.

When you incorporate the fundamentals of the Torah into standard daily operating procedures - specifically, in the way you think when you daven - you will become more effective, and your studies will be more effective. You will deal with others on a higher level, with more freedom, choices, control, respect and assistance.

You are a person with different parts: you have a mind, feelings, and you can get things done. So it's important that your standard daily operating procedures incorporate exercises for your mind, feelings, and power of action.

This guide book is called **Soulwaze**. Your soul has intellectual, emotional and practical aspects, thus, every soul path (way) includes exercises focused on your mind, heart and action. It's your responsibility to tailor your own standard operating procedures based on the guidelines and rules you will learn in this guide book and Tanya.

As you learn things in this guide book, continually ask yourself: "How can I incorporate this in my standard daily operation procedures? How can I continually upgrade these procedures as I learn more about these subjects from other *Sefarim* and teachers? How can I make these fundamentals simple and effective to do?"

WHY THE NEED FOR A FOUNDATION?

Before you learn some of the fundamentals, there is a foundation. A foundation is the base for everything you learn and do in your life.

Why is such a foundation crucial to everything in your life? If you build a house without a level foundation, then every door, wall and window built on top will be crooked.

Let's take one personal example of how a foundation is crucial:

Is intelligence a virtue or is it sometimes a liability? At first you might answer that intelligence is always a virtue, however, it has a downside. Intelligence is like a pillar, as everything one understands is based on a previous understanding. Thus, when one makes a small mistake or distortion lower in the pillar, then the more intelligent one is, the more distorted the pillar can become. The smarter you are, the more mistaken you can become. Intelligence can be so useful; it can enable you to help others, to make the world a better place, like a candle in a dark room. But how can you protect intelligence from the downside?

The downside is largely mitigated by creating a solid bedrock foundation for everything you do, study and experience.

THE SOLID BEDROCK FOUNDATION

The core of reality is in a different dimension than the way we know it. **This core is everything and everything is this core**.

Everything includes all intelligence including yours, all feelings including yours, and all objects and how they behave. Time and space are also creations of this core. This is difficult for our intellect to relate to, however, our Divine Soul/Neshama is a spark of Hashem and does understand.

Everything you study or experience teaches you something unique about this core. This core is literally a core; if it would not exist, everything would cease to exist.

Go back and read the foundation another time.

Picture a green tree in your mind. Your mind is the core of this mental green tree, and if your mind would stop to exist, so would this tree. The way you designed this green tree teaches us something about you and your tastes.

Now, apply the above metaphor to the core. Like pictures inside a mind, the entire reality is inside the core, and also the core is inside everything. This is a good metaphor to illustrate how we are inside Hashem.

IN THE HOLY WORDS OF THE RAMBAM;

MISHNEH TORAH, THE FOUNDATIONS OF THE TORAH, PEREK ALEPH

א יְסוֹד הַיְסוֹדוֹת וְעַמּוּד הַחָכְמוֹת לֵידַע שֶׁיֵּשׁ שָׁם מָצוּי רִאשׁוֹן. וְהוּא מַמְצִיא כָּל נִמְצָא. וְכָל הַנִּמְצָאִים מִשָּׁמַיִם וָאָרֶץ וּמַה שֶּׁבֵּינֵיהֶם לֹא נִמְצְאוּ אֶלָּא מֵאֲמִתַּת הִמָּצְאוֹ:

1:1 The foundation of foundations and firmest pillar of all wisdom is, to know that there is a First Being, that He caused all beings to be (He is everything), and that all beings in heaven and earth, and between them, maintain their existence from the truth of His Own Being (everything is Him and everything teaches something specific about Him).

ב וְאִם יַעֲלֶה עַל הַדַּעַת שֶׁהוּא אֵינוֹ מָצוּי אֵין דָּבָר אַחֵר יָכוֹל לְהִמָּצְאוֹת:

1:2 Thus, supposing that He is not, none else could have been called into existence.

ג וְאִם יַעֲלֶה עַל הַדַּעַת שֶׁאֵין כָּל הַנִּמְצָאִים מִלְּבַדּוֹ מְצוּיִים הוּא לְבַדּוֹ יִהְיֶה מָצוּי. וְלֹא יִבָּטֵל הוּא לְבִטּוּלָם. שֶׁכָּל הַנִּמְצָאִים צְרִיכִין לוֹ וְהוּא בָּרוּךְ הוּא אֵינוֹ צָרִיךְ לָהֶם וְלֹא לְאֶחָד מֵהֶם. לְפִיכָךְ אֵין אֲמִתָּתוֹ כַּאֲמִתַּת אֶחָד מֵהֶם:

1:3 Conversely, suppose something could be alone, then they would be non-existent, His Being alone remains; for, He does not cease to be because of their non-existence, as all beings are dependent upon Him, but He, blessed is He, is not dependent upon them nor upon a single one of them; therefore, the real truth of His Being is incomparable to the truth of any other individual being.

MAKE FUNDAMENTALS PRACTICE YOUR HABIT
Pause 3x Daily

INTRODUCTION

When you commit to make fundamentals your habit, you become an emissary of Hashem by bringing the core of Judaism into daily practice.

You become a warrior of Hashem.

Practice of the fundamentals helps keep you safe and the Jewish people safe.

It is written;

עַל כִּי אֵין אֱלֹקַי בְּקִרְבִּי מְצָאוּנִי הָרָעוֹת הָאֵלֶּה:

It is because our G-d is not in our midst that these evils have befallen us.

DEVARIM 31:17

Practicing fundamentals as a habit will result in Hashem being revealed in you, thus protecting you.

Even when life's surprises come, the fundamentals will be a source of stability for you.

Making fundamentals a habit connects you with friends in a global community. It also gives you a sense of pride and humility, as you know what you have is all a gift from Hashem.

It will give you a sense of stealth in plain sight. All you need to do is learn Chassidus to get fuel, and pause three times, to do three thinking strategies, while doing the regular things you probably do already.

An outsider will not notice that you are doing three specific thinking strategies when you pause three times. However, you will likely be able to tell when someone practices fundamentals as a habit and you will know that they too belong to a group of special warriors with a mission to reveal this gift in everyone in the world.

Everything living needs to grow, and the habit of fundamentals will be a basis for your personal growth, in the way you interact with people and your growth in relating to Hashem. You will always be able to take strength from your habit of fundamentals.

Now we are ready to practice some of the fundamentals. You will learn one thinking strategy for Yirah, one for Ahava, and one for Rachamim.

INSTRUCTIONS FOR YIRAH THINKING STRATEGY:

1. Anchor what you are about to do in practical action, give a coin to *Tzedaka* right now.

2. (On the following page) read from "It is important..." until "... before a king" out loud so you can hear the words you're saying.

3. Read it a second time, quietly, and think what it means practically.

The best standard operating procedure for these specific fundamentals is to practice them daily as a moment of silence, a moment you pause. However, first read them out loud because this will help you understand the meaning and its implications better.

At the end after thinking over the entire quote, take a moment to visualize three scenarios:

A) Visualize yourself in front of an important person, and then visualize yourself doing something different later today with the spirit of how you would behave in front of an important person. Envision doing a good action, doing something in a better way, or avoiding something negative.

   Imagine the feeling you are going to feel when you do this.

B) Visualize yourself spending time with people who will encourage you and limiting your exposure to people who discourage you.

   Visualize yourself being a positive inspiration to someone else.

C) Visualize yourself changing something in your surroundings that will make it easier to do the good behavior or make it harder to do the bad behavior.

THE FUNDAMENTALS   IN PRACTICE

MAKE FUNDAMENTALS PRACTICE YOUR HABIT
Pause 3x Daily

REVEAL YIRAH (PAUSE #1)
FROM TANYA, CHAPTER 41

Pause and think about the text below one time each day.

It is important to remind myself constantly

what actually is the beginning of service

and its core and (living) root.

Even though fear (of G-d) is the root of turning from evil

and love (is the root) of doing good,

nevertheless, it is not sufficient to awaken love alone

to do good

and it is important to first awaken

at least the natural fear

which is hidden in the heart of all of Israel

which leads one to refrain from rebelling

against the King of kings

the Holy One, blessed be He, as mentioned above,

that this awe be revealed in my heart

or at least in my mind.

This means to at least reflect in my thoughts,

the greatness of G-d A-lmighty

and His Kingship (rules)

which extend to all the words,

both higher and lower.

He fills all worlds

and is also in a higher dimesion in all worlds

as it is written

"Do I not fill heaven and earth?" (Yirmeyahu 23:24)

Yet, He leaves aside (the creatures of) the higher (worlds)

and (the creatures of) the lower (worlds)

and he uniquely bestows His Kingship

upon His people Israel, in general,

and upon me in particular,

for man is obligated to say

"For my sake the world is created" (Sanhedrin 4:5).

I, in turn,

accept His Kingship upon myself,

that He will be King over me,

to serve Him and do His Will

in all kinds of work required of a servant.

And, behold, G-d is standing over him (me),"

and "The whole world is filled with His Glory,"

and He is watching you,

and is checking (my) innermost thoughts and feelings

that I serve Him properly.

Therefore, I serve in His Presence

with awe and fear

as I would, when standing before a King.

**Now, you are ready to practice the next basic fundamental, the second pause.
In contrast to Yirah in which the most effective technique is to practice it as a moment of silence, the best technique for this easy Ahava is to say it out loud so you can hear yourself.**

REVEAL AHAVA (PAUSE #2)
FROM TANYA, CHAPTER 44

Read from "And this is what…" until "Do we not have One Father" out loud.

And this is what's written in the Zohar (Vol. 3, pg. 68a)

on the Pasuk (Yeshayahu 26:9)

"My soul, I desire You (Hashem) at night…"

(the Zohar says) "Love Hashem,

with the love for the soul and spirit

when they are attached to the body,

the body loves them (the soul and spirit)…"

(In other words,) this is what the verse,

"My soul, I desire You," is saying.

"Since You, G-d, are my true energy and life,

therefore I desire You."

That is to say, "I long for and yearn for You (Hashem)

like a man who craves the life of his soul."

And when I am weak and exhausted,

I long and yearn for my soul to revive me.

Likewise, when I go to sleep,

I long and yearn for my soul to return to me

when I wake up from my sleep.

The same way, I long and yearn

for the light of the Infinite One,

blessed is He,

the true Life of life,

to be drawn into me

through my occupation in Torah (study),

when I awaken from my sleep during the night.

For the Torah and the Holy One, blessed be He,

are one and the same.

Like the Zohar says (ibid.)

"A man is required,

out of love for the Holy One, blessed be He,

to rise each night

and exert himself in His service until the morning…"

**Note that the upgraded Ahava is a much higher form than the basic Ahava.
You can reveal both through reading out loud regularly. Continue on next page. »**

UPGRADED AHAVA
FROM TANYA, CHAPTER 44

"Like a son who exerts himself

for his father and mother,

whom he loves

more than self,

his Nefesh, Ruach etc..

for "Do we not have One Father"?

THE FUNDAMENTALS IN PRACTICE

Immediately make an anchor by reading this chapter of Tehillim straight away:
(This chapter of Tehillim is chosen as a tactic, since many people know it well. However, you can make an anchor in practical action with any Torah study.)

TEHILLIM, CHAPTER 20

1: To the lead musician, a composition by David.	א: לַמְנַצֵּחַ מִזְמוֹר לְדָוִד:
2: May the L-RD answer you in time of trouble, May the name of the G-d of Jacob's keep you safe.	ב: יַעַנְךָ ה' בְּיוֹם צָרָה יְשַׂגֶּבְךָ שֵׁם אֱלֹקֵי יַעֲקֹב:
3: May He send you help from the sanctuary, and support you from Zion.	ג: יִשְׁלַח עֶזְרְךָ מִקֹּדֶשׁ וּמִצִּיּוֹן יִסְעָדֶךָּ:
4: May He remember all your offerings, and favor your burnt offerings. For ever.	ד: יִזְכֹּר כָּל מִנְחֹתֶךָ וְעוֹלָתְךָ יְדַשְּׁנֶה סֶלָה:
5: May He grant you your heart's desire, and fulfill your every plan.	ה: יִתֶּן לְךָ כִלְבָבֶךָ וְכָל עֲצָתְךָ יְמַלֵּא:
6: May we shout for joy in your victory, and raise our banner in the name of our G-d. May the L-RD fulfill your every wish.	ו: נְרַנְּנָה בִּישׁוּעָתֶךָ וּבְשֵׁם אֱלֹקֵינוּ נִדְגֹּל יְמַלֵּא ה' כָּל מִשְׁאֲלוֹתֶיךָ:
7: Now I know that the L-RD will give victory to His anointed, will answer him from His holy heavens with the mighty saving power of His right arm.	ז: עַתָּה יָדַעְתִּי כִּי הוֹשִׁיעַ ה' מְשִׁיחוֹ יַעֲנֵהוּ מִשְּׁמֵי קָדְשׁוֹ בִּגְבֻרוֹת יֵשַׁע יְמִינוֹ:
8: They come on chariots, and others on horses, but we call on the name of the L-RD our G-d.	ח: אֵלֶּה בָרֶכֶב וְאֵלֶּה בַסּוּסִים וַאֲנַחְנוּ בְּשֵׁם ה' אֱלֹקֵינוּ נַזְכִּיר:
9: They were brought to their knees and fell, but we rally and gather strength.	ט: הֵמָּה כָּרְעוּ וְנָפָלוּ וַאֲנַחְנוּ קַּמְנוּ וַנִּתְעוֹדָד:
10: G-d, grant victory! May the King answer us when we call.	י: ה' הוֹשִׁיעָה הַמֶּלֶךְ יַעֲנֵנוּ בְיוֹם קָרְאֵנוּ:

Experience has shown that when you practice the Ahava fundamental as part of your standard daily personal operating procedures, you will probably experience the enthusiasm within seven consecutive days of reading the above out loud, so commit now to do it for seven days.

STRATEGY FOR RACHAMIM:

The next fundamental we are going to practice is called Rachamim (you will learn more about it in unit three).

What is *Rachamim*? *Rachamim* means compassion, we all need compassion and it is powered by the trait of *Tiferes* (beauty). *Tiferes* is a powerful mixture of *Chessed* (kindness) and *Gevura* (strictness). The way to evoke compassion is through a thinking strategy in which you focus on the bigger reality, specifically on the "extreme contrast" of a given situation.

For example, when you see a child and you think about where they are now and where they could be in the future when they get the right support, this causes you to feel compassion, and when you feel compassion, Hashem responds with Divine compassion to your request.

The Rachamim/mercy/compassion pause leads to a feeling of compassion which leads to a request powered by compassion which lead to a compassionate response from Hashem.

INSTRUCTIONS FOR RACHAMIM THINKING STRATEGY:

We are going to learn the mental compassion thinking strategy through reading the following quote from the Siddur which we recite every morning, and we will say it now to help reveal Rachamim.

In Paragraph One focus on the wider picture of reality, what seems important and what is truly important in the long run. In this paragraph, ask Hashem for Divine compassion.

In the first section of this paragraph, focus on one side of the contrast, the things that we may look up to that are really not significant.

PARAGRAPH 1, PART 1

Master of all the worlds,	רִבּוֹן כָּל הָעוֹלָמִים
not because of our righteousness do we bring our requests to you,	לֹא עַל צִדְקוֹתֵינוּ אֲנַחְנוּ מַפִּילִים תַּחֲנוּנֵינוּ לְפָנֶיךָ
but because of Your abundant mercies.	כִּי עַל רַחֲמֶיךָ הָרַבִּים.
What are we?	מָה אָנוּ,
What is our life?	מֶה חַיֵּינוּ,
What is our kindness?	מֶה חַסְדֵּנוּ,

PARAGRAPH 1, PART 1 (CONTINUED)

What is our righteousness?	מַה צִּדְקֵינוּ,
What is our strength?	מַה כֹּחֵנוּ,
What is our might?	מַה גְּבוּרָתֵנוּ.
What could we say before you,	מַה נֹּאמַר לְפָנֶיךָ
L-rd, our G-d and the G-d of our fathers?	ה׳ אֱלֹקֵינוּ וֵאלֹקֵי אֲבוֹתֵינוּ,
Aren't all strong men	הֲלֹא כָּל הַגִּבּוֹרִים
nothing before You,	כְּאַיִן לְפָנֶיךָ,
and the famous people as if they have never been,	וְאַנְשֵׁי הַשֵּׁם כְּלֹא הָיוּ,
and the wise men as if without knowledge,	וַחֲכָמִים כִּבְלִי מַדָּע,
and the men of understanding without intelligence?	וּנְבוֹנִים כִּבְלִי הַשְׂכֵּל,
For most of their actions are nothing,	כִּי רוֹב מַעֲשֵׂיהֶם תֹּהוּ,
and their days of their lives are worthless to you.	וִימֵי חַיֵּיהֶם הֶבֶל לְפָנֶיךָ,
And man is no better than an animal	וּמוֹתַר הָאָדָם מִן הַבְּהֵמָה אָיִן,
because everything is worthless.	כִּי הַכֹּל הָבֶל:

In **Part Two of Paragraph One**, focus on the high side of the contrast: what is important and significant in the bigger picture of reality?

PARAGRAPH 1, PART 2

Except the pure soul	לְבַד הַנְּשָׁמָה הַטְּהוֹרָה
which is destined to give	שֶׁהִיא עֲתִידָה לִתֵּן
an account and reckoning	דִּין וְחֶשְׁבּוֹן
before the Throne of Your glory.	לִפְנֵי כִסֵּא כְבוֹדֶךָ.
All the nations are as nothing before You,	וְכָל הַגּוֹיִם כְּאַיִן נֶגְדֶּךָ.
as it is written:	שֶׁנֶּאֱמַר
"After all, nations are as a drop from a bucket;	הֵן גּוֹיִם כְּמַר מִדְּלִי
no more than dust upon the scales	וּכְשַׁחַק מֹאזְנַיִם
are they considered!	נֶחְשָׁבוּ,
Indeed, He can blow away islands like dust."	הֵן אִיִּים כַּדַּק יִטּוֹל:

It is common practice to do a gratitude thinking strategy right after the compassion thinking strategy.

> In **Paragraph Two**, focus on a few specific good things Hashem A-lmighy has done for you.

PARAGRAPH 2

But we are Your nation,	אֲבָל אֲנַחְנוּ עַמְּךָ
the people of Your covenant:	בְּנֵי בְרִיתֶךָ,
the children of Avraham Your beloved,	בְּנֵי אַבְרָהָם אֹהַבְךָ,
to whom You swore on Mount Moriah;	שֶׁנִּשְׁבַּעְתָּ לּוֹ בְּהַר הַמּוֹרִיָּה,
the descendents of Yitzchak, his only son,	זֶרַע יִצְחָק יְחִידוֹ,
who was bound upon the altar;	שֶׁנֶּעֱקַד עַל גַּבֵּי הַמִּזְבֵּחַ,
the community of Yaakov, Your firstborn,	עֲדַת יַעֲקֹב בִּנְךָ בְּכוֹרֶךָ,
because of Your love for him	שֶׁמֵּאַהֲבָתְךָ שֶׁאָהַבְתָּ אוֹתוֹ,
and Your delight in him	וּמִשִּׂמְחָתְךָ שֶׁשָּׂמַחְתָּ בּוֹ,
You named him Yisrael and Yeshurun.	קָרָאתָ אֶת שְׁמוֹ יִשְׂרָאֵל וִישֻׁרוּן:

> In **Paragraph Three**, which is a call to action, focus on how you respond to this Divine kindness.

PARAGRAPH 3, PART 1

Therefore, we are obligated to thank You,	לְפִיכָךְ אֲנַחְנוּ חַיָּבִים לְהוֹדוֹת לְךָ,
praise You, and glorify You,	וּלְשַׁבֵּחֲךָ וּלְפָאֶרְךָ
to bless, to sanctify	וּלְבָרֵךְ וּלְקַדֵּשׁ
and to offer praise and thanksgiving to Your Name.	וְלִתֵּן שֶׁבַח וְהוֹדָיָה לִשְׁמֶךָ:
Fortunate are we!	אַשְׁרֵינוּ,
How good is our portion,	מַה טּוֹב חֶלְקֵנוּ,
how pleasant our lot,	וּמַה נָּעִים גּוֹרָלֵנוּ,
and how beautiful our heritage!	וּמַה יָּפָה יְרֻשָּׁתֵנוּ,
Fortunate are we	אַשְׁרֵינוּ,
who early and late,	שֶׁאָנוּ מַשְׁכִּימִים וּמַעֲרִיבִים
evening and morning,	עֶרֶב וָבֹקֶר,
declare twice each day:	וְאוֹמְרִים פַּעֲמַיִם בְּכָל יוֹם:

When you say the first line of the Shema, accept upon yourself to fulfill Torah and Mitzvos wherever you may be in the four directions of the world. (See page 164 for a graphic of this.)

The Daled (ד) from the word אחד has the numerical value of four which represents that you commit to keep Torah and Mitzvos wherever you may be in the four directions of the world.

The numerical value of Ches (ח) is eight which represents the seven heavens and one earth.

When you say the Ches (ח) from the word אחד, ask yourself why your soul descended so far, from the seven heavens all the way to this earth. It is for this unique special mission and purpose to keep Torah and Mitzvos wherever you may be in the four directions of the world.

PARAGRAPH 3, PART 2

Hear, Yisrael,	שְׁמַע יִשְׂרָאֵל
G-d is our L-rd,	ה' אֱלֹקֵינוּ
the G-d is One.	ה' אֶחָד:

Say the following sentence quietly:

Blessed be the name of	בָּרוּךְ, שֵׁם
His glorious kingdom,	כְּבוֹד מַלְכוּתוֹ,
forever and ever.	לְעוֹלָם וָעֶד:

Cotinue in regular voice:

You should love the G-d your L-rd	וְאָהַבְתָּ אֵת ה' אֱלֹקֶיךָ,
with all your heart,	בְּכָל לְבָבְךָ,
with all your soul,	וּבְכָל נַפְשְׁךָ,
and with all your might.	וּבְכָל מְאֹדֶךָ:
Let these words	וְהָיוּ הַדְּבָרִים הָאֵלֶּה
which I command you today	אֲשֶׁר אָנֹכִי מְצַוְּךָ הַיּוֹם
be upon your heart.	עַל לְבָבֶךָ:
You should teach them thoroughly to your children	וְשִׁנַּנְתָּם לְבָנֶיךָ
and you should speak of them,	וְדִבַּרְתָּ בָּם,
when you sit in your house,	בְּשִׁבְתְּךָ בְּבֵיתֶךָ,

when you walk on the way,	וּבְלֶכְתְּךָ בַדֶּרֶךְ,
when you lie down and when you rise.	וּבְשָׁכְבְּךָ וּבְקוּמֶךָ:
You should bind them as a sign	וּקְשַׁרְתָּם לְאוֹת
on your arm,	עַל יָדֶךָ,
and as an ornament	וְהָיוּ לְטֹטָפֹת
between your eyes.	בֵּין עֵינֶיךָ:
And you should write them	וּכְתַבְתָּם
on the doorposts of your homes,	עַל מְזֻזוֹת בֵּיתֶךָ,
and your gates.	וּבִשְׁעָרֶיךָ:

It turns out that in the Siddur, this fundamental *Rachamim* thinking strategy leads to the fundamental of commitment that you practiced in the *Yiras Shamayim* thinking strategy.

UPGRADED RACHAMIM

Traditionally, the thinking strategy to evoke the fundamental emotion of *Rachamim* focuses on the lowliness of the body and the loftiness of the *Neshama* (see the beginning of Tanya chapter 32). However, we will practice an upgraded version of the contrast by focussing on a more global contrast.

The contrast is;

ONE) The revelation of the Divine (*Giluy Elokus*) that existed in the Beis Hamikdash, and

TWO) the fact that we are now lacking this revelation, we do not perceive Hashem openly.

This something your Neshama cares about.

In order for this upgraded *Rachamim* strategy to be effective, it's important you learn about Divine revelation (*Giluy Elokus*), and when something becomes understandable, then most probably there are ways to measure it.

In fact, when you *Daven* (Pray) properly, this causes a mini Divine revelation (*Giluy Elokus*) in your soul. Since there is a way to measure a lack in effective Tefillah (prayer work) (see HaYom Yom Iyar 23), therefore there is a way to appreciate the mini personal *Giluy Elokus* and contrast it to when it is lacking. When you understand this contrast well, it will help you effectively ask for Divine compassion that there be *Giluy Elokus* in your life and the world.

THE FUNDAMENTALS IN PRACTICE

MAKE FUNDAMENTALS PRACTICE YOUR HABIT
Pause 3x Daily

The following six indicators can be used to measure your personal mini *Giluy Elokus*. Give yourself a score of 1-10, 1 represents very little and 10 represents a lot.

It does not matter what number you score yourself. The very fact that your attention is on *Giluy Elokus* and the lack of it, will help you to ask for Divine compassion for it, during Tefilla.

SCORE

- [ ] You feel warm and refreshed
- [ ] Mitzvos feel easy to do even when challenged
- [ ] You feel tranquil when you do things
- [ ] You feel pleasure in Torah study
- [ ] The atmosphere around you is refined
- [ ] You are a positive influence on others

Make an anchor by reading out loud the following request to Hashem

וְתֶחֱזֶינָה עֵינֵינוּ בְּשׁוּבְךָ לְצִיּוֹן בְּרַחֲמִים[1]

May our eyes see Your return to Zion with compassion.

This request refers the revelation of Hashem in the Jewish people as the verse says:

וְלֵאמֹר לְצִיּוֹן עַמִּי-אָתָּה:

Have said to Zion: You are My people! *Yeshayahu 51:16*

How does this request make sense? Hashem is everywhere, like is it written "Do I not fill heaven and earth?" (Yirmeyahu 23:24) why are we asking that He return to us when he is with us now?

The answer is in the wording of our request **"May our eyes behold"** We want to see and perceive Hashem in an open revealed way. This is the request we make at least three times a day in the Siddur.

Say the request again with meaning;

וְתֶחֱזֶינָה עֵינֵינוּ בְּשׁוּבְךָ לְצִיּוֹן בְּרַחֲמִים

May our eyes see Your return to Zion with compassion.

---

1. And (we) request three times every day ומבקש ג' פעמים בכל יום (או יותר) ותחזינה עינינו בשובך לציון ברחמים, שאז יהיה גילוי אלקות ועד לגילוי העצמות (or more) May our eyes see Your return to Zion with compassion. That then there will be a revelation of the divine and even the revelation of the essence. ואתה תצוה קונטרס פורים-קטן תשנ"ב

FUNDAMENTALS PRACTICE CHECKLIST

Put a check by the days you completed all the steps of the fundamentals

Fundamentals	Day 1	Day 2	Day 3	Day 4	Day 5	Day 6	Day 7
Rachamim							
Yirah							
Ahava							
Upgraded Ahava							

MAKE FUNDAMENTALS PRACTICE YOUR HABIT

Describe the changes these fundamentals made to your day.

	How did it change you?	What did you do differently?
Day 1		
Day 2		
Day 3		
Day 4		
Day 5		
Day 6		
Day 7		

FORWARD

FLYING IN BUSINESS CLASS

Riga, Latvia, 5758 (1998). Yehuda, a yeshivah student from Brooklyn, came for the summer to be head counselor in the local Gan Yisroel camp. One Shabbos afternoon, he meets a business executive who introduced himself as David. David had a distinct Spanish accent, and appeared to be around sixty years old. He explained that his company, based in Florida, was renovating many of the city's historic buildings, some of which were hundreds of years old. in one building, for instance, the workers found a cannonball still stuck in the wall from the Swedish invasion of Riga in the early 1700's, and now it is displayed in a glass showcase in the building.

Yehuda was intrigued as to David's specific mission, and David explained that he reviews all the work and releases the funds to pay the workers. Yehuda was surprised, "You just flew in, and you must be exhausted. How are you able to have the clarity of mind to make these decisions where there is so much at stake?"

"I flew business class," David explained. "My company can't afford that an executive walk into an important meeting tired and unfocused. Therefore, they buy me a seat in business class where the seats are wider and there is more legroom. It is like a reclining armchair where it is easy to sleep during the flight. That way, I arrive well rested and I can make better decisions."

Many times, Yehuda had heard his friends talking about getting upgraded to business class when they flew. Now, he understood that it's not only about a better travel experience; it's about making the best use of the travel time, staying your best self, and being able to make better decisions. The passenger in business class shares the same plane and experiences the same turbulence as the other passengers, yet he maintains a considerable advantage.

Life is a journey, and some people get an upgrade that gives them an advantage in their life experiences and ability to make the best decisions. Imagine that the key to getting this upgrade is now in your hands. It's only a few hours of reading, together with a few days of focused practice. You will continue to have the same challenges, however, it's going to be different as you will experience the benefit of the upgrade.

The journey of life can sometimes seem like flying in the air, and sometimes it seems like traveling on ground. Is it possible to fly and have your feet grounded in reality at the same time? Yes! But to unlock this possibility, it is not enough to just study, or to know more information. This can only be achieved by doing certain activities regularly, which will be within your grasp in just a few hours. "Soulwaze" was created to help you navigate the road to revealing your soul.

A LESSON FROM AERODYNAMICS

Throughout history, man has been fascinated with flying, and only in 1903 did Hashem allow two brothers to uncover the formula to fly a plane. Their discovery wasn't based on knowledge or study alone. They tried and tested their ideas over a few years in a homemade wind tunnel and later tested their ideas in an open field.

Something similar applies to an upgrade of spirit. It does not come from study alone. You have to practice an exercise, and if it does not bring the desired results, the exercise must be slightly modified while remaining faithful to the principle of the topic.

Often, there are a few ways to get to your destination. This handbook will guide you in your journey, while leaving you with the flexibility of a few paths. Some of the methods could even be traveled almost simultaneously, because the spirit has different boundaries than the physical.

Only after the Wright brothers successfully got their aircraft to fly did they began to really understand how it works. They realized something interesting: drag, the aerodynamic force that opposes an aircraft's motion through the air, actually causes the plane to lift.

A similar idea can be applied to the journey of life. The opposing force can actually help you lift. It is very important to overcome the opposing force, however its very existence gives the opportunity for flight. Battling and being victorious over our internal drive to do bad actually helps us lift, similar to the way the raging waters of Noach's flood lifted his Teivah above all the mountains.

However, before going into a strategic conflict, it's important to know you will win with your superior strategy. By reading and implementing this handbook, you will learn how to upgrade and use the superior strategy combination as taught in Tanya.

A JOINT EFFORT

Another lesson we can learn from the discovery of the airplane is that it came from two people working together. Similarly, the most effective way to use and implement this handbook is together with a partner. Your partner will keep you accountable to do the exercises and you will keep them accountable. You will also help each other tailor your strategies to be effective.

If, as you are reading the handbook, there is a word you do not understand, be sure to look it up in the glossary. If you do not understand the Hebrew footnotes that do not have Nikud (vowels), this will not stop you from understanding and being able to implement the skills of this course.

Don't miss out on the experience by only *studying* the course. Make sure to do the exercises as well, and that will help you achieve the desired goals. We wish you much success as you go through "Soulwaze," and navigate the journey to revealing your G-dly soul.

INTRODUCTION

THREE FIGHTING FORCES

On *Erev Shabbos*, 22 Teves 5573 (1812), two days before his passing, the Alter Rebbe explained to his grandson the Tzemach Tzedek a technique how to win over the *Yetzer Hara*. This was a lesson he had heard from R' Avraham Hamalach, son of the Mezritcher Magid, derived from a famous war called "The Seven Years' War."

This war, spanning the seven-year period from 1756 to 1763, involved almost every European great power of the time. Its effects also reached the Americas, West Africa, India, and the Philippines.

One of the monumental battles was the battle of Leuthen, which demonstrated that a smaller force can win over a bigger force if it maneuvers three fighting forces to attack one fighting force at the same time. R' Avraham explained that the same idea applies to the fight against the *Yetzer Hara*: one will be victorious by attacking with multiple fighting forces at the same time. These fighting forces are Ahava (אַהֲבָה), Yirah (יִרְאָה) and Rachamim (רַחֲמִים), which are all explained by the Alter Rebbe in Tanya.

The story of the battle is as follows, Frederick the great of Prussia had arrived in the area of Silesia on November 28, 1757 to find that the primary city in Silesia, Breslau (now Wrocław, Poland), had just fallen to the Austrians and that at the village of Leuthen the Austrian army was twice the size of his own.

He realized that he must either win a great victory or suffer a major defeat.

On December 5, 1757 (5518) Frederick marched directly toward the Austrian army with its center at Leuthen, the Austrian army was stretched over a line of 4 miles.

Frederick first marched to face the Austrian right flank (side) appearing as though it would act as a spearhead for a right flank attack. Then he swiftly moved his well-disciplined infantry toward the Austrian left in columns.

The infantry marched southward, out of sight of the Austrians, behind a line of low hills.

The whole Prussian army ended up in line of battle at nearly a right angle to the left flank of the Austrian position. The Prussian infantry, arrayed in the conventional two lines of battle, then advanced and rolled up the Austrian flank.

The determined Prussians, in 40 minutes, took the village.

The three fighting forces explained in Tanya — Ahava, Yirah and Rachamim — correspond to the three *Avos*, Avraham Yitzchak and Yaakov. Avraham's prime service is Ahava, Yitzchak - Yirah, and Yaakov - Rachamim.

Tanya is written to be learned beginning from its introduction, chapter by chapter in order, and there are many guides that will help you do this.

The uniqueness of this guide is that it is focused on helping you acquire and implement the skills explained in the Tanya. It will help you unlock these skills so that even if you have not yet learned the the entire Tanya in order, when you do, you will be able to recognize keywords, and what they mean to you in practical action. In this way, you will be able to actually live Tanya.

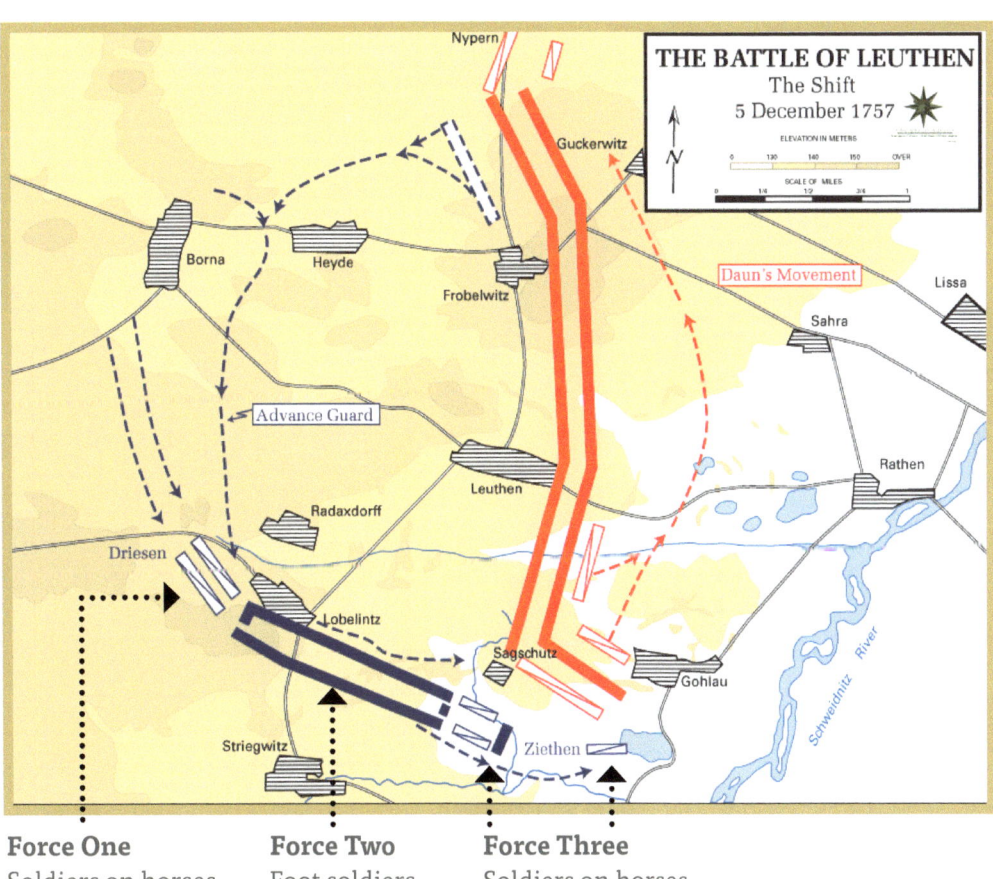

The two dark lines represent two lines of foot soldiers. The two white columns on both sides represent cavalry, soldiers on horses.

Force One
Soldiers on horses

Force Two
Foot soldiers

Force Three
Soldiers on horses

THIS COURSE TEACHES YOU HOW TO REVEAL אהבה ויראה מסותרת

COURSE PREREQUISITES

To gain the full benefits from this curriculum, it is important to first fulfill the prerequisites. This guide may be partially effective without doing the prerequisites first.

1. ACTION

Being observant in Torah and Mitzvos. Including: Shabbos Observance, Kosher food, *Tefillos*, Kosher media exposure.

2. DAILY STUDY

For example; Study of *Chitas* for at least one year.

Chitas includes;

- Daily Chumash Study
- Daily Tanya Study
- Daily Rambam Study
  (or have studied the Yahadus curriculum or Sefer HaMitzvos)

Daily Study Options

Chayenu.org Publication	Chabad.org/ dailystudy	Learn on your own or with a partner	Learn in a class especially a Tanya class

3. EXPERIENCE

Have experienced a task-based achievement system like the missions in Tzivos Hashem youth.

COURSE INSTRUCTIONS

A person has an internal drive towards good as well as a drive towards bad. The drive towards good is called the *Yetzer Tov* (good adviser) and the drive towards bad is called the *Yetzer Hara* (bad adviser). Part of our life mission is overcoming our internal drive towards bad, this struggle can be described as two generals fighting to rule one city, i.e. your body, specifically your thought, speech and action.

When fighting an infection, there are two paths of treatment, direct and indirect.

1. Directly fighting the infection
2. Indirect by strengthening the body so the entire body will overcome the infection.

In this training guide, you will learn six skills in the indirect approach. You will learn how to feed your good drive with calculated inspiration to the point that the *Yetzer Hara* will be starved and overwhelmed.

In future guides, we intent to teach you how to even transform parts of your *Yetzer Hara* to support the *Yetzer Tov*, however initially its important to overwhelm it with inspiration towards good using the techniques taught in this guide.

The skills are very simple to understand and only take a few hours to read. However, the implementation of these skills require small nuances, it takes trial and error, discussion with friends and guidance from those who have done it.

Before passenger planes became popular, people did not understand why passenger planes could be useful, why do I need to travel? What am I missing? After people started to travel, it become apparent how traveling in a plane enriches their lives, e.g. by visiting distant family, new experiences etc...

Similarly, when the first mobile phones came out, people did not understand the value of a mobile phone. People said I have a phone in my office, why do I need one with me?!? Only when people started to try mobile phones did they realize how useful they can be.

This course will enrich your life in ways you can not yet imagine. However, once you do this course properly, you will gain skills which you will use your entire life. It will open up a world that you never imagined existed, it will change the path of your life.

To get these benefits, it is not sufficient just to study this guide, be sure to do the activities and mission checklists towards the end of this guide. The mission checklists will help you experience the full benefits of what you will gain.

To help you make and recognize the developmental changes you will undergo, there is a progress diary towards the end of this guide. After each day you study and practice this guide, jot down in what way the experience changed you.

REFLECT ON THESE QUESTIONS BEFORE STARTING UNIT ONE:

1. What is the Mitzvah of loving Hashem? Start by defining love.

2. What do you practice to fulfill it?

3. How does it enhance your life?

4. How do you measure your success in this Mitzvah?

5. How do you teach others to fulfill it?

UNIT 1

THE FIRST FIGHTING FORCE
AN ARMY AGAINST THE YETZER HARA

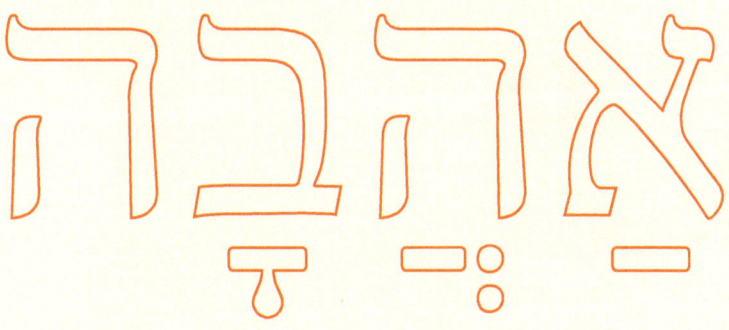

GOAL

A thinking strategy makes it second nature to fulfill the commandment of loving Hashem.

TANYA – CHAPTER 44
INTRODUCTION

UNIT 1 / INTRODUCTION

The Mitzvah of Ahavas Hashem

(RAMBAM) MITZVAH 4

מִצְוָה לְאָהֲבוֹ

LOVE HASHEM

וְאָהַבְתָּ אֵת ה' אֱלֹקֶיךָ

(דברים ו, ה)

You shall love Hashem your G-d

Think about the greatness of Hashem and all that He does for us to bring us to love Him.

How is it possible to command anybody to love something?

Either they like it or they don't like it.

The Torah answers this question by explaining that the Mitzvah to love Hashem is asking you to think about Hashem. When you think about Hashem in the ways you will learn in this unit, you fulfill this great Mitzvah.

In the words of the Rambam:

> **FROM THE SOURCE**
>
> וְהֵיאַךְ הִיא הַדֶּרֶךְ לְאַהֲבָתוֹ וְיִרְאָתוֹ? בְּשָׁעָה שֶׁיִּתְבּוֹנֵן הָאָדָם בְּמַעֲשָׂיו וּבְרוּאָיו הַנִּפְלָאִים הַגְּדוֹלִים וְיִרְאֶה מֵהֶן חָכְמָתוֹ שֶׁאֵין לָהּ עֵרֶךְ וְלֹא קֵץ, מִיָּד הוּא אוֹהֵב וּמְשַׁבֵּחַ וּמְפָאֵר וּמִתְאַוֶּה תַּאֲוָה גְדוֹלָה לֵידַע הַשֵּׁם הַגָּדוֹל.
>
> What is the path [to attain] **love** and fear of Him? When a person **contemplates** His wondrous and great deeds and creations and appreciates His infinite wisdom that surpasses all comparison, he will immediately love, praise, and glorify [Him], yearning with tremendous desire to know [G-d's] great name.
>
> THE FOUNDATIONS OF TORAH CHAPTER 2:2

☞ SUMMARY

The Mitzvah to love Hashem is a Mitzvah to set aside time to think about things that will bring you to feel love to Hashem.

Why does thinking about Hashem bring you to love Hashem?

The reason we like something is because deep down we "think" that this thing is good.

The way we think affects the way we feel because the mind naturally rules over the heart.

👉 IS THERE MORE THAN ONE TYPE OF LOVE?

Actually, there are different types of love. The love to a family member is different than the way you like your friend.

Tanya explains that there are many different types of love one can have to Hashem, e.g. a love passionate like fire, a relaxed love like water, a reciprocal love like water reflects a face, and more.

In this chapter, we will learn the thinking strategy that reveals the love called,

"כִּי הוּא חַיֶּיךָ"

"For He is your life,"

which Moshe Rabeinu explained in Devarim 30:20.

It was further explained by Yeshayahu HaNavi and it became known by the name,

"נַפְשִׁי אִוִּיתִיךָ"

"My soul, I am speaking to you, I desire you."

It was further explained by Rabbi Shimon Bar Yochai in the Zohar (3, 68a) and then clearly explained by the Alter Rebbe in Tanya chapter 44.

The reason we chose to teach you this thinking strategy first, is because it is so easy and straight forward to do. It only has 4-5 parts and you will be fulfilling the Mitzvah of Ahavas Hashem, so in addition to learning Tanya, you will be living and experiencing it.

UNIT 1 / INTRODUCTION

Tanya at a Glance

When learning something new, we usually start at the beginning. So why dive right into perek Mem Daled?

This chapter will teach you a key skill of Tanya: How to fulfill the Mitzvah of Ahavas Hashem. After learning this unit, every other perek will take on a whole new meaning.

You are here

THE 53 CHAPTERS OF TANYA AT A GLANCE

Intro | **1-5** Spiritual Anatomy

6-8 Spiritual Anatomy | **9-11** Conquering Ourselves

12-17 Conquering Ourselves

18-23 Revealing Hidden Love

24-25 Revealing Hidden Love | **26-29** Reaching Happiness

30-31 Reaching Happiness | **32** Ahavas Yisroel | **33-34** Reaching Happiness | **35** Implementation

36-40 Implementation | **41** Skill: Fearing Hashem

42 Skill: Fearing Hashem | **43** Skill: Loving & fearing Hashem | **44** Skill: Loving Hashem | **45** Awakening Compassion | **46-47** Becoming Effective

48-50 Becoming Effective | **51-53** Implementation

THE PARADIGM SHIFT

In this section, you will learn a four-part thinking strategy to reveal Ahava.

In Love with Life

Take a deep breath. Look around at all the beauty in this world. Don't you love being alive?

Think about the last time you were tired—or maybe you're tired right now. Doesn't it feel good to go to sleep after a long day? And doesn't it feel even better to wake up refreshed after a good night's sleep? That's you feeling your life.

Stop for a moment and think about the source of life, where our energy comes from. Loving life means loving the Life of life, Hashem.

The source of life is even deeper than life as we know it. Our days on this earth are numbered, while Hashem is beyond time, unlimited. Our love for life brings us to a desire to connect to the root of eternal life, Hashem. Studying Torah and performing Mitzvos is how we can tap into this power. When we leave this world, our "life" as we know it will be left behind, while the everlasting strength of Torah and Mitzvos will carry on.

chapter 44
ליקוטי אמרים, פרק מד

The lighter areas represent the text of Tanya covered in this section translated on pages 46-47.

ליקוטי אמרים סג

ואהבת עולם והיא שוה לכל נפש מישראל וירושה לנו מאבותינו. והיינו מ"ש הזהר ע"פ נפשי איויתך בלילה וגו' דירחים לקב"ה רחימותא דנפשא ורוחא כמה דאתדבקו אילין בגופא וגופא רחים לון וכו'. וז"ש נפשי איויתך כלומר מפני שאתה ה' נפשי וחיי האמיתים לכך איויתיך פי' שאני מתאוה ותאב לך כאדם המתאוה לחיי נפשו וכשהוא חלש ומעונה מתאוה ותאב שתשוב נפשו אליו וכן כשהוא הולך לישן מתאוה וחפץ שתשוב נפשו אליו כשיעור משנתו כך אני מתאוה ותאב לאור א"ס ב"ה חיי החיים האמיתיים להמשיכו בקרבי ע"י עסק התורה בהקיצי משנתי בלילה דאורייתא וקב"ה כולא חד. כמ"ש הזהר שם דבעי בר נש מרחימותא דקב"ה למיקם בכל לילא לאשתדלא בפולחניה עד צפרא כו'. ואהבה רבה וגדולה מזו והיא מסותרת ג"כ בכל נפש מישראל בירושה מאבותינו היא מ"ש בר"מ כברא דאשתדל בתר אבוי ואימיה דרחים לון יתיר מגרמיה ונפשיה ורוחיה כו' כי הלא אב אחד לכולנו. ואף כי מי הוא זה ואיזהו אשר ערב לבו לגשת להשיג אפי' חלק אחד מני אלף ממדרגת אהבת רעיא מהימנא. מ"מ הרי אפס קצהו ושמץ מנהו מרב טובו ואורו מאיר לכללות ישראל בכל דור ודור כמ"ש בתיקונים דאתפשטותיה בכל דרא ודרא לאנהרא לון וכו' רק שהארה זו היא בבחי' הסתר והעלם גדול בנפשות כל בית ישראל ולהוציא אהבה זו המסותרת מהעלם והסתר אל הגילוי להיות בהתגלות לבו ומוחו לא נפלאת ולא רחוקה היא אלא קרוב הדבר מאד בפיך ובלבבך דהיינו

THE FOUR PARADIGM SHIFTS

1. You love your life.

👉 **LIST 5 THINGS YOU LIKE:**

A_____

B_____

C_____

D_____

E_____

When you are asleep, can you enjoy them?

So if you like those 5 things, you certainly love being awake and alive.

Being alive gives you the ability to experience these things!

2. The feeling of yearning when you are tired or weak is your natural love of life.

👉 **DESCRIBE 2 SPECIFIC TIMES WHEN YOU REALLY FELT YOUR URGE TO LIVE = LOVE OF LIFE:**

A_____

_____

_____

_____

B_____

_____

_____

_____

3. Hashem is your life.

Like the Pasuk says "כִּי הוּא חַיֶּיךָ" - Devarim 30:20.

So if you love your life – you love Hashem.

☞ **EXPLAIN THIS IDEA IN YOUR OWN WORDS:**

_____

_____

_____

4. Hashem is not only life; He is the Life of life.

☞ **HOW CAN YOU CONNECT TO UNLIMITED LIFE, WHEN YOU ARE STILL ALIVE IN THIS WORLD? HINT: WHAT DOES A NESHAMA KEEP EVEN AFTER LEAVING THIS WORLD?**

_____

So if you love life, it makes sense to go further and love the Life of life.

And the way to connect is specifically through Torah and Mitzvos.

☞ **WHICH ONE OF THE 4 PARADIGM SHIFTS MAKES YOU WANT TO ACTIVELY DO SOMETHING? EXPLAIN WHY.**

_____

_____

_____

Exercise

☞ **EXPLAIN THE FOUR PARADIGM SHIFTS TO A FRIEND. ASK YOUR FRIEND TO GIVE YOU A GRADE OUT OF 10 ON HOW WELL YOU EXPLAINED THEM.**

(There is a fifth paradigm shift, that is crucial to fulfill this Mitzvah, which you will learn in part two.)

> **Quote from Tanya chapter 44**

And this is what's written in the Zohar (Vol. 3, pg. 68a)	וְהַיְינוּ מַה שֶּׁכָּתַב הַזֹּהַר
on the Pasuk (Yeshayahu 26:9)	עַל פָּסוּק
"My soul, I desire You (Hashem) at night…"	נַפְשִׁי אִוִּיתִיךָ בַּלַּיְלָה וְגוֹ'
(the Zohar says) "Love Hashem,	דְּיַרְחִים לְקוּדְשָׁא בְּרִיךְ הוּא
with the love for the soul and spirit	רְחִימוּתָא דְנַפְשָׁא וְרוּחָא
just as they are attached to the body,	כְּמָה דְאִתְדַּבְּקוּ אִילֵּין בְּגוּפָא
and the body loves them (the soul and spirit)…"	וְגוּפָא רָחִים לוֹן וְכוּ'.
(In other words,) this is what the verse,	וְזֶהוּ שֶׁכָּתוּב
"My soul, I desire You," is saying.	נַפְשִׁי אִוִּיתִיךָ, כְּלוֹמַר
"Since You, G-d, are my true energy and life,	מִפְּנֵי שֶׁאַתָּה ה' נַפְשִׁי וְחַיַּי הָאֲמִתִּים
therefore I desire You."	לְכָךְ אִוִּיתִיךָ
That is to say, "I long for and yearn for You (Hashem)	פֵּירוּשׁ שֶׁאֲנִי מִתְאַוֶּה וְתָאֵב לְךָ
like a man who craves the life of his soul."	כְּאָדָם הַמִּתְאַוֶּה לְחַיֵּי נַפְשׁוֹ
And when he is weak and exhausted,	וּכְשֶׁהוּא חַלָּשׁ וּמְעוּנֶּה
he longs and yearns for his soul to revive him.	מִתְאַוֶּה וְתָאֵב שֶׁתָּשׁוּב נַפְשׁוֹ אֵלָיו
Likewise, when he goes to sleep,	וְכֵן כְּשֶׁהוּא הוֹלֵךְ לִישֹׁן
he longs and yearns for his soul to return to him	מִתְאַוֶּה וְחָפֵץ שֶׁתָּשׁוּב נַפְשׁוֹ אֵלָיו
when he wakes up from his sleep.	כְּשִׁיעוּר מִשְּׁנָתוֹ

◂ KEY TERMS ▸

Love	יַרְחִים
Weak and exhausted	חַלָּשׁ וּמְעוּנֶּה
Life of life (Hashem)	חַיֵּי הַחַיִּים
Upon awakening from sleep	כְּשִׁיעוּר מִשְּׁנָתוֹ
Occupation in Torah (study)	עֵסֶק הַתּוֹרָה
And exert himself in his service	לְאִשְׁתַּדְּלָא בְּפוּלְחָנֵיהּ

> Quote from Tanya chapter 44

The same way, I long and yearn	כָּךְ אֲנִי מִתְאַוֶּה וְתָאֵב
for the light of the Infinite One,	לְאוֹר אֵין סוֹף
blessed is He,	בָּרוּךְ הוּא
the true Life of life,	חַיֵּי הַחַיִּים הָאֲמִתִּיִּים
to be drawn into me	לְהַמְשִׁיכוֹ בְּקִרְבִּי
through my occupation in Torah (study),	עַל יְדֵי עֵסֶק הַתּוֹרָה
when I awaken from my sleep during the night.	בַּהֲקִיצִי מִשְּׁנָתִי בַּלַּיְלָה
For the Torah and the Holy One, blessed be He,	דְּאוֹרַיְיתָא וְקוּדְשָׁא בְּרִיךְ הוּא
are one and the same.	כּוּלָּא חַד.
Like the Zohar says (ibid.)	כְּמוֹ שֶׁכָּתַב הַזֹּהַר שָׁם
"A man is required,	דְּבָעֵי בַּר נַשׁ
out of love for the Holy One, blessed be He,	מֵרְחִימוּתָא דְקוּדְשָׁא בְּרִיךְ הוּא
to rise each night	לְמֵיקַם בְּכָל לֵילָא
and exert himself in His service until the morning…"	לְאִשְׁתַּדְּלָא בְּפוּלְחָנֵיהּ עַד צַפְרָא כו'.

FROM THE SOURCE

נַפְשִׁי אִוִּיתִיךָ בַּלַּיְלָה
My soul, I desire You at night

— YESHAYAHU 26:9

SEE THE WORDS

כִּי הֵם חַיֵּינוּ
For they (the words of Torah) are our life

תְּפִלַּת עַרְבִית — SIDDUR

👉 **TAKE NOTE**

Notice when the Alter Rebbe uses the third person "him" or "he," he actually means "you." In *Lashon Kodesh*, the third person is a respectful way of communication.

UNIT 1 / THE FIRST FIGHTING FORCE - AHAVA   PART 1 / TANYA – CHAPTER 44

MAKE FUNDAMENTALS PRACTICE YOUR HABIT
Pause 3x Daily

SAY IT REGULARLY לִהְיוֹת רָגִיל עַל לְשׁוֹנוֹ וְקוֹלוֹ

SEE THE WORDS

BIRCHOS KRIAS SHEMA IN TEFILAS MAARIV

TANYA CHAPTER 44 ON THE MEANING OF THE WORDS בפיך ובלבבך **FROM THE POSUK OF** כי קרוב.

PAUSE

1. **THINK**
2. **SAY**
3. **DO**

DAILY TORAH STUDY PUBLICATION

👉 INSTRUCTIONS

Set a reminder to come to come to Maariv 3 minutes early to **think** about the the Ahava Thinking Strategy and then **verbalize** your intent when you say כי הם חיינו and immediately **learn** a paragraph of Torah after Maariv to anchor the love in practical action.

48

HAYOM YOM, 12 CHESHVAN

Hear O Israel (means)	שְׁמַע יִשְׂרָאֵל
a *Yid* deeply recognizes that	אַ אִיד דֶערְהֶערְט
The Eternal L-rd is our G-d (meaning;)	הוי' אֱלֹקֵינוּ
that our power and life energy actually stems from higher than nature;	אַז כּוֹחֵנוּ וְחַיּוּתֵנוּ אִיז דָאס לְמַעְלָה מִן הַטֶּבַע
and The Eternal L-rd is One.	אוּן הוי' אֶחָד.

FIND OUT MORE

אהבה הייסט, א המשכה צו דעם גוט וואס ער האט פארשטאנען און געפילט אין זיין שכל, ווען בא איהם ווערט אט די המשכה (דער ציה צו דער גוטער זאך וואס ער האט פארשטאנען) ווערט איהם זעהר געשמאק און עס לאזט אין איהם איבער א געוויסן רושם אין מדות און הנהגות טובות, און מדת היראה ווירקט אויף איהם מואס זיין ברע.

ליקוטי דיבורים ח"ב ע' שז

☞ HALACHA

The Alter Rebbe's Shulchan Aruch (Orach Chayim 1:3) explains that one who wakes up early to study the Oral Torah during the night is considered a servant of Hashem.

Some, like Rabbi Akiva, would rise at midnight. If a person cannot do this, the next best option is to rise at the beginning of the last third of the night. However, the middle path would be to at least wake up sometime before morning.

Here is a quote from the first *Halacha* in the Alter Rebbes Shulchan Aruch;

"It is imperative on every man, to overcome his *Yetzer* in the morning like a lion and rise from his sleep before the light of the morning for the service of his Creator, in order that he will awaken the morning, like it is written, "I will awaken the morning"-I will awaken the morning and the morning will not wake me, and this is the path for the regular person."

Tanya is Sefer shel Beinonim, a guidebook for the average person, so the Alter Rebbe advises his readers to arise before morning to study Torah.

In a case when waking up at midnight would hinder the next day's energetic pursuit of meticulous observance, Rabbi Avraham of Butchatch writes not to wake up later than needed to daven with the *tzibbur*.

FIND OUT MORE

Aishel Avrohom 1:2; Shulchan Aruch, Orach Chayim 1:1; Likkutei Sichos, Vol 16, p. 361

KEEP IN MIND

LIKKUTEI TORAH, SHLACH 42B

As you reflect on	לִכְשֶׁיִּתְבּוֹנֵן
how you love	אֵיךְ הוּא אוֹהֵב
the life of your soul	חַיֵּי נַפְשׁוֹ
and want very much	וְרוֹצֶה מְאֹד
your life to continue—	בְּקִיּוּם חַיּוּתוֹ
that (your life) shouldn't disconnect from you, G-d forbid—	שֶׁלֹּא יִפָּסֹק מִמֶּנּוּ חַס וְשָׁלוֹם,
place this idea into your heart:	וְזֹאת יָשִׂים הָאָדָם אֶל לִבּוֹ
He, the blessed One,	כִּי הוּא יִתְבָּרֵךְ
His very self is the life inside of you,	הִנֵּה הוּא עַצְמוֹ הַחַיּוּת שֶׁבְּקִרְבּוֹ
And He is your real life.	וְחַיָּיו מַמָּשׁ

⮘ KEY TERMS ⮕

Reflect (in your mind)	יִתְבּוֹנֵן
Place into your heart	יָשִׂים אֶל לִבּוֹ
power and life	כּוֹחֵנוּ וְחַיּוּתֵנוּ
deeply recognizes	דֶערְהֶערְט
Higher than nature	לְמַעְלָה מִן הַטֶּבַע
Alone, only	לְבַדּוֹ

LIKKUTEI TORAH, SHEMINI ATZERES 92D

To love the L-rd your G-d	לְאַהֲבָה אֶת ה' אֱלֹקֶיךָ
with all your heart	בְּכָל לְבָבְךָ
and with all your soul	וּבְכָל נַפְשְׁךָ
because of your life;	לְמַעַן חַיֶּיךָ
This means (love Him)	כְּלוֹמַר
because He alone	לְמַעַן כִּי ה' לְבַדּוֹ
is all of your life.	הוּא כָּל חַיֶּיךָ

MAKE FUNDAMENTALS PRACTICE YOUR HABIT
Pause 3x Daily

You have started to become a special warrior of Hashem by making fundamentals your habit.

You have contributed to your safety and the safety of the Jewish people and the entire world by revealing Hashem inside you by practicing the fundamentals, the habit of Pause 3x.

Most probably, when you were uncertain about something you were able to fall back on the fundamentals as a source of personal stability.

You have joined a global growing community of people who made fundamentals practice a habit, people who practice don't stick out, yet through their good example of a high level of personal conduct, they are bringing Pause 3x to the world.

You have started to use Pause 3x as a basis for personal, social and spiritual growth.

FUNDAMENTALS PRACTICE:

INSTRUCTIONS:

1. **Start with anchoring in action, give some money to *Tzedaka*.**

2. **Read from Tanya 41 (on the next page) quietly in your mind.**

As you read, notice when the intellectual reflection leads into emotional commitment and when this becomes a practical visualization. This practice that reveals Yirah is actually comprised of three fundamentals. Mental reflection, then emotional commitment and then a visualization of practical behavior.

3. **Say the first line of the Shema where indicated on the Tanya page.**

Once you committed to be *Mekabel Ol Machus Shamayim*, you are now going to actually *Mekabel Ol Machus Shamayim* by saying Shema on the spot.

4. **When you get to the end of the Tanya 41 page,**

A) **Visualize yourself in front of an important person, and then visualize yourself doing something different later today with the spirit of how you would behave in front of an important person. Envision doing something good or avoiding something or doing something better.**

Imagine the feeling you are going to feel when you do this.

B) **Visualize yourself spending time with people who will encourage you and limiting your exposure to people who discourage you.**

Visualize yourself being a positive inspiration to someone else.

C) **Visualize yourself changing something in your surroundings that will make it easier to do the good behavior or make it harder to do the bad behavior.**

THE FUNDAMENTALS　　IN PRACTICE

MAKE FUNDAMENTALS PRACTICE YOUR HABIT
Pause 3x Daily

PAUSE #1: YIRAH - TAKE RESPONSIBILITY
FROM TANYA, CHAPTER 41

Instructions on previous page.

It is important to remind myself constantly

what actually is the beginning of service

and its core and (living) root.

Even though fear (of G-d) is the root of turning from evil

and love (is the root) of doing good,

nevertheless, it is not sufficient to awaken love alone

to do good

and it is important to first awaken

at least the natural fear

which is hidden in the heart of all of Israel

which leads one to refrain from rebelling

against the King of kings

the Holy One, blessed be He, as mentioned above,

that this awe be revealed in my heart

or at least in my mind.

This means to at least reflect in my thoughts,

the greatness of G-d A-lmighty

and His Kingship (rules)

which extend to all the words,

both higher and lower.

He fills all worlds

and is also in a higher dimesion in all worlds

as it is written

"Do I not fill heaven and earth?" (Yirmeyahu 23:24)

Yet, He leaves aside (the creatures of) the higher (worlds)

and (the creatures of) the lower (worlds)

and he uniquely bestows His Kingship

upon His people Israel, in general,

and upon me in particular,

for man is obligated to say

"For my sake the world is created" (Sanhedrin 4:5).

I, in turn,

accept His Kingship upon myself,

that He will be King over me,

to serve Him and do His Will

in all kinds of work required of a servant. **Say שְׁמַע**

And, behold, G-d is standing over him (me),"

and "The whole world is filled with His Glory,"

and He is watching you,

and is checking (my) innermost thoughts and feelings

that I serve Him properly.

Therefore, I serve in His Presence

with awe and fear

as I would, when standing before a King.

52

PAUSE #2: AHAVA - REVEAL ENTHUSIASM
FROM TANYA, CHAPTER 44

Read the following out loud:

And this is what's written in the Zohar (Vol. 3, pg. 68a)

on the Pasuk (Yeshayahu 26:9)

"My soul, I desire You (Hashem) at night…"

(the Zohar says) "Love Hashem,

with the love for the soul and spirit

when they are attached to the body,

the body loves them (the soul and spirit)…"

(In other words,) this is what the verse,

"My soul, I desire You," is saying.

"Since You, G-d, are my true energy and life,

therefore I desire You."

That is to say, "I long for and yearn for You (Hashem)

like a man who craves the life of his soul."

And when I am weak and exhausted,

I long and yearn for my soul to revive me.

Likewise, when I go to sleep,

I long and yearn for my soul to return to me

when I wake up from my sleep.

The same way, I long and yearn

for the light of the Infinite One,

blessed is He,

the true Life of life,

to be drawn into me

through my occupation in Torah (study),

when I awaken from my sleep during the night.

For the Torah and the Holy One, blessed be He,

are one and the same.

Like the Zohar says (ibid.)

"A man is required,

out of love for the Holy One, blessed be He,

to rise each night

and exert himself in His service until the morning…"

**Immediately make an anchor by learning Torah;
read the following short paragraph from Tehillim:**

TEHILLIM, CHAPTER 117

**1: Praise the L-RD, all you nations;
give tribute to Him, all you peoples.**

**2: for great is His steadfast love toward us;
the faithfulness of the L-RD endures forever.
Praise the L-rd.**

א: הַלְלוּ אֶת ה' כָּל גּוֹיִם
שַׁבְּחוּהוּ כָּל הָאֻמִּים:

ב: כִּי גָבַר עָלֵינוּ חַסְדּוֹ
וֶאֱמֶת ה' לְעוֹלָם
הַלְלוּיָ-הּ:

THE FUNDAMENTALS   IN PRACTICE

MAKE FUNDAMENTALS PRACTICE YOUR HABIT
Pause 3x Daily

PAUSE #3: RACHAMIM - HAVE COMPASSION

Make the evaluation below. Give yourself a score of 1-10, 1 represents very little and 10 represents a lot. Notice that even if you score highly, since your *Giluy Elokus* (experience of Hashem in your life) is not in the entire world, then even what you have is not a revelation of the real essence of Hashem.

SCORE

- [ ] You feel warm and refreshed
- [ ] Mitzvos feel easy to do even when challenged
- [ ] You feel tranquil when you do things
- [ ] You feel pleasure in Torah study
- [ ] The atmosphere around you is refined
- [ ] You are a positive influence on others

Make an anchor by reading the following request to Hashem

וְתֶחֱזֶינָה עֵינֵינוּ בְּשׁוּבְךָ לְצִיּוֹן בְּרַחֲמִים

May our eyes see Your return to Zion with compassion.

You are asking that Hashem be revealed in the Jewish people as the verse says:

וְלֵאמֹר לְצִיּוֹן עַמִּי-אָתָּה:

Have said to Zion: You are My people! *Yeshayahu* 51:16

☞ WE NEED TO ASK

אז ניט קוקנדיק אויף די תפלות ובקשות וואס זיינען געווען ביז איצטער, דארף מען נאכאמאל און ווידעראמאל מתפלל זיין און בעטן בא דעם אויבערשטן "עד מתי".

That not looking at all the prayers and requests that have been until now, We need to again and again pray and ask Hashem "Until when?"

ספר השיחות ה'תשנ"א ש"פ דברים, שבת חזון ת"ב (נדחה) ע' 730

די איינציקע זאך אויף וואס מ'ווארט איז - אז א איד זאל געבן נאך א געשריי, מיט נאך א בקשה ותביעה און נאך א דערמאנונג:"עד מתי?!

The only thing we are waiting for is, that a Jew will give another shout, with another request and demand and another mention "Until when?"...

שם ע' 735

STRATEGY PAGE - YOUR ONE-PAGE SUMMARY

Go to the beginning of this guide book and notice every time you put a dot in the margin.

In the left column below, record all the key ideas to marked. In the right column, explain the big ideas and how they affect your life.

List the key ideas:	Explain how they affect your life:
_____	_____
_____	_____
_____	_____
_____	_____
_____	_____
_____	_____
_____	_____

THREE EASY HABITS I CAN IMPLEMENT RIGHT AWAY:

1. _____
2. _____
3. _____

When will I do them? _____
_____

How can I track them on a score sheet? _____
_____

BECOMING OUTWARD FACING

In the previous section, we learned how we naturally love life, and since Hashem is our life; it is natural to love Hashem.

We also learned that Hashem is the Life of life which we connect to when we learn Torah and do a Mitzvah.

Now we are going to learn that real love is not only about connecting; it is about giving.

In the beginning of the previous section we were centered on ourselves; now we make the center outside of ourselves.

Thinking of You

Loving someone means wanting what's best for them. Hashem loves us and has our best interests in mind, knowing what we need most and what experiences will be good for us.

We know we love our life, and recognizing that Hashem is the source of life means we also have a strong love for Hashem. A deeper level of love means taking the focus off what we need and thinking about Hashem. Our love becomes selfless, with the goal of bringing happiness to Hashem.

chapter 44
ליקוטי אמרים, פרק מד

The lighter areas represent the text of Tanya covered in this section translated on page 60.

126 ליקוטי אמרים

דהיינו להיות רגיל על לשונו וקולו לעורר כוונת לבו ומוחו להעמיק מחשבתו בחיי החיים א"ס ב"ה כי הוא אבינו ממש האמיתי ומקור חיינו ולעורר אליו האהבה כאהבת הבן אל האב · וכשירגיל עצמו כן תמיד הרי ההרגל נעשה טבע · ואף אם נדמה לו לכאורה שהוא כח דמיוני לא יחוש מאחר שהוא אמת לאמיתו מצד עצמו בבחי' אהבה מסותרת רק שתועלת יציאתה אל הגילוי כדי להביאה לידי מעשה שהוא עסק התורה והמצות שלומד ומקיים ע"י זה כדי לעשות נחת רוח לפניו ית' כבן העובד את אביו · ועל זה אמר מחשבה טובה הקב"ה מצרפה למעשה להיות גרפין לפרחא כנ"ל · והנחת רוח הוא כמשל שמחת המלך מבנו שבא אליו בצאתו מבית האסורים כנ"ל או להיות לו דירה בתחתונים כנ"ל והנה גם לבחי' נפשי אויתיך הנ"ל קרוב הדבר מאד להוציאה מההעלם אל הגילוי ע"י ההרגל תמיד בפיו ולבו שוין · אך אם אינו יכול להוציאה אל הגילוי בלבו אעפ"כ יכול לעסוק בתורה ומצות לשמן ע"י ציור ענין אהבה זו במחשבתו שבמוחו ומחשבה טובה הקב"ה מצרפה כו' : והנה ב' בחי' אהבות אלו אף שהן ירושה לנו מאבותינו וכמו טבע בנפשותינו וכן הוראה הכלולה בהן שהיא לירא מליפרד ח"ו ממקור חיינו ואבינו האמיתי ב"ה אעפ"כ אינן נקראות בשם דחילו ורחימו טבעיים אלא כשהן במוחו ומחשבתו לבד ותעלומות לבו ואז מקומן בי"ס דיצירה ולשם הן מעלות עמהן התורה והמצות הבאות מחמתן ובסיבתן · אבל כשהן בהתגלות לב נק' רעותא דלבא בזוהר ומקומן בי"ס דבריאה ולשם הן מעלות עמהן

TAKING / GIVING

👉 **1. DESCRIBE A TIME WHEN YOU DID SOMETHING BECAUSE YOU HAD THAT PERSON'S BEST INTEREST IN MIND, EVEN THOUGH IT WAS NOT SO COMFORTABLE FOR YOU PERSONALLY.**

_____

_____

👉 **2. DESCRIBE A TIME WHEN SOMEBODY GAVE OR DID SOMETHING THAT MEANT A LOT TO YOU AND HOW YOU FELT TOWARDS THAT PERSON.**

_____

_____

👉 **3. WHICH OF THE TWO LOVES ABOVE ARE MORE MATURE? EXPLAIN WHY.**

_____

_____

👉 **4. DO YOU NEED TO GO THROUGH A LESS MATURE LOVE TO BE ABLE TO UPGRADE TO A MORE MATURE LOVE? EXPLAIN WHY.**

_____

_____

👉 **5. WOULD YOU SAY THAT IF YOU JUMP TO THE MORE MATURE LOVE WITHOUT WORKING ON THE LESS MATURE LOVE, THEN THE LOVE WILL BE LESS AUTHENTIC?**

_____

☞ **6. EXPLAIN HOW YOU FELT WHEN YOU DID SOMETHING WITH THE OTHER PERSON'S BEST INTEREST IN MIND WITHOUT EXPECTING ANYTHING IN RETURN.**

_____

_____

☞ **7. EXPLAIN A TIME WHEN YOU DID SOMETHING TO GIVE SOMEBODY NACHAS AND YOU WERE NOT LOOKING FOR RECOGNITION FOR IT?**

_____

_____

☞ **8. EXPLAIN HOW IT FELT?**

_____

_____

Congratulations!
Now you know the five parts of the thinking strategy that fulfills this important Mitzvah.

Exercise 1

☞ **EXPLAIN ALL FIVE PARTS OF THE THINKING STRATEGY TO A FRIEND.**

Exercise 2

Do a Mitzvah now with the specific intention to give *nachas* to Hashem!

☞ **WHAT DID YOU DO?** _____

For example: Learn Torah, give a coin to *Tzedaka*, say a *kapital* Tehilim with specific intention to give Nachas to Hashem.

Did you do it? Now that you took action, you now know that you fulfilled the Mitzvah of Ahavas Hashem!

Quote from Tanya chapter 44

The benefit of bringing out (this love hidden in your heart)	שֶׁתּוֹעֶלֶת יְצִיאָתָהּ
to be revealed,	אֶל הַגִּילוּי
is in order to bring (the feeling) to (result in) practical action:	כְּדֵי לַהֲבִיאָהּ לִידֵי מַעֲשֶׂה
This is the occupation in Torah and Mitzvos	שֶׁהוּא עֵסֶק הַתּוֹרָה וְהַמִּצְוֹת
that you learn and fulfill	שֶׁלּוֹמֵד וּמְקַיֵּים
through this (the inspiration from this love).	עַל יְדֵי זֶה
With the intention to bring *nachas ruach* (satisfaction) before Him, blessed is He.	כְּדֵי לַעֲשׂוֹת נַחַת רוּחַ לְפָנָיו יִתְבָּרֵךְ
Like a son who wants to serve his father…	כְּבֵן הָעוֹבֵד אֶת אָבִיו...
And the *nachas ruach* (satisfaction) you give is	וְהַנַּחַת רוּחַ הוּא
like the metaphor of a king's happiness	כִּמְשַׁל שִׂמְחַת הַמֶּלֶךְ
when his son returned to him	מִבְּנוֹ שֶׁבָּא אֵלָיו
after leaving captivity.	בְּצֵאתוֹ מִבֵּית הָאֲסוּרִים

Think about a king who is overjoyed to have his son released from captivity and come home to him. This metaphor helps us focus on Hashem, and direct our love toward Him.

FROM THE SOURCE

נַחַת רוּחַ לְפָנַי, שֶׁאָמַרְתִּי וְנַעֲשָׂה רְצוֹנִי

(G-d says;) It gives me great satisfaction when I asked and my desire was done.

-RASHI SHEMOS 29:18

THE POWER OF NACHAS
HAYOM YOM, 8 KISLEV

Part of a person's regular meditations includes (this thought):	אַ מֶענְשׁ זָאל זִיךְ מִתְבּוֹנֵן זַיְין
How great is the kindness of the Creator to us personally.	וְוִי גְרוֹיס חַסְדֵי הַבּוֹרֵא בָּרוּךְ הוּא זַיְינֶען,
That the "smallest of the small,"	אַז אַזאַ קָטָן שֶׁבִּקְטַנִים
—as a person is—	וְוִי דֶער מֶענְשׁ אִיז,
Can cause great pride	קֶען עֶר מַאכֶען אַ נַחַת רוּחַ גָּדוֹל
for the "Greatest of the great" (Hashem)	צוּם גָּדוֹל הַגְּדוֹלִים
about whom it is written, "His greatness cannot be fathomed" (Tehillim 145:3).	וּכְמוֹ שֶׁכָּתוּב וְלִגְדוּלָתוֹ אֵין חֵקֶר,
Then, (after realizing this,) a person will always be	דַאךְ דֶער מֶענְשׁ זַיְין תָּמִיד
high-spirited	בַּאגַיְיסְטֶערְט
and do their service (of Hashem) with a motivated heart and spirit.	אוּן טָאן דִי עֲבוֹדָה בְּלֵב וָנֶפֶשׁ חֲפֵצָה

↘ KEY TERMS ↙

Revealed	גִּילּוּי
Action	מַעֲשֶׂה
Satisfaction	נַחַת רוּחַ
High-spirited	בַּאגַיְיסְטֶערְט

☞ KEEP ON LEARNING

The love described here is in the category of "love like water."[1] Just like water gives life to plants, this love gives life to your speech and action of Torah and mitzvos.

There is another form of love in the category of fire, explained in other chapters of Tanya. A person loves Hashem with a fiery passion, like a flame flickering upward, striving to connect to its source. And just like fire purifies metal, this kind of love purifies a person's character traits.

---

1 כסף אהבה כמים (תורה אור תצוה פד,א)

IMPLEMENTATION

How to make this Mitzvah part of your life.

In the previous sections, we learned the paradigm shifts necessary to fulfill this Mitzvah.

Now, we will learn how to implement the thinking strategy so it will be effective. We will also learn ways to make this Mitzvah part of our daily schedule so that we will fulfill this fundamental Mitzvah regularly.

Let's take it a level further and apply the information of the Tanya that we've learned until now. Through a practical thinking strategy, we'll learn how to initiate our Ahavas Hashem by making it a regular habit.

ליקוטי אמרים

דהיינו להיות רגיל על לשונו וקולו לעורר כוונת לבו ומוחו להעמיק מחשבתו בחיי החיים א"ס ב"ה כי הוא אבינו ממש האמיתי ומקור חיינו ולעורר אליו האהבה כאהבת הבן אל האב. וכשירגיל עצמו כן תמיד הרי ההרגל נעשה טבע. ואף אם נדמה לו לכאורה שהוא כח דמיוני לא יחוש מאחר שהוא אמת לאמיתו מצד עצמו בבחי' אהבה מסותרת רק שתועלת יציאתה אל הגילוי כדי להביאה לידי מעשה שהוא עסק התורה והמצות שלומד ומקיים ע"י זה כדי לעשות נחת רוח לפניו ית' כבן העובד את אביו. ועל זה אמרו מחשבה טובה הקב"ה מצרפה למעשה להיות גרפין לפרחא כנ"ל. והנחת רוח הוא כמשל שמחת המלך מבנו שבא אליו בצאתו מבית האסורים כנ"ל או להיות לו דירה בתחתונים כנ"ל והנה גם לבחי' נפשי אויתיך הנ"ל קרוב הדבר מאד להוציאה מההעלם אל הגילוי ע"י ההרגל תמיד בפיו ולבו שוין. אך אם אינו יכול להוציאה אל הגילוי בלבו אעפ"כ יכול לעסוק בתורה ומצות לשמן ע"י ציור ענין אהבה זו במחשבה שבמוחו ומחשבה טובה הקב"ה מצרפה כו': והנה ב' בחי' אהבות אלו אף שהן ירושה לנו מאבותינו וכמו טבע בנפשתינו וכן היראה הכלולה בהן שהיא לירא מליפרד ח"ו ממקור חיינו ואבינו האמיתי ב"ה אעפ"כ אינן נקראות בשם דחילו ורחימו טבעיים אלא כשהן במותו ומחשבתו לבד ותעלומות לבו ואז מקומן בי"ס דיצירה ולשם הן מעלות עמהן התורה והמצות הבאות מחמתן ובסיבתן. אבל כשהן בהתגלות לבו נק' רעותא דלבא בזוהר ומקומן בי"ס דבריאה ולשם הן מעלות עמהן

SCHEDULE THE MITZVAH

The Mitzvah of Ahavas Hashem is one of the Six Mitzvos *Temidios*, six Mitzvos that apply to all people in all places and at all times.

So we can't tell you to do this at any specific time to the exclusion to other times because it applies all the time. However, it is good to schedule specific times for this Mitzvah to ensure that you actually fulfill it.

The Alter Rebbe explains in Tanya chapter 44 that when Moshe Rabeinu said the words "בְּפִיךָ וּבִלְבָבְךָ - in your mouth and in your heart" in the *Pasuk* כִּי קָרוֹב (Devarim 30:14), he was saying that the ideas he just taught are to be "regular on your tongue and voice." In other words, when these ideas are regular on your tongue and voice, then you will reveal the love of Hashem that is already hidden in your heart.

There are various options regarding what to make

"Regular on your tongue and voice":

☛ **OPTION 1:** If you read and think about the *Pesukim* which speak about "כִּי הוּא חַיֶּיךָ" (Devarim 30:20)
Will you be fulfilling this Mitzvah? Yes!

14: Rather,[this] thing is very close to you; it is in your mouth and in your heart, so that you can fulfill it.	יד: כִּי קָרוֹב אֵלֶיךָ הַדָּבָר מְאֹד **בְּפִיךָ וּבִלְבָבְךָ** לַעֲשֹׂתוֹ:
15: Behold, I have set before you today life and good, and death and evil,	טו: רְאֵה נָתַתִּי לְפָנֶיךָ הַיּוֹם **אֶת הַחַיִּים וְאֶת הַטּוֹב** וְאֶת הַמָּוֶת וְאֶת הָרָע:
19: .....And choose life, so that you and your offspring will live;	יט: ....**וּבָחַרְתָּ בַּחַיִּים** לְמַעַן תִּחְיֶה אַתָּה וְזַרְעֶךָ:
20: To love the L-rd your G-d, to listen to His voice, and to cleave to Him. For that is your life and the length of your days...	כ: לְאַהֲבָה אֶת ה' אֱלֹקֶיךָ לִשְׁמֹעַ בְּקֹלוֹ וּלְדָבְקָה בוֹ **כִּי הוּא חַיֶּיךָ** וְאֹרֶךְ יָמֶיךָ....

👉 OPTION 2: If you read the *Pasuk* of נַפְשִׁי אִוִּיתִיךָ (My soul, I desire You - Yeshayahu 26:9) and think about what is means, will you fulfill the same Mitzvah? Yes!

👉 OPTION 3: If you read the Zohar that explains the Pasuk of נַפְשִׁי אִוִּיתִיךָ and think about it, will you fulfill the Mitzvah? Yes!

👉 OPTION 4: If you read the Tanya that explains the Zohar and think about it, will you fulfill the same Mitzvah? Yes!

👉 OPTION 5: If you verbally say the parts of the thinking strategy in your own words, or as explained in any *Maamar* would you fulfill the same Mitzvah. Also Yes!

👉 OPTION 6: If you think about how Hashem is your life etc and say words from the *Siddur* that express this idea, will you fulfill this Mitzvah? For sure! If you do not choose to do anything and do not make a regular time to do it, will you fulfill this Mitzvah? No.

We suggest practicing the part of Tanya that explains the Zohar printed in the first section of this unit, which is from Tanya chapter 44 (page 25), until you know it *Baal Peh*, no matter where you are or what time it is, you will be able to repeat the Tanya and remind yourself of the five points. Learning these few lines *Baal Peh* will equip you with the skills to do this Mitzvah anywhere and everywhere.

How can you exercise this regularly?

Schedule a specific time; otherwise, you might end up being busy with other things and won't get around to do it regularly.

Just like you have options regarding what to say you have options when to schedule it:

An opportune time to think and speak about this Mitzvah is before *Davening*.

You decide to think about these ideas before every *Tefillah*.

Another option is to say this thinking strategy before *Krias Shema* when going to sleep. This makes sense because it's a time when you anyway feel tired and recognize your natural love of life, and in extension, your love for Hashem, so it is an opportune time to practice this Mitzvah.

We suggest the exercise of repeating the Tanya quoted in Section One (page 25) before *Krias Shema She'al Hamitah*, however you can choose any option within the guidelines of the Tanya.

HOW CAN WE USE OUR ABILITIES TO FULFILL THIS MITZVAH?

Different people respond to different methods of learning. Some people have great sensitivity to sounds, while other people respond more to pictures.

In this section, you will see that the Alter Rebbe gives the option of fulfilling this Mitzvah by visualizing and picturing the metaphor explained in this chapter.

We want to use all the gifts that Hashem has given us for *Avodas* Hashem. Use your ability to visualize and picture the metaphor explained in this chapter of Tanya and fulfill the Mitzvah of Ahavas Hashem.

Exercise

Visualize how the scene would look when a king's only son would returns to his father the king after leaving jail. What would the expression on their faces look like?

☞ DESCRIBE:

_____

_____

_____

How does a person look like when he is exhausted, and what does he look like when he is revived and happy to be alive?

_____

_____

If you are skilled in physical activity, you can easily relate to the feeling of your body being tired, and then follow the 5 step thinking strategy to fulfill this Mitzvah.

You also have the ability to make sure that your strategy leads to *Maaseh BePoel*, practical action in Torah and Mitzvos, which is the real way to measure your success in doing this Mitzvah.

TIMELINE
TEACHINGS OVER TIME FOR THIS MITZVAH

Year	Event	Torah teachings related to this Ahava	Source
2448-2488	Moshe teaches Torah for 40 years until he passes away	וְאָהַבְתָּ, אֵת ה' אֱלֹקֶיךָ	Devarim 6:5
2488	Moshe teaches Sefer Devarim	כִּי קָרוֹב אֵלֶיךָ הַדָּבָר מְאֹד בְּפִיךָ וּבִלְבָבְךָ לַעֲשֹׂתוֹ	Devarim 30:14
2488	Moshe teaches Sefer Devarim	לְאַהֲבָה אֶת ה' אֱלֹקֶיךָ לִשְׁמֹעַ בְּקֹלוֹ וּלְדָבְקָה בוֹ **כִּי הוּא חַיֶּיךָ וְאֹרֶךְ יָמֶיךָ**	Devarim 30:20
Around 3150	Yeshayahu says Nevua	נַפְשִׁי אִוִּיתִךָ בַּלַּיְלָה	Yeshayahu 26:9
Around 4000	Rabbi Shimon Bar Yochai writes the Zohar HaKadosh	נַפְשִׁי אִוִּיתִיךָ... וְאָהַבְתָּ אֶת ה' אֱלֹקֶיךָ וְגוֹ' דְּיַרְחִים לֵיהּ לְקֻבָּ"ה רְחִימוּתָא דְנֶפֶשׁ מַמָּשׁ... צַפְרָא	Zohar 3 68a
5540-5550	The Alter Rebbe compiles the Tanya	וְהַיְינוּ מַה שֶּׁכָּתוּב בְּזֹהַר עַל פָּסוּק נַפְשִׁי אִוִּיתִיךָ	Tanya 44 page סג

> **Quote from Tanya chapter 44**

To take out	וּלְהוֹצִיא
this hidden love (that every Jew has)	אַהֲבָה זוֹ הַמְסוּתֶּרֶת
from its (current) hidden state to a revealed one,	מֵהַעֲלֵם וְהַסְתֵּר אֶל הַגִּילוּי
so that it will be revealed in your heart and mind	לִהְיוֹת בְּהִתְגַּלּוּת לִבּוֹ וּמוֹחוֹ
is not beyond you and is not far (from you).	לֹא נִפְלֵאת וְלֹא רְחוֹקָה הִיא
Rather, this thing is very close	**אֶלָּא קָרוֹב הַדָּבָר מְאֹד**
"In your mouth and in your heart,"	**בְּפִיךָ וּבִלְבָבְךָ**
meaning, to make this a regular activity	**דְּהַיְינוּ לִהְיוֹת רָגִיל**
on your tongue and voice	**עַל לְשׁוֹנוֹ וְקוֹלוֹ**
to arouse the concentration of your heart and mind,	**לְעוֹרֵר כַּוָּנַת לִבּוֹ וּמוֹחוֹ**
to deepen your thought	**לְהַעֲמִיק מַחֲשַׁבְתּוֹ**
regarding the Life of life, the Infinite One, blessed be He....	בְּחַיֵּי הַחַיִּים אֵין סוֹף בָּרוּךְ הוּא...
When you constantly train yourself in this way,	וּכְשֶׁיַּרְגִּיל עַצְמוֹ כֵּן תָּמִיד
the result of this training becomes natural in you.	הֲרֵי הַהֶרְגֵּל נַעֲשֶׂה טֶבַע
And even if it seems to you	וְאַף אִם נִדְמֶה לוֹ לִכְאוֹרָה
that this (experience)	שֶׁהוּא
is (coming from) your power of imagination,	כֹּחַ דִּמְיוֹנִי
do not worry,	לֹא יָחוּשׁ
because this (perhaps self-made) experience is aligned	מֵאַחַר שֶׁהוּא
with what is real and true on its own	אֱמֶת לַאֲמִיתּוֹ מִצַּד עַצְמוֹ

❖ KEY TERMS ❖

Love for Hashem hidden in your heart	אַהֲבָה הַמְסוּתֶּרֶת
In your mouth and in your heart	בְּפִיךָ וּבִלְבָבְךָ
To do regularly	רָגִיל
Power of your imagination	כֹּחַ דִּמְיוֹנִי
To awaken	לְעוֹרֵר
Visualization	צִיּוּר

> Quote from Tanya chapter 44

the hidden love (inside each Jew)...	בִּבְחִינַת אַהֲבָה מְסוּתֶּרֶת...
...regarding this love called "my Soul, I desire You" that was explained above,	...לִבְחִינַת נַפְשִׁי אִוִּיתִיךָ הַנִּזְכָּר לְעֵיל
this thing is very near to you	קָרוֹב הַדָּבָר מְאֹד
to bring it from concealment to revelation	לְהוֹצִיאָהּ מֵהֶעְלֵם אֶל הַגִּילוּי
through consistent practice	עַל יְדֵי הַהֶרְגֵּל תָּמִיד
where you align your words with (the feelings of) your heart.	בְּפִיו וְלִבּוֹ שָׁוִין
However if you are (still) unable	אַךְ אִם אֵינוֹ יָכוֹל
to reveal this love in your heart,	לְהוֹצִיאָהּ אֶל הַגִּילוּי בְּלִבּוֹ
you can still learn Torah and do Mitzvos with the correct intention	אַף-עַל-פִּי-כֵן יָכוֹל לַעֲסוֹק בַּתּוֹרָה וּמִצְוֹת לִשְׁמָן
through **visualizing the idea of this love**	עַל יְדֵי צִיּוּר עִנְיַן אַהֲבָה זוֹ
with thoughts that are in your mind,	בַּמַּחֲשָׁבָה שֶׁבְּמוֹחוֹ
and "A good thought (like this),	וּמַחֲשָׁבָה טוֹבָה
Hashem attaches to your good deeds..." (thus elevating them).	הַקָּדוֹשׁ בָּרוּךְ הוּא מְצָרְפָהּ כו'

↘ KEY TERMS ↙

A good thought .... מַחֲשָׁבָה טוֹבָה

Torah and Mitzvos done with the correct intention .... בַּתּוֹרָה וּמִצְוֹת לִשְׁמָן

Audible voice awakens attention* .... קוֹל מְעוֹרֵר הַכַּוָּנָה

Regular repetition becomes nature .... הֶרְגֵּל נַעֲשָׂה טֶבַע

Constant training .... הַהֶרְגֵּל תָּמִיד

FIND OUT MORE

ווען איינער הארעוועט ביגיעת בשר ויגיעת נפש אין א סוגיא...נאכדעם ווי דער ענין לייגט זיך ביי איהם גוט אפ, קוקט ער אויף דעם ענין ווי איינער קוקט אויף א דבר המצויר...בדוגמת דבר ווי א ציור הנראה לעינים.

ליקוטי דיבורים ח"א ע' קנז

איינע פון די זאכען וואס אנשי שלומנו ותלמידי התמימים שיחיו בעדארפען זיך מרגיל זיין, איז ציור

שם ע' 314

---

*This is the concept behind the prime strategy of revealing Ahava.

FROM THE SOURCE

כִּי קָרוֹב אֵלֶיךָ הַדָּבָר מְאֹד בְּפִיךָ וּבִלְבָבְךָ לַעֲשׂוֹתוֹ

It is very near to you, this thing, in your heart and in your mind, to fulfill it.

DEVARIM 30:14

מַחֲשָׁבָה טוֹבָה הַקָּדוֹשׁ בָּרוּךְ הוּא מְצָרְפָהּ לְמַעֲשֶׂה

A good intention Hashem joins with deed

TALMUD BAVLI, KIDDUSHIN 40a

☞ THE RESULTS

On the next page, when you read the 3 levels of fulfilling this Mitzvah, have in mind the following 4 points:

A) Which exercises did you choose to do; verbal, picturing, or both?

B) How often do you do it?

C) How does it affect you?

D) How does it affect your Torah and Mitzvos?

There are three levels in fulfilling this Mitzvah of this Ahava for Hashem:

1. צִיּוּר בְּמַחֲשָׁבָה שֶׁבְּמוֹחוֹ

Visualizing this love with your thoughts.

Without feeling anything, you still fulfill the Mitzvah of loving Hashem, and your Torah and Mitzvos are elevated as if you had actual feelings of love toward Hashem. מַחֲשָׁבָה טוֹבָה הַקָּדוֹשׁ בָּרוּךְ הוּא מְצָרְפָהּ לְמַעֲשֶׂה - "A good thought (like this), Hashem attaches to your good deeds."

2. מְעוֹרֵר הָאַהֲבָה לְגִילוּי עַל יְדֵי הַהֶרְגֵּל

Awakening love for Hashem through regular repetition

This process involves multiple senses working together simultaneously: speech, hearing, and thinking.

At this stage it is possible that this experience that comes from regular training, is created by your imagination and still needs Hashem to join your intention to your action so that your Torah and Mitzvos will be elevated. מַחֲשָׁבָה טוֹבָה הַקָּדוֹשׁ בָּרוּךְ הוּא מְצָרְפָהּ לְמַעֲשֶׂה - "A good thought (like this), Hashem attaches to your good deeds."

3. וְגִילוּי מַמָּשׁ

Actual revelation of love

Authentic enthusiasm for Hashem, previously hidden inside our hearts, is revealed and infused into Torah and Mitzvos.

A GOOD TIME

As the night wears on, and the hour gets later, we feel more and more tired. "My soul, I desire You (Hashem) at night…" teaches us that this is the perfect time to take a moment to reflect on our love for Hashem.

FIND OUT MORE

מ"מ הגהות והערות קצרות פרק מ"ד

RESULTS

WHAT RESULTS ARE YOU RESPONSIBLE FOR?

1. Are you responsible to do the strategies that reveal Ahava?
☞ YES/NO

Are you responsible to feel Ahava?
☞ YES/NO

Are you responsible to do the Mitzvos that Ahava leads to?
☞ YES/NO

2. After doing the strategies that lead to Ahava, you may end up feeling:

A. An authentic feeling of the real Ahava that was hidden in your heart.

B. A feeling created by your imagination which is not the authentic Ahava.

Will you be able to tell the difference?
☞ YES/NO

3. Does one still fulfill the Mitzvah if one only achieved B?
☞ YES/NO

Why?_____

4. What does Hashem do if you got B as a result?

_____

5. In which 2 situations does Hashem connect your thinking strategy to elevate your Mitzvos?

A) _____

B) _____

6. Which method always requires that Hashem connects your thinking strategy to your Mitzvos?

_____

7. What is the power of habit able to achieve more than visualization alone?

_____

8. If the feeling of Ahava happens by itself and you will not know if it is authentic, yet you still fulfill the Mitzvah by doing the strategy, why would it make sense to focus on the practical action that Ahava is supposed to enthuse. Explain?

_____

9. If a person thinks that they feel something, yet they do not do a practical Mitzvah to give Hashem *Nachas*, how authentic do you think their feeling is?

_____

10. What is the best way to measure your success?

_____

CONCLUSION

Be aware of what you feel, and let the feelings come by themselves. Ahava is really a gift from Hashem and feeling Ahava is not fully up to you. You are responsible for your part, so put your main attention **on what you can do!**

The Alter Rebbe explains that for a love of Hashem to become second nature, the feeling needs to be revealed regularly. Why not make Ahavas Hashem part of your nightly routine? Before *Shema*, say the words "נַפְשִׁי אִוִּיתִיךָ בַּלַּיְלָה" (My soul, I desire You) out loud, with conviction. Your voice will arouse your mind's intention, making *Kriyas Shema* more passionate. After a few weeks your enthusiasm for Hashem will become naturally revealed.

Chazal teach us אֵין חָכָם כְּבַעַל הַנִּסָּיוֹן—there is no wise man like the person who experiences something. You will only find out if you will feel enthusiasm or מַחֲשָׁבָה טוֹבָה (A good thought) once you practice this Mitzvah regularly.

כָּל עַצְמוֹתַי תֹּאמַרְנָה   תהילים 35:10

USE ALL YOUR ABILITIES TO SERVE HASHEM

Your mind has many abilities, and all are part of *Machshava* (thought).

1. Focus attention on goal (of learning Torah and doing Mitzvos)

When you think towards achieving a goal, like making sure your thinking strategy leads to practical action, this can be described as a high level of thinking, or thought within thought (*Machshava* within *Machshava*).

2. Hear the words you are saying

When you think about words you are saying, this can be described as speech within thought (*Dibbur* within *Machshava*).

3. Picture the metaphors - *Maaseh* within *Machshava*

When you actually picture this, it can be described as action within thought (*Maaseh* within *Machshava*).

    a) Feeling tired

    b) Feeling weak

    c) A king's happiness when his child returns

4. Become aware of your body's exhaustion (think about how you feel)

When you notice how you are feeling it can be called *Midos* within *Machshava*.

OUTCOMES

1. Fulfill the Mitzvah of Ahavas Hashem
2. Increase enthusiasm in Torah and Mitzvos
3. Elevate Torah and Mitzvos to the category of *lishma*
4. Cause Hashem satisfaction

A GOOD WAY TO DESCRIBE THIS LOVE

Ahava is translated "love", however a good way to describe it is "enthusiasm." This feeling comes from a spark of Hashem within you, as explained in Tanya chapters 18-24.

KEEP IT UP

Loving Hashem is not enough to strengthen ourselves against the *Yetzer Hara*. We also need to learn the skill of Yiras Hashem.

TWO WINGS OF A BIRD

Just like a bird cannot fly with one wing, authentic Ahava includes Yiras *Cheit*, and *Kabolas Ol Malchus Shamayim* requires the Ahava of כִּי הוּא חַיֶּיךָ ("for it is your life") so it will not be a burden, like we read in Shacharis: "מְקַבְּלִים עֲלֵיהֶם עֹל מַלְכוּת שָׁמַיִם .... בְּאַהֲבָה" ("They accept upon themselves the yoke of heaven with love").

POWER OF SIMCHA

Love is sometimes potent and at other times more hidden, resulting in varying degrees of enthusiasm in serving Hashem. Joy in doing a Mitzvah (שמחה של מצוה) causes the Ahava to be strong and stable.

FIND OUT MORE

במדת אהבה וחסד, בה נכלל גם כן מדת הגבורה ויראה - יראת-חטא.
שירא לנפשו שלא ליפרד מיחודו ואחדותו על ידי שום חטא ועון...
לקוטי תורה מסעי פח, ד

יקבל עליו עול מלכות שמים באהבה ורצון ולא יהיה העול עליו למשא,
כמו שכתוב "לאהבה את ד' אלקיך - כי הוא חייך."
שם פט, א

שינויים והנפילה מעבודת ה' מגדלות לקטנות גם הנפילה בתאוות שזהו ענין ועבדת את אויבך כ"ז הוא רק תחת אשר לא עבדת בשמחה כ"א בבחי' יש מי שאוהב ומשיג שהוא בחי' לגרמיה ומזה נמשך הנפילה כו' אבל ע"י השמחה בה' לא יהיו שינוים אלו
ליקוטי תורה תזריע כ, ג

Unit 1
NOTES

Educating and Teaching Others

In the section of Tanya which focuses on education of youth called חינוך קטן, the Alter Rebbe mentions that in a person's *Avoda* when they are adults there are ups and downs between one level and the next.

Between levels, a person will fall back and be inspired and motivated by the way they learned to love Hashem as a child.[1]

The Alter Rebbe explains that one of the enthusiasm strategies learnt while young is נַפְשִׁי אִוִּיתִיךָ[2] and he says that this is the reason the book of שער היחוד והאמונה is printed next, because a love like נַפְשִׁי אִוִּיתִיךָ is based on *Emuna*, and שער היחוד והאמונה will strengthen a person's *Emuna*.

The Alter Rebbe explains that this training which includes training someone in נַפְשִׁי אִוִּיתִיךָ, is part of the requirement of חינוך[3] which is a מצוה on its own, as explained in Shulchan Aruch Orach Chaim chapter 343.

When you practice the strategy yourself, you fulfill the מצות עשה of אהבת ה', and when you train someone else to do it, you fulfill מצות חינוך.

Feeling Fortunate

The difference between the thinking strategy described in Tanya and the one outlined in Hayom Yom is:

In Tanya, the focus is that your intention before and during learning Torah and doing Mitzvos is to cause satisfaction to Hashem and uses the power of visualization to enthuse the intention.

In the Hayom Yom, the focus is on how fortunate you are and how kind Hashem is to give you the opportunity to cause Him satisfaction.

The Hayom Yom is revealing the natural human attribute of reciprocity.

Wanting to cause satisfaction to someone in general is a uniquely human characteristic, one could likely say that this trait most probably stems from the deep need implanted in our soul to cause Hashem satisfaction. How fortunate we are and how kind Hashem is to give us this opportunity.

---

1. שהאדם נקרא מהלך ולא עומד וצריך לילך ממדרגה למדרגה ולא לעמוד במדרגה אחת לעולם ובין מדרגה למדרגה טרם שיגיע למדרגה עליונה ממנה הוא בבחי' נפילה ממדרג' הראשון' אך כי יפול לא יוטל כתיב...כי נשאר...מאהבה שנתחנך והורגל בה מנעוריו. (תניא - חינך קטן)

2. כשיתבונן היטב בעומקא דלבא בדברים המעוררים את האהבה לה' בלב כל ישראל. הן דרך כלל כי הוא חיינו ממש וכאשר האדם אוהב את נפשו וחייו. כן יאהב את ה' כאשר יתבונן וישים אל לבו כי ה' הוא נפשו האמיתית וחייו ממש כמ"ש בזהר ע"פ נפשי אויתיך וגו'. (שם)

3. ומצות החינוך היא ג"כ במ"ע כמ"ש בא"ח סימן שמ"ג. (שם)

This התבוננות helps you center yourself away from yourself even more.

The specific Ahava explained here is one that requires us to have the intention of giving Hashem *nachas*.

Think about it, when can you behave really selfless? When you first validate your self. Validate that you love life. Yes it is self centered, however once you recognize that ingrained trait you can then choose to go beyond yourself, choose to serve Hashem and in extension serving family, work and life mission in a healthy way. If you miss the first step, you may think you're selfless yet you build up resentment, and you are still not really intending to serve outside of yourself. Doing the third intention is really liberating when you experience it correctly and third in order.

They tell you on a plane, to put your oxygen mask first, and only then, help others.

Regarding Reciprocity

In unit 2 we will explain that just like service is an ingrained need and trait of a human being, so is reciprocity. As explained in Tanya 46-49, if somebody smiles you smile back; when somebody does you a favor you just want to do something for them.

That is why Hashem took us out of Egypt, so we can experience the power of reciprocity, and use it as a motivating basis of our service to Him. The entire Judaism is built on this base.

In the Hayom Yom, the Rebbe is using two human traits in one strategy. He is saying to meditate to evoke the human trait of reciprocity for the gift of opportunity to fulfill the other human trait of serving to give satisfaction to Hashem.

When a child brings a cup of water to a parent, the child fulfills a deep human need to give satisfaction to a parent. It's a deep need and the child needs it so much more than the parent needs the water.

The Rebbe is using the power of two human traits at once to help maintain a person's powerful enthusiasm in doing their *avoda*.

The Tanya is saying "what" to intend and uses a "visualization" to infuse emotion into the intention. Hayom Yom evokes "reciprocity" to infuse the emotion into the intention.

The difference between צִיּוּר Visualization, and דִמְיוֹן Imagination

צִיּוּר is a conscious visualization, where you know for sure that you have yet not tapped into your hidden love. You recognize that it is a visualization that is generated by your imagination.

דִמְיוֹן is like a mirage; you think it may be real however you suspect the experience is a mirage. Specifically because you are training regularly, you do experience some enthusiasm, however you suspect it is not the authentic experience of נַפְשִׁי אִוִּיתִיךָ rather the experience is created by your imagination and repetition. Even if the experience is not the authentic love and is your imagination, you still fulfill the Mitzvah and your training has truth to it because you do have an authentic hidden enthusiasm.

STRATEGY PAGE - YOUR ONE-PAGE SUMMARY

Go to the beginning of this guide book and notice every time you put a dot in the margin.

In the left column below, record all the key ideas to marked. In the right column, explain the big ideas and how they affect your life.

List the key ideas	Explain how they affect your life
_____	_____
_____	_____
_____	_____
_____	_____
_____	_____
_____	_____
_____	_____
_____	_____

THREE EASY HABITS I CAN IMPLEMENT RIGHT AWAY

1. _____
2. _____
3. _____

When will I do them? _____
_____

How can I track them on a score sheet? _____
_____

QUESTIONS BEFORE STARTING THE NEXT SECTION:

1. What is a *Chossid*?
2. What is *Chassidishkeit*?
3. What does a *Chossid* do that makes them different?
4. What is the difference between *Chassidishkeit* and *Yiddishkeit*?
5. What is the difference between Chabad and being a *Chossid*?
6. How are they connected?
7. Which type of Ahava helps bring Moshiach and why?

TANYA CHAPTER 44

BONUS PART

UNIT 1 / THE FIRST FIRST FIGHTING FORCE

HOW TO UPGRADE YOUR AHAVA TO THAT OF A REAL CHOSSID

Introduction

In sections 1-3, you have learned how to fulfill the fundamental Mitzvah of Ahavas Hashem and make it part of the regular regime of Mitzvos you perform daily.

The hidden love for Hashem that you already have in your heart comes from Avraham Avinu. In this section, you will learn how to upgrade the love of כִּי הוּא חַיֶּיךָ to a greater level of maturity and enthusiasm by connecting to the level of מֹשֶׁה רַבֵּינוּ inside of you.

ENTHUSIASM OF A CHOSSID

By connecting to the extension of מֹשֶׁה רַבֵּינוּ in each generation, our love for Hashem becomes enthused with a great power of בִּיטוּל and מְסִירַת נֶפֶשׁ resulting in enthusiasm expressing itself in your entire body, and spreading Torah and Mitzvos to others as well, to make the entire world a place where Hashem feels comfortable.

Chassidishkeit is about going beyond the letter of the law, doing what Hashem really deeply wants.

Revealing this love inside you will help you fulfill not only *Yiddishkeit* and *Chassidishkeit* as well.

The holy Zohar tells the story of various ways people serve Hashem. When the רַעֲיָא מְהֵימְנָא (the Shepherd of the generation) explained that he serves Hashem like a son who totally dedicates himself to save his mother and father from captivity even if it will cost him his life, the holy Zohar says that Hashem was so pleased with this response that Hashem kissed the רַעְיָא מְהֵימְנָא.

The Tanya in chapter 44 explains that we alone can not even achieve one thousandth of this level. We can, however, tap into some of it through our connection to the רַעְיָא מְהֵימְנָא.

The father and mother metaphors both refer to Hashem. The father is a metaphor for the level called Z"A or *Zeir Anpin* of the world of *Atzilus*, which is Hashem expressing Himself through His *Midos*, it refers to what Hashem really wants.

Mother, however, refers to the *Shechina*, the Divine presence of Hashem, it's Hashem speaking and creating our world.

Taking the mother and father out of captivity is about taking the *Shechina* out of *galus*. To connect Hashem speaking (*Shechina*) with what Hashem (*Kudsha Brich Hu*) really wants, i.e. to be openly revealed in the world and in our minds.

When we put effort and enthusiasm to spread Torah and Mitzvos wherever we are, we connect *Kudsha Brich Hu* to the *Shechina*. When an *aveira* is done Ch"V, it keeps the *Shechina* in *galus*, it remains in captivity inside our mind.

The Tanya Chapter 44 explains that with "regular attention," we will reveal the spark of רַעְיָא מְהֵימְנָא inside ourselves, empowering us with the motivation to accomplish our mission and overcome obstacles and temptations.

What is the meaning behind the son who puts himself in danger to save his mother and father? The Gemara (Nidah 17a) explains that a *Chossid* will put himself in definite detriment to even perhaps help another *Yid*. This is like a person condensing their personal time to study Torah in order to go out and do *Mivtzoyim* or to teach Torah to others.

Seemingly, when he goes out of the atmosphere of the *Yeshiva* and takes away from his own time to study Torah and goes out to do *mivtzoyim*, he puts himself in spiritual danger.

Even though a *chossid* will put themselves in spiritual danger for another, in reality, when one helps another their own heart and mind become refined a thousand times, meaning that what would take a thousand hours to achieve will now take one hour.

> **Quote from Tanya chapter 44**

And a greater love	וְאַהֲבָה רַבָּה
And more expansive than this	וּגְדוֹלָה מִזּוֹ
Which is also hidden within every soul of Israel	וְהִיא מְסוּתֶּרֶת גַּם כֵּן בְּכָל נֶפֶשׁ מִיִּשְׂרָאֵל
As an inheritance from our forefathers	בִּירוּשָׁה מֵאֲבוֹתֵינוּ
Is what is written in "Raya Mehemna"	הִיא מַה שֶּׁכָּתוּב בְּרַעֲיָא מְהֵימְנָא
"Like a son who exerts himself for his father and mother, whom he loves more than himself,	**כִּבְרָא דְּאִשְׁתַּדֵּל בָּתַר אֲבוֹי וְאִימֵּיהּ דְּרָחִים לוֹן יַתִּיר מִגַּרְמֵיהּ**
His *Nefesh*, *Ruach* etc.	**וְנַפְשֵׁיהּ וְרוּחֵיהּ כו'**
For "Do we not have One Father" (therefore we all can attain this love)	**כִּי הֲלֹא אָב אֶחָד לְכוּלָּנוּ.**

HOW DO YOU REVEAL IT?

The Tanya explains that you will reveal it using the same method as the first love.

☞ **YOU CAN ACTUALLY READ BOTH QUOTES OF TANYA ONE AFTER ANOTHER.**

Where does this enthusiasm come from?

> Quote from Tanya chapter 44

And although, who could possibly say that he,	וְאַף כִּי מִי הוּא זֶה וְאֵיזֶה
"has prepared his heart to come close to"	אֲשֶׁר עָרַב לִבּוֹ לָגֶשֶׁת
And attain even one thousandth of the level of love of the *Raya Mehemna* (faithful shepherd)	אֲפִילוּ חֵלֶק אֶחָד מִנֵּי אֶלֶף מִמַּדְרֵגַת אַהֲבַת רַעְיָא מְהֵימְנָא.
Nevertheless,	מִכָּל מָקוֹם
The very edge of (Vayikra 23:13)	הֲרֵי אֶפֶס קָצֵהוּ
And "remote whisper of " (Iyov 4:12)	וְשֶׁמֶץ מֶנְהוּ
(this love) shines in every generation to all Yisroel from Moshe's abundant good light	מֵרַב טוּבוֹ וְאוֹרוֹ מֵאִיר לִכְלָלוּת יִשְׂרָאֵל בְּכָל דּוֹר וָדוֹר
As is written in Tikunei Zohar (112a)	כְּמוֹ שֶׁכָּתוּב בַּתִּיקוּנִים
"An extension of him (Moshe) reaches	דְּאִתְפַּשְׁטוּתֵיהּ
into every single generation	בְּכָל דָּרָא וְדָרָא
to give (our souls) light"	לְאַנְהָרָא לוֹן וכו'
Only, this light is extremely hidden and covered up within the souls of all the house of Israel	רַק שֶׁהֶאָרָה זוֹ הִיא בִּבְחִינַת הֶסְתֵּר וְהֶעְלֵם גָּדוֹל בְּנַפְשׁוֹת כָּל בֵּית יִשְׂרָאֵל
And, to take out this hidden and concealed love to make it revealed	וּלְהוֹצִיא אַהֲבָה זוֹ הַמְסוּתֶּרֶת מֵהֶעְלֵם וְהֶסְתֵּר אֶל הַגִּילוּי
Palpably in your heart and mind	לִהְיוֹת בְּהִתְגַּלּוּת לִבּוֹ וּמוֹחוֹ
"It's not beyond you, nor is it far away" (Devarim 30:11)	לֹא נִפְלֵאת וְלֹא רְחוֹקָה הִיא
Rather "the thing is very much within reach for you, in your mouth and in your heart" (ibid.14)	אֶלָּא קָרוֹב הַדָּבָר מְאֹד בְּפִיךָ וּבִלְבָבְךָ
Namely, by regularly accustoming your mouth,	דְּהַיְינוּ לִהְיוֹת רָגִיל עַל לְשׁוֹנוֹ
With "audible vocalization" (that stimulates concentration-Shaloh HaKadosh Sukkah)	וְקוֹלוֹ

When you read the entire chapter 44 of Tanya, you will see that the method of בְּפִיךָ וּבִלְבָבְךָ will be effective to reveal both levels of enthusiasm explained in Tanya chapter 44.

EXERCISE

👉 DISCUSS THE FOLLOWING WITH A FRIEND

1. Is this a gift or a loan? What is the difference?

2. Does it need to be renewed? How often?

3. On whom can you recognize some of this enthusiasm from the רַעֲיָא מְהֵימְנָא?
   a) Working Professionals
   b) Teachers
   c) Shluchim
   d) Kollel students

4. How have you experienced it when you went on *Mivtzoyim*?

5. Does this enthusiasm transform your *Nefesh Habehamis*?

6. In addition to this enthusiasm, what key behavior is required to transform your *Nefesh Habehamis*? (Study *Chassidus* with effort and reflect on it)

7. How long does it take to reveal the enthusiasm of this section?

8. Discuss the difference between this enthusiasm and the earlier enthusiasm.

Notice how this enthusiasm spreads to the entire body, and all your body becomes involved.

👉 NOTE

Revealing Ahava *Rabba* has a connection with bringing the *Geulah Shleima*, as the famous *Sicha* in 28 Nissan 5751 says:

ויהי רצון שסוף כל סוף ימצאו עשרה מישראל ש"יתעקשו" שהם מוכרחים לפעול אצל הקב"ה, ובודאי יפעלו אצל הקב"ה - כמ"ש "כי עם קשה עורף הוא (למעליותא, ולכן) וסלחת לעווננו ולחטאתנו ונחלתנו" - להביא בפועל את הגאולה האמיתית והשלימה תיכף ומיד ממש.

"May there arise a new Divine will that finally there will be found ten Yidden who will be "stubborn" in that they feel it's imperative that they affect the Holy One Blessed be He, and for sure they will. As it is written "that they are a stiff necked people (this being a virtue, therefore) pardon our iniquity and our sin, and take us for Your own" Shmos 34:9 to actually bring the real and complete redemption immediately now!"

The meaning of עם קשה עורף ("stiff necked nation") is explained in Likutei Torah Bamidbar 88d.

"יֵשׁ לָהֶם אַהֲבָה-רַבָּה בְּטִבְעָם וְלָכֵן נִקְרָאִים "עַם קְשֵׁה עוֹרֶף"

"They have the great love hidden deeply in their nature, thats why they are called a stiff necked people."

In this unit, you have learned how to implement Tanya 44 and reveal not only Ahava of כי הוא חייך, rather a spark of אהבה רבה as well, to bring the *Geula Shleima*!

BASIC AHAVA

AHAVA TO HASHEM MADE SIMPLE

Meditate On Each Idea Below	Core Concepts
You love your life	כִּי הוּא חַיֶּיךָ
Hashem is unlimited life	חַיֵּי הַחַיִּים
Connect to unlimited life through Torah etc.	עֵסֶק הַתּוֹרָה
Intend to give Hashem Nachas	לַעֲשׂוֹת נַחַת רוּחַ

UPGRADED AHAVA

AHAVA OF MOSHE MADE SIMPLE

Act On Each Idea Below	Core Concepts
Connect to the Moshe	הִתְקַשְּׁרוּת
Look at the world from Hashem's perspective	דִּירָה בַּתַּחְתּוֹנִים
Do whatever it takes	כְּבָרָא דְאִשְׁתַּדֵּל

MAKE AHAVA 3-POINT TURN

Step One	Step Two	Step Three
Face IN	**Face OUT**	**Make 180 turn** Look at world from Hashem's perspective
Reveal love; You love life. Love Life of life Connect with Torah	Intent to give **Nachas**! Imagine son returning from jail	**Reveal upgraded love;** Like a son who loves parents **more than self**

Ahava is simple and easy to remember when you follow the three stages of;

1. **Face In** (explained in Unit 1, Part 1)
2. **Face Out** (explained in Unit 1 part 2)
3. **Make 180 Degree Turn** and look at the world from the perspective of Hashem.

Naturally, a Neshama does not want to be disconnected from Hashem and therefore wants to do Torah and Mitzvos, however, when you put effort to make the 180 degree turn and look at the world from the perspective of Hashem, then the Torah and Mitzvos that you do will be done with even more enthusiasm and attention.

Looking at the world from the perspective of Hashem is what a Rebbe naturally does and what a Chossid strives to do when connecting to a Rebbe. The 180 degree turn can also be termed "Commander's intent," when you understand the commander's intent the commands Mitzvos are done with the intention of fulfilling the goal of the commander.

The strategy is the way you will fulfill the goal and the tactics are what exactly you are going to do on a practical level. Tactics describes tasks and strategy describes the function of those tasks.

It is interesting that the English word for goal sounds similar to the Hebrew word *Geula*.

Your Service	Neshama's Intent	Commander's Intent
The Goal	To stay connected to Hashem	To stay connected to Hashem AND to make a Dirah BaTachtonim.
Strategy	To learn Torah and do Mitzvos	To learn Torah and do Mitzvos, AND to spread Torah and Mitzvos to the world
Tactics	Keep Dinim	Keep Dinim AND go beyond the letter of the law

EVALUATE YOUR PERSONAL PROGRESS

1. What is the most important thing you have learned so far?

2. What skills have you learned?

3. What specific things do you intend to do differently from now on?

4. Have your goals become enriched since you started this guide book? In what way?

5. How do you define love?

6. How do you practice the Mitzvah of loving Hashem?

7. Which specific type of love helps bring Moshiach?

☞ **COMPARE YOUR ANSWERS TO HOW YOU ANSWERED SIMILAR QUESTIONS EARLIER IN THIS GUIDE BOOK.**

WHERE IS YOUR CHABAD?

Chabad is an acronym referring to the three parts of your mind:

1. **Chochma** - Insight. This part of your mind is mainly situated on the right side of your brain. You can recognize it when you get a flash of an idea.

2. **Binah** - Understanding. This is mainly situated on the left side of your brain, and is the detailed thinking part of your mind. Countdown from ten and you will be using your *Binah* brain. Notice how thinking in detail has a calming effect.

3. **Daas** - Focus. This is mainly situated in the back of your brain, directly corresponding to your forehead. When you clear your mind of distractions and decide what to focus on, you are using *Daas*. Notice that when someone asks you a question and you do not know how to answer straight away, you will often pause for a moment. That pause is when your *Daas* is dominant.

WHEN DO YOU USE CHABAD?

Any time you study a subject matter successfully, you will use all three parts of Chabad.

WHY IS CHABAD IMPORTANT?

Our mind can only grasp what we experience with our senses. Since the Divine is abstract, we tend to relate to Hashem with belief and not with understanding.

Hashem asked us to relate to Him with understanding in addition to belief, as it is written:

וְיָדַעְתָּ הַיּוֹם וַהֲשֵׁבֹתָ אֶל לְבָבֶךָ כִּי ה' הוּא הָאֱלֹקִים בַּשָּׁמַיִם מִמַּעַל וְעַל הָאָרֶץ מִתָּחַת אֵין עוֹד:

Know therefore this day and keep in mind and place on your heart that the L-RD alone is G-d in heaven above and on earth below; there is no other.
(Devarim 4:39)

דַּע אֶת אֱלֹקֵי אָבִיךָ וְעָבְדֵהוּ בְּלֵב שָׁלֵם

Know the G-d of your father, and serve Him with single mind and fervent heart. (Divrei HaYamim 28:9)

What is more real to you, something that you believe or something that you understand?

But how can we understand the abstract? The answer is: because a metaphor is concrete, the mind is able to grasp the metaphor and understand the inner message.

For example:

Sunlight itself has many colors. However, when you lift a blue glass to the sunlight, the blue glass actually blocks the other colors and only lets the blue light through.

Similarly, Hashem is everywhere, yet He blocks the perception of most aspects of Himself and only allows us to perceive very specific aspects of Himself in various ways. For example, when we see a chair, Hashem is actually fully present around and in the chair. But in order to create the chair, Hashem covered all the infinite aspects of Himself that are not the chair and only revealed the limited aspects of Himself that allow us to see and experience the chair. The same idea applies to every creation. This metaphor illustrates how Hashem remains only One, yet at the same time He is the source of all the many things in our world.

The practice of understanding Hashem with metaphors was passed down throughout the generations from teacher to student. We are taught that King Shlomo had three thousand metaphors, yet today we have no known written record of them.

About a thousand years ago, the *Chovos HaLevavos* explained that traditionally people worked to understand Hashem as best as they could through analyzing the creations of Hashem.

This system can be understood through the metaphor of a bedroom. If you go into someone's room, even if you never actually met them, you can still understand a lot about them through the way they chose to arrange their room.

The father of the Jewish people, Avraham Avinu, analyzed nature around him to recognize Hashem using his understanding.

The Alter Rebbe, father of the Chabad movement, taught the *Pnimiyus HaTorah*, the hidden Torah, (also known as the soul of the Torah) in his works Tanya, *Torah Ohr* and *Likutei Torah*. In these works, he gave us multiple concrete metaphors so all people can actually understand Hashem.

Later *Maamarim* (*chassidic* discourses), that were taught by all of the seven Chabad leaders, usually explained and elaborated on a specific section of *Torah Ohr* or *Likutey Torah*. These works are called with the name *Chassidus*, derived from *Chessed*-kindness because by using this system one is kind to Hashem.

The reason why the Alter Rebbe compiled such a comprehensive system is to prepare the world for Moshiach, as the Rambam tells us:

וּבְאוֹתוֹ הַזְּמַן לֹא יִהְיֶה שָׁם לֹא רָעָב וְלֹא מִלְחָמָה. וְלֹא קִנְאָה וְתַחֲרוּת. שֶׁהַטּוֹבָה תִּהְיֶה מֻשְׁפַּעַת הַרְבֵּה. וְכָל הַמַּעֲדַנִּים מְצוּיִין כֶּעָפָר. וְלֹא יִהְיֶה עֵסֶק כָּל הָעוֹלָם אֶלָּא לָדַעַת אֶת ה' בִּלְבַד.

At that time there will be no famines and no wars, no envy and no competition. For the Good will be very abundant. All the delicacies will be as readily available as is dust. The world will only be engaged in knowing G-d. (Rambam, Mishneh Torah, Kings and Wars, 12:5)

WHAT IS THE FLAGSHIP TOOL OF CHABAD?

Hisbonenus (התבוננות) is the practice of using *Binah*, the left brain, to understand in detail.

The double "N" or " נ " in the word *Hisbonenus* hints that you go over each idea in your mind more than once. In English, *Hibonenus* means reflection.

Hisbonenus has been core to the practice of Judaism for thousands of years.

Like it is written:

וַהֲשֵׁבֹתָ אֶל לְבָבֶךָ...

Place on your heart... (Devarim 4:39)

Weakness in the practice of *Hisbonenus* leads to negative consequences, like it is written:

עַמִּי לֹא הִתְבּוֹנָן:

My people takes no thought. (Yeshayahu 1:3)

Anybody that practices *Hisbonenus* knows that it is not practiced in the order of Chabad, *Chochma*, *Binah*, *Daas*, rather in the order of *Binah*, *Daas*, *Chochma*. You study something in detail, then you focus on it, and then the flash of inspiration comes.

In fact, experience has shown than the best way to reach *Chochma* is through slight but not complete distraction.

Some explain that the reason for the need of a slight distraction is that the innermost part of *Daas*/focus needs time to focus on all the details. When your external focus is distracted, the inner *Daas* can function without interruption and the best insight - *Chochma*, comes by itself.

So if that's the case, why is Chabad not called *Badach*? Because once the insight flashes, it immediately goes to *Binah* to clarify it and to think of a way to anchor the insight in actual action and experience. Once the proper action is taken, you really know it, *Daas*.

So in fact, before insight, the order is *Binah*, *Daas*, *Chochma*, and when it is being implemented, the order is *Chochma*, *Binah*, *Daas*.

Without action to anchor the flash of insight, the flash will disappear. That is why Reb Hillel Paritcher practiced many *Hiddurim* in Mitzvos. With each *Hiddur* Mitzvah - actions that beautify a Mitzvah, he would anchor an insight of *Chochma*.

In fact, Reb Hillel would first do *Hisbonenus* on how to implement a concept even **before** he fully understood it. Reb Hillel imagined the key outcome and the desired end state based on the apparent theme of the *Maamar* Chassidus.

Better faster action based on amateur understanding than proper insight and delayed action.

So the best order is *Daas* (experience through action) and then *Binah* (study and reflection), then *Daas* (focus on meaning of words in *Tefilla*), *Chochma* (flash of insight during *Tefilla*), then *Bina* (how to implement), and finally *Daas* (implementation).

SUMMARY

Goal: To connect to Hashem in a real, internalized way

Strategy: Chabad

Tactics: *Hisbonenus*

Outcome / Desired End State: *Yirei Shamayim, Benoni,* Chossid, *Oved* Hashem

Notice how there can be more than one strategy to achieve a goal, and even more options of tactics to reach an outcome or desired end state. You can build your own tactics to achieve an outcome based on the fundamentals you learned in this guide book.

HOW TO BE A CHABADNIK TODAY?

Begin by learning some Chassidus and jotting down around seven specific details about what you learned in the *Maamar*. Writing is a technique that will help you use your *Binah* (thinking in detail) and Daas (focus), because writing will help you focus.

When learning the *Maamar*, locate a line in the Siddur that captures the core idea of the *Maamar* of Chassidus. Learn the translation of that verse and how its meaning hints to the ideas of the *Maamar* you studied.

Under regular circumstances, the only time a person can have an experience of the Divine is during prayer. The insight of Chochma can take place when saying the line that captures the core concept of the *Maamar* Chassidus.

Here are some tactical steps that will enable you to be a *Chabadnik* today:

1. **Study some Chassidus** (about 30 minutes).
2. **Write down** around 7 details about the *Maamar* Chassidus (5-10 minutes) BINAH, DAAS.
3. **Slightly distract yourself** through preparing for prayers (*Tzedaka, Mikvah* etc.).
4. **Read one line in the Siddur** and keep in mind the meaning that captures the core idea of the *Maamar* Chassidus (20 seconds). Perhaps now you will receive a flash of CHOCHMA; do not intend on it, just allow whatever happens to happen.
5. **Think and visualize** how to anchor the insight of *Chochma* in action, even if you did not get a flash of insight.
6. **Take action** (real *Daas*). Do something small and easy straight away.

A *Chabadnik* is like an iceberg in that most of an iceberg is hidden under the water and all that is apparent is the tip of the iceberg. So too, most of the practice of a *Chabadnik* is internal and not apparent to others; all that you see is some of the actions that he does.

That is perhaps why Chabad houses are famous mainly for the actions they facilitate in helping people.

THE FUNDAMENTALS

The goal of this guide book is to help you experience the most basic fundamentals. Even when you reach advanced levels of insight, you will constantly build on and practice fundamentals.

Hisbonenus using your Chabad is only one fundamental component. Actually, each path in serving Hashem has three parts:

1. Intellectual reflection - Chabad
2. Emotional commitment/preparation - *Chagas*
3. Practical Visualization (How) - *Nehi*

In fact, each section of the path also has its own intellectual, emotional and practical components. However, the dominant theme will be one of the three.

There is a saying that men think like waffles and women like spaghetti: men divide everything into separate compartments and women connect everything together like spaghetti. The reality is that there is truth to both approaches.

The fundamentals have distinct functions with specific outcomes and they are also interconnected.

Ahava, *Yirah* and *Rachamim* each have these three components. Additionally, the path of a Chossid which upgrades the three paths to another level also has the same three components.

In total, there are twelve general fundamentals. This guide book helps you experience specifically six of these fundamentals. This is enough to help you be effective.

It is important to become proficient in all areas: Intellectual reflection, emotional preparation, practical implementation and at least one fundamental, from each of the paths of *Ahava*, *Yirah*, *Rachamim* and Chossid.

AHAVA	YIRAH	RACHAMIM	CHOSSID
1. INTELLECTUAL	4. INTELLECTUAL	7. INTELLECTUAL	10. INTELLECTUAL
2. EMOTIONAL	5. EMOTIONAL	8. EMOTIONAL	11. EMOTIONAL
3. PRACTICAL	6. PRACTICAL	9. PRACTICAL	12. PRACTICAL

The above can be better understood with a metaphor of glass containers, some of which are wider on the bottom, and some are wider on the top. Each container represents the character traits of a person. The container that is wider on the bottom represents a person whose focus is practical action; his primary impact is in getting things done. The container which is larger on top represents a person whose contribution is largely intellectual; he guides other people. What is important is that all the vessels, no matter the shape, be filled to the top.

Some people need more action, others more understanding. What's important is that each person does all three completely according to their own personal capacity.

No matter the person's focal contribution, intellectual, emotional or practical action, everybody begins to fill their personal vessel from the bottom, which represents practical action. Even an intellectual person starts his connection to Hashem with some practical action.

WORKSHEET

Explain the following to the best of your ability:

1. Commander-in-chief's intent.

2. Goal

3. Strategy

4. Tactics

5. Outcome. Desired end state

6. How will you measure your success?

REFLECT ON THESE QUESTIONS BEFORE STARTING UNIT 2:

1. What does Chabad mean to you?

2. What is the flagship practice of Chabad, and in what order is it done?

3. How do you practice it and how often?

4. What is the goal of the flagship practice of Chabad?

5. What result comes from practicing it?

UNIT 2

THE SECOND FIGHTING FORCE
AN ARMY AGAINST THE YETZER HARA

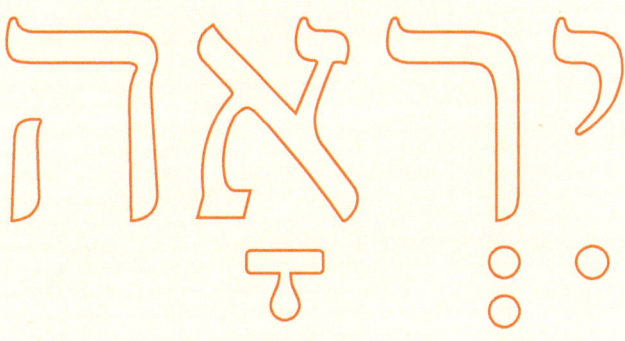

GOAL

The thinking strategy that reveals your inner Yiras Shamayim and power to take responsibility.

TANYA – CHAPTER 41
INTRODUCTION

The Mitzvah of Yiras Hashem

(RAMBAM)
MITZVAH 5

לְיִרְאָה מִמֶּנּוּ

FEAR HASHEM

אֶת-ה' אֱלֹהֶיךָ תִּירָא

(דברים י, כ)

You shall fear the L-rd your G-d

Fear Hashem.

How is it possible to keep Hashem's rules, enjoy them, and maintain this feeling constantly?

The Torah answers this question by explaining that the Mitzvah to fear Hashem, which will motivate you to keep the rules of the Torah, is fulfilled by thinking about Hashem in the way you will learn in this unit.

In the words of the Rambam:

> **FROM THE SOURCE**
>
> וְהֵיאַךְ הִיא הַדֶּרֶךְ לְאַהֲבָתוֹ וְיִרְאָתוֹ? בְּשָׁעָה שֶׁיִּתְבּוֹנֵן הָאָדָם בְּמַעֲשָׂיו וּבְרוּאָיו הַנִּפְלָאִים הַגְּדוֹלִים וְיִרְאֶה מֵהֶן חָכְמָתוֹ שֶׁאֵין לָהּ עֵרֶךְ וְלֹא קֵץ, מִיָּד הוּא אוֹהֵב וּמְשַׁבֵּחַ וּמְפָאֵר וּמִתְאַוֶּה תַּאֲוָה גְדוֹלָה לֵידַע הַשֵּׁם הַגָּדוֹל.
>
> What is the path [to attain] love and **fear** of Him? When a person **contemplates** His wondrous and great deeds and creations and appreciates His infinite wisdom that surpasses all comparison, he will immediately love, praise, and glorify [Him], yearning with tremendous desire to know [G-d's] great name.
>
> THE FOUNDATIONS OF TORAH CHAPTER 2:2

☞ SUMMARY

The Mitzvah to fear Hashem is a Mitzvah to make a time to think about things that will bring you to keep the rules of Hashem.

What do I fear when I fear Hashem?

The reason we like something is because deep down we "think" that this thing is good.

The way we think affects the way we feel because the mind naturally rules over the heart.

When you realize that someone put a lot of effort to do something good for you, you will probably feel some connection to this person and will naturally NOT want to do something that will break that connection or mess up the very thing that they did for you.

When you feel you have a personal relationship, you will want to live up to your responsibility. Not only does it motivate you to avoid doing something bad that will ruin the relationship; it gets you to keep **doing** your responsibilities in the relationship.

In this case, you are afraid of messing up the relationship. This fear is called יִרְאַת אֱלֹקִים ("Fear of the A-lmighty") in contrast to יִרְאַת חֵטְא ("Fear of sin"), in which you fear the negative effect of the sin itself.

What do I fear when I fear sin?

On the most basic level, a person who fears sin, fears the punishment that will come after doing the sin. In this case, the fear stems from his inner drive to protect himself; his focus is protecting himself and not the relationship.

After understanding that punishments of the Torah are not to cause harm G-d forbid to the person, rather for the purpose of cleansing the soul from the blemish caused to it by the sin, one's fear is on a more mature level. His fear is of the automatic negative result that is triggered by the sin.

You naturally possess a hidden Yiras Shamayim deep inside your heart, as an inheritance from the *Avos*, specifically Yitzchak Avinu. This hidden fear is revealed and activated to affect your actions through your connection to Moshe Rabeinu and his extension in every generation.

Activated Yiras Shamayim means that your desire to

maintain your Yiras Shamayim and not be a *Rasha* is stronger than any and every temptation you might feel. When you have activated Yiras Shamayim, your mind is calm and tranquil because your desire to keep this tranquil state overpowers the intensity of any urges to break the Torah rules.

The Hebrew name for Jerusalem, Yerushalayim, can be divided into two words: *Yirah* (fear) and *Shalem* (complete), hinting to complete fear of Hashem. Those who experience activated Yiras Shamayim could describe it as a feeling of completeness and confidence, when you know you are doing the right thing and you have no strong urges to do otherwise.

When a person G-d forbid stumbles and consciously does something against the Torah, it becomes impossible for him to feel Yiras Shamayim. He will have to do *Teshuvah* before he can get the Yiras Shamayim back with hard effort.

It turns out that when you fear sin, you fear the immediate loss of the Yiras Shamayim state. When a person loses his Yiras Shamayim, he becomes susceptible to receiving *Tuma* which will give him strong desires which may be very difficult to resist. They may be so strong that it feels like the person lost his gift of free choice, G-d forbid.

A person that loses his Yiras Shamayim becomes closer to an animal that only follows its impulses and programs.

In summary, the fear of sin itself is the fear of becoming a *rasha* immediately and all its negative immediate repercussions.

☞ ARE THERE A FEW TYPES OF YIRAS SHAMAYIM?

Tanya (ch. 43) explains that there is a lower fear (יִרְאָה תַּתָּאָה) and a higher fear (יִרְאָה עִילָאָה).

The lower fear (יִרְאָה תַּתָּאָה) itself is divided into two grades: basic (קַטְנוּת) and advanced (גַדְלוּת).

What is the difference between the basic and advanced levels?

It depends on how many details on the topic of "how the world is dependent on Hashem" you reflect on. The more you learn, the more details you incorporate into your thinking strategy to reveal, maintain and grow your Yiras Shamayim.

The higher fear (יִרְאָה עִילָאָה) is a much deeper recognition of reality than the two grades of יִרְאָה תַּתָּאָה, and it can only come to a person after first learning Torah and doing Mitzvos with אַהֲבָה and יִרְאָה תַּתָּאָה.

Tanya at a Glance

In the beginning of Tanya ch. 41, you will learn the skill how to fulfill the Mitzvah of Yiras Hashem, how to have reverence for Hashem.

It is crucial that you master this skill because Yiras Hashem is the beginning of your *Avodas* Hashem.

You are here

THE 53 CHAPTERS OF TANYA AT A GLANCE

MAKE FUNDAMENTALS PRACTICE YOUR HABIT
— *Pause 3x Daily* —

Make being a special warrior of Hashem part of you by committing to pause 3x while doing the easy thinking strategies learned in this guide.

Contribute to your safety and the safety of the Jewish people by practicing the fundamentals.

In the following fundamentals, make a commitment to guide what you stare at with your eyes, and Hashem will respond and protect you like a person protects their own eyes.

Your daily schedule may sometimes be hectic with the many things you want to do, as well as uncertainties and some surprises. So stop and Pause 3x daily to reconnect to your source of stability. See every situation as a Divine challenge to apply your fundamentals. Your mission gets chosen for you in the form of your personal situation, the fundamentals will empower you to respond to your situation in the most honorable way.

It's important to remember that you are part of a growing global community. These fundamentals have been a source of strength for the Jewish people for thousands of years. What's different now is that you are becoming empowered to access your inner spark through conscious thinking strategies rather than a Jewish soul gut reaction to severe challenge, like in past history.

The habit of Pause 3x daily opens you up to the opportunity of growth that was not so easily accessible to you before learning Soulwaze.

FUNDAMENTALS PRACTICE:

INSTRUCTIONS:

1. **Start with anchoring in action, give some money to Tzedaka.**
2. **Read from Tanya 41 (on the opposite page) quietly in your mind.**

Notice when the intellectual reflection leads into emotional commitment and when this becomes a visualization.

3. **Mentally list the four concepts in the intellectual part of this thinking strategy. These four points are listed right after the instructional part finishes in the Tanya quote itself.**
4. **Say the first line of the Shema when you are Mekabel Ol Machus Shamayim (indicated on the Tanya page).**

When you get to the end, visualize yourself in front of an important person, and then visualize yourself doing something different later today with the spirit of how you would behave in front of an important person. Envision doing something good or avoiding something or doing something better.

Imagine the feeling you are going to feel when you do this.

5. **Visualize yourself spending time with people who will encourage you and limiting your exposure to people who discourage you.**

Visualize yourself being a positive inspiration to someone else.

6. Visualize yourself changing something in your surroundings that will make it easier to do the good behavior or make it harder to do the bad behavior.

- Visualize yourself coming 5 min early to Maariv to pause and reveal Ahava.
- Visualize yourself coming 5 min early to Mincha to pause and reveal Yirah.
- Visualize yourself coming 5 min early to Shacharis to pause and arouse mental Rachamim

NOTE: When you take on something new, run it by your Rov/Mashpia

PAUSE #1: YIRAH - TAKE RESPONSIBILITY
FROM TANYA, CHAPTER 41

It is important to remind myself constantly

what actually is the beginning of service

and its core and (living) root.

Even though fear (of G-d) is the root of turning from evil

and love (is the root) of doing good,

nevertheless, it is not sufficient to awaken love alone

to do good

and it is important to first awaken

at least the natural fear

which is hidden in the heart of all of Israel

which leads one to refrain from rebelling

against the King of kings

the Holy One, blessed be He, as mentioned above,

that this awe be revealed in my heart

or at least in my mind.

This means to at least reflect in my thoughts,

the greatness of G-d A-lmighty

and His Kingship (rules)

which extend to all the words,

both higher and lower.

He fills all worlds

and is also in a higher dimesion in all worlds

as it is written

"Do I not fill heaven and earth?" (Yirmeyahu 23:24)

Yet, He leaves aside (the creatures of) the higher (worlds)

and (the creatures of) the lower (worlds)

and he uniquely bestows His Kingship

upon His people Israel, in general,

and upon me in particular,

for man is obligated to say

"For my sake the world is created" (Sanhedrin 4:5).

I, in turn,

accept His Kingship upon myself,

that He will be King over me,

to serve Him and do His Will

in all kinds of work required of a servant. **Say** שְׁמַע

And, behold, G-d is standing over him (me),"

and "The whole world is filled with His Glory,"

and He is watching you,

and is checking (my) innermost thoughts and feelings

that I serve Him properly.

Therefore, I serve in His Presence

with awe and fear

as I would, when standing before a King.

THE FUNDAMENTALS IN PRACTICE

MAKE FUNDAMENTALS PRACTICE YOUR HABIT
Pause 3x Daily

PAUSE #2: AHAVA - REVEAL ENTHUSIASM
FROM TANYA, CHAPTER 44

Read from "And this is what…" until "Do we not have One Father" out loud.

And this is what's written in the Zohar (Vol. 3, pg. 68a)

on the Pasuk (Yeshayahu 26:9)

"My soul, I desire You (Hashem) at night…"

(the Zohar says) "Love Hashem,

with the love for the soul and spirit

when they are attached to the body,

the body loves them (the soul and spirit)…"

(In other words,) this is what the verse,

"My soul, I desire You," is saying.

"Since You, G-d, are my true energy and life,

therefore I desire You."

That is to say, "I long for and yearn for You (Hashem)

like a man who craves the life of his soul."

And when I am weak and exhausted,

I long and yearn for my soul to revive me.

Likewise, when I go to sleep,

I long and yearn for my soul to return to me

when I wake up from my sleep.

The same way, I long and yearn

for the light of the Infinite One,

blessed is He,

the true Life of life,

to be drawn into me

through my occupation in Torah (study),

when I awaken from my sleep during the night.

For the Torah and the Holy One, blessed be He,

are one and the same.

Like the Zohar says (ibid.)

"A man is required,

out of love for the Holy One, blessed be He,

to rise each night

and exert himself in His service until the morning…"

UPGRADED AHAVA
FROM TANYA, CHAPTER 44

"Like a son who exerts himself

for his father and mother,

whom he loves

more than self,

his Nefesh, Ruach etc.

for "Do we not have One Father"?

Immediately make an anchor by learning Torah;
read the following short paragraph from Tehillim:

TEHILLIM, CHAPTER 117

1: Praise the L-RD, all you nations;
give tribute to Him, all you peoples.

א: הַלְלוּ אֶת ה' כָּל גּוֹיִם
שַׁבְּחוּהוּ כָּל הָאֻמִּים:

2: for great is His steadfast love toward us;
the faithfulness of the L-RD endures forever.
Praise the L-rd.

ב: כִּי גָבַר עָלֵינוּ חַסְדּוֹ
וֶאֱמֶת ה' לְעוֹלָם
הַלְלוּ-יָ-הּ:

PAUSE #3: RACHAMIM - HAVE COMPASSION

Make the following evaluation.
Notice that even if you score highly, since your *Giluy Elokus* (experience of Hashem in your life) is not in the entire world, then even what you have is not a revelation of the real essence of Hashem.

SCORE

- [ ] You feel warm and refreshed
- [ ] Mitzvos feel easy to do even when challenged
- [ ] You feel tranquil when you do things
- [ ] You feel pleasure in Torah study
- [ ] The atmosphere around you is refined
- [ ] You are a positive influence on others

Make an anchor by reading the following request to Hashem

וְתֶחֱזֶינָה עֵינֵינוּ בְּשׁוּבְךָ לְצִיּוֹן בְּרַחֲמִים
May our eyes see Your return to Zion with compassion.

You are asking that Hashem be revealed in the Jewish people as the verse says:
וְלֵאמֹר לְצִיּוֹן עַמִּי-אָתָּה:
Have said to Zion: You are My people! *Yeshayahu 51:16*

TANYA CHAPTER 41

UNIT 2 / THE SECOND FIGHTING FORCE

THE PARADIGM SHIFT

What you are about to learn is the beginning of *Avodas* Hashem.

What is Avodas Hashem?

Avoda means work and service. In Hebrew, the word עֲבוֹדָה (*Avoda*) has the same root as עִבּוּד עוֹרוֹת (*ibud oros*), which means transforming and improving raw hide into useful leather.

From the Hebrew meaning of the word עֲבוֹדָה we understand Hashem wants us to transform and improve ourselves and the world around us, like a tanner improves skin into leather.

The general need for service (*Avoda*) is deeply rooted in people. People intrinsically feel a need to serve and make improvement. All around, we see people serving one thing or another; for example, their job, hobby, health.

Hashem wants us to take our natural drive to serve and direct it only to Hashem, improving ourselves and the world in this direction. Everything we do ought to be incorporated in this service, in that we do it לְשֵׁם שָׁמַיִם (for Hashem's sake). Everything we experience is part of learning about Hashem, בְּכָל דְּרָכֶיךָ דָעֵהוּ (know Him in all your ways).

chapter 41

ליקוטי אמרים, פרק מא

The lighter areas represent the text of Tanya covered in this section translated on pages 114-115.

אינו מובן דמי שהוא צמא ומתאוה ללמוד פשיטא שילמוד מעצמו ולמה לו לנביא לצעוק עליו הוי וכמ"ש במ"א באריכות:

פרק מא ברם צריך להיות תמיד זכרון ראשית העבודה ועיקרה ושרשה. והוא כי אף שהיראה היא שרש לסור מרע והאהבה לעשה טוב. אעפ"כ לא די לעורר האהבה לבדה לעשה טוב ולפחות צריך לעורר תחלה היראה הטבעית המסותרת בלב כל ישראל שלא למרוד בממ"ה הקב"ה כנ"ל שתהא בהתגלות לבו או מוחו עכ"פ דהיינו להתבונן במחשבתו עכ"פ גדולת א"ס ב"ה ומלכותו אשר היא מלכות כל עולמים עליונים ותחתונים ואיהו ממלא כל עלמין וסובב כל עלמין וכמ"ש הלא את השמים ואת הארץ אני מלא ומניח העליונים ותחתונים ומיחד מלכותו על עמו ישראל בכלל ועליו בפרט כי חייב אדם לומר בשבילי נברא העולם והוא גם הוא מקבל עליו מלכותו להיות מלך עליו ולעבדו ולעשות רצונו בכל מיני עבודת עבד. והנה ה' נצב עליו ומלא כל הארץ כבודו ומביט עליו ובוחן כליות ולב אם עובד כראוי

112 ליקוטי אמרים

כראוי. ועל כן צריך לעבוד לפניו באימה וביראה כעומד לפני המלך ויעמיק במחשבה זו ויאריך בה כפי יכולת השגת מוחו ומחשבתו וכפי הפנאי שלו לפני עסק התורה או המצוה כמו לפני לבישת טלית ותפילין וגם יתבונן איך שאור אין סוף ב"ה הסובב כל עלמין וממלא כל עלמין הוא רצון העליון הוא מלובש באותיות וחכמת התורה או בציצית ותפילין אלו ובקריאתו או בלבישתו הוא ממשיך אורו ית' עליו דהיינו על חלק

THE THREE-PART CHALLENGE

THE CHALLENGE OF YIRAS SHAMAYIM HAS THREE PARTS;

ONE **Attaining** Yiras Shamayim has two parts;

1. **Asking Hashem for it;** asking for Divine compassion (רַחֲמִים) that Hashem should help you make the internal changes required for *Teshuvah* and Yiras Shamayim (this will be explained more in detail in Unit 3).
2. **Doing the thinking strategy** explained in Tanya ch. 41 so that you will merit that Hashem should give you the gift of Yiras Shamayim.

TWO **Maintaining** Yiras Shamayim is about keeping the thinking strategy in your short-term memory (לְזִכָּרוֹן תָּמִיד).

The difference between long-term and short-term memory is: Long-term memory contains things you understand, that are already part of you. Items in your short-term memory are things that you recently thought about.

Even if you understand the many details explained in this unit, these concepts alone will not help you maintain the gift of Yiras Shamayim. **It is important to think about these ideas daily** so that it's easy to remind yourself of them throughout the entire day.

THREE **Protecting** Yiras Shamayim is about **engaging in immediate combat on your borders.**

As soon as you recognize a thought from the *Yetzer Hara* entering in your mind, immediately **combat it by immersing in something else**. Do not talk and argue with the *Yetzer Hara*, rather immediately think of something else. As long as you still have Yiras Shamayim, the evil urge will not be so intense, and your desire to keep your Yiras Shamayim will overpower it. (What you can do is, in your thoughts scream at the *Yetzer Hara*, calling him a stupid *Rasha*, and immediately get busy with something productive.)

Being constantly busy with good things is a major skill in protecting your Yiras Shamayim.

It is important to be on guard when a thought comes from the *Yetzer Hara*. If you don't immediately start thinking about something else, and instead you G-d forbid consciously continue thinking about it, you are prone to losing your Yiras Shamayim. In such a case, you must go to back to stage one of attaining Yiras Shamayim; request Divine compassion (רַחֲמִים) and assistance to do *Teshuvah* and get your Yiras Shamayim back.

Imagine a border guard protecting a country from terrorists. Once a terrorist is inside the country, they are more difficult to remove. It is much better to **catch the terrorist by the border.** The terrorist may look cute and innocent, however, have no doubt that they want to kill someone. The terrorist may want to stay dormant for a while before they kill that person, or they may want to first do things that will weaken them and only then kill them.

Yiras Shamayim will help you keep the combat at your border, at the edge of your thoughts. Once the *Yetzer Hara* has infected a person's speech or action, it will be harder to deal with. The urges and bad habits will become more intense, and your thoughts may be so infected that your best course of action is to strengthen the areas which are straightforward to strengthen. This is your **power of physical action**. So just do a physical Mitzvah and then go to stage one; to attain Yiras Shamayim once again.

Yiras Shamayim will take effort, however, it is more straightforward that combating the *Yetzer Hara* in your thoughts, speech and action. When you have activated Yiras Shamayim, then your good speech and action will be easier to maintain, and it will be also easier to maintain healthy thoughts.

When the evil nation of *Amalek* attacked the Yidden when they left *Mitzrayim*, the *Pasuk* says that the *Yidden* were tired and not G-d fearing. This teaches us that **when we are weak and tired, we are susceptible to losing the gift of Yiras Shamayim.** It is important to constantly work on our *Simcha*, and when we are tired, we must make sure to do things that will give us extra protection.

REVEALING YIRAS SHAMAYIM

Discuss the following questions (you can look for clues by flipping later in this unit):

1. What four ideas are you supposed to think about to reveal your Yiras Shamayim?

☛ **ONE WORD ANSWERS:**

A_____

B_____

C_____

D_____

2. In the first page of Tanya ch. 41, by which words does the instructional section end and the thinking strategy start?

_____

_____

3. How would you divide this thinking strategy into 3 parts; A. Thinking; B. Emotional; C. Action?

☛ **WRITE THE BEGINNING AND END OF EACH SECTION:**

A_____

B_____

C_____

4. What two things do you need to do to attain Yiras Shamayim?

A_____

B_____

5. After you reveal your Yiras Shamayim, what two things must you do to keep it?

A_____

B_____

6. How will you know that you have revealed Yiras Shamayim?

_____

7. If you G-d forbid did something that is אָסוּר (prohibited according to Torah law), thus losing your gift of Yiras Shamayim, what must you immediately do?

_____

_____

_____

8. Discuss how the four ideas lead to action of Yiras Shamayim:

_____

_____

_____

> Quote from Tanya chapter 41

Tanya Chapter 41	תניא פרק מא
It is highly imperative to remind yourself constantly	בְּרַם צָרִיךְ לִהְיוֹת לְזִכָּרוֹן תָּמִיד
what actually is the beginning of service	רֵאשִׁית הָעֲבוֹדָה
and its core and (living) root.	וְעִיקָרָהּ וְשָׁרְשָׁהּ.
Even though fear (of G-d) is the root of turning from evil	וְהוּא כִּי אַף שֶׁהַיִּרְאָה הִיא שֹׁרֶשׁ לְסוּר מֵרָע
and love (is the root) of doing good,	וְהָאַהֲבָה לְוַעֲשֵׂה טוֹב.
nevertheless, it is not sufficient to awaken love alone	אַף עַל פִּי כֵן לֹא דַי לְעוֹרֵר הָאַהֲבָה לְבַדָּהּ
to do good	לְוַעֲשֵׂה טוֹב
and it is imperative to first awaken at least	וּלְפָחוֹת צָרִיךְ לְעוֹרֵר תְּחִלָּה
the natural fear which is hidden	הַיִּרְאָה הַטִּבְעִית הַמְסוּתֶּרֶת
in the heart of all of Israel	בְּלֵב כָּל יִשְׂרָאֵל
(which leads one) not to rebel against	שֶׁלֹּא לִמְרוֹד
the King of kings	בְּמֶלֶךְ מַלְכֵי הַמְּלָכִים
the Holy One, blessed be He, as mentioned above,	הַקָּדוֹשׁ בָּרוּךְ הוּא, כַּנִּזְכָּר לְעֵיל
that it should be revealed in your heart	שֶׁתְּהֵא בְּהִתְגַּלּוּת לִבּוֹ
or at least in your mind.	אוֹ מוֹחוֹ עַל כָּל פָּנִים
This means to reflect in your thoughts, at least,	דְּהַיְינוּ לְהִתְבּוֹנֵן בְּמַחֲשַׁבְתּוֹ עַל כָּל פָּנִים
the greatness of G-d A-lmighty	גְּדוּלַת אֵין סוֹף בָּרוּךְ הוּא
and His Kingship (rules) which extend to all the words,	וּמַלְכוּתוֹ אֲשֶׁר הִיא מַלְכוּת כָּל עוֹלָמִים
both higher and lower.	עֶלְיוֹנִים וְתַחְתּוֹנִים
He fills all worlds	וְאִיהוּ מְמַלֵּא כָּל עָלְמִין
and is around (everywhere) all words	וְסוֹבֵב כָּל עָלְמִין
as it is written	וּכְמוֹ שֶׁכָּתוּב
"Do I not fill heaven and earth?" (Yirmeyahu 23:24)	הֲלֹא אֶת הַשָּׁמַיִם וְאֶת הָאָרֶץ אֲנִי מָלֵא
Yet, He leaves aside (the creatures of) the higher (worlds)	וּמַנִּיחַ הָעֶלְיוֹנִים
and (the creatures of) the lower (worlds)	וְתַחְתּוֹנִים
and he uniquely bestows His Kingship	וּמְיַיחֵד מַלְכוּתוֹ
upon His people Israel, in general,	עַל עַמּוֹ יִשְׂרָאֵל בִּכְלָל

> Quote from Tanya chapter 41

וְעָלָיו בִּפְרָט	and upon you in particular,
כִּי חַיָּיב אָדָם לוֹמַר	for man is obligated to say
בִּשְׁבִילִי נִבְרָא הָעוֹלָם	"For my sake the world is created" (Sanhedrin 4:5).
וְהוּא גַם הוּא	You, in turn,
מְקַבֵּל עָלָיו מַלְכוּתוֹ	accept His Kingship upon yourself,
לִהְיוֹת מֶלֶךְ עָלַי	that He will be King over you,
וּלְעָבְדוֹ וְלַעֲשׂוֹת רְצוֹנוֹ	to serve Him and do His Will
בְּכָל מִינֵי עֲבוֹדַת עֶבֶד.	in all kinds of work required of a servant.
וְהִנֵּה ה' נִצָּב עָלָיו	And, behold, G-d is standing over him (you),"
וּמְלֹא כָל הָאָרֶץ כְּבוֹדוֹ	and "The whole world is filled with His Glory,"
וּמַבִּיט עָלָיו	and He is watching you,
וּבוֹחֵן כְּלָיוֹת וָלֵב	and is checking (your) innermost thoughts and feelings
אִם עוֹבְדוֹ כָּרָאוּי.	[to see] if you are serving Him properly.
וְעַל כֵּן צָרִיךְ	Therefore, you must
לַעֲבוֹד לְפָנָיו בְּאֵימָה וּבְיִרְאָה	serve in His Presence with awe and fear
כְּעוֹמֵד לִפְנֵי הַמֶּלֶךְ	as if you were standing before the King.

►KEY TERMS◄

Fear	יִרְאָה
Fear of Hashem, Reverence for Hashem	יִרְאַת ה'
Fear of the A-lmighty	יִרְאַת אֱ-לֹהִים
Fear of (the master of) heaven	יִרְאַת שָׁמַיִם
Fear of sin (breaking Torah rules)	יִרְאַת חֵטְא
Accepting the yoke (to focus your abilities)	קַבָּלַת עוֹל

FROM THE SOURCE

לְךָ ה' **הַגְדֻלָּה** וְהַגְּבוּרָה וְהַתִּפְאֶרֶת וְהַנֵּצַח וְהַהוֹד כִּי כֹל בַּשָּׁמַיִם וּבָאָרֶץ לְךָ ה' הַמַּמְלָכָה וְהַמִּתְנַשֵּׂא לְכֹל לְרֹאשׁ.

Yours, L-rd, is the greatness, the power, the splendor, the victory, and the glory, everything in the heaven and earth [is Yours]. Yours, L-rd, is the kingship and the exaltedness over all rulers.

DIVREI HAYAMIM I 29:11

לְךָ ה' הַגְדֻלָּה: זוֹ מַעֲשֵׂה בְרֵאשִׁית וְכֵן הוּא אוֹמֵר (איוב ט, י) עֹשֶׂה **גְדֹלוֹת** עַד אֵין חֵקֶר

Yours, L-rd, is the greatness; this is the act of creation, as it says (Iyov 9:10): **"Who does great things beyond comprehension."**

TALMUD, BRACHOS 58A

⇘ KEY TERMS ⇙

Taking off the yoke, (being unfocused and open to receive from many places) . . . פְּרִיקַת עוֹל

Service . . . . עֲבוֹדָה

To reflect in your mind . . . . לְהִתְבּוֹנֵן

Greatness (Kindness, Goodness) of the Unlimited One . . . . גְּדוּלַת אֵין סוֹף בָּרוּךְ הוּא

His kingship (Rules) . . . . מַלְכוּתוֹ

He fills all worlds . . . . מְמַלֵּא כָּל עָלְמִין

is around (everywhere) all words . . . . סוֹבֵב כָּל עָלְמִין

WHAT IS GEDULA (גְּדוּלָה)?
SHAAR HAYICHUD VEHAEMUNA CHAPTER 4

The meaning of "The Great (One)"	וּפֵירוּשׁ הַגָּדוֹל
refers to (G-d's) attribute of Kindness	הִיא מִדַּת חֶסֶד
and the spreading of the life-force into all the worlds	וְהִתְפַּשְּׁטוּת הַחַיּוּת בְּכָל הָעוֹלָמוֹת
and creations, without end or limit,	וּבְרוּאִים לְאֵין קֵץ וְתַכְלִית
so that they be created from nothing to something	לִהְיוֹת בְּרוּאִים מֵאַיִן לְיֵשׁ
and exist	וְקַיָּימִים
with unearned kindness.	בְּחֶסֶד חִנָּם
The reason it is called "greatness"	וְנִקְרֵאת גְּדוּלָה
is because it spreads from the Greatness	כִּי בָּאָה מִגְּדוּלָתוֹ
of the Holy One, blessed be He	שֶׁל הַקָּדוֹשׁ בָּרוּךְ הוּא
from Himself in all His glory,	בִּכְבוֹדוֹ וּבְעַצְמוֹ
for Hashem is Great	כִּי גָדוֹל ה'
and no one can fathom His greatness.	וְלִגְדוּלָתוֹ אֵין חֵקֶר
Therefore, He also gives life	וְלָכֵן מַשְׁפִּיעַ גַּם כֵּן חַיּוּת
and existence from nothing to something	וְהִתְהַוּוּת מֵאַיִן לְיֵשׁ
for the words and creations to no end	לְעוֹלָמוֹת וּבְרוּאִים אֵין קֵץ
for the nature of good is to do goodness.	שֶׁטֶּבַע הַטּוֹב לְהֵטִיב

◂ KEY TERMS ▸

Spreading	הִתְפַּשְּׁטוּת
Kindness without expecting a return / even if undeserving	חֶסֶד חִנָּם
From intangible to tangible / From abstract to concrete	מֵאַיִן לְיֵשׁ
Gives sustenance	מַשְׁפִּיעַ
Nature of good is to do goodness	טֶבַע הַטּוֹב לְהֵטִיב

LIKKUTEI TORAH, NASO 20D

And this is the idea of reflection	וְהוּא עִנְיַן הַהִתְבּוֹנְנוּת
on the Greatness of Hashem,	בִּגְדוּלַּת ה'
how all the worlds,	אֵיךְ שֶׁכָּל הָעוֹלָמוֹת כּוּלָם
(Including) the higher *Gan Eden*	גַּן עֵדֶן עֶלְיוֹן
and the lower *Gan Eden*,	וְתַחְתּוֹן
and also what will be in the seventh millennium	וְגַם מַה שֶּׁעָתִיד לִהְיוֹת בְּאֶלֶף הַשְּׁבִיעִי
in the time that will come…	לֶעָתִיד לָבוֹא…
all of them went up in one thought	כּוּלָם עָלוּ בְּמַחֲשָׁבָה א' לְבַד
before the essence of G-d,	קַמֵּי' עַצְמוּתוֹ יִתְבָּרֵךְ
like the statement,	וְכַמַּאֲמָר
"He looks and sees until the end of all generations." (Ritva Taanis 15a)	צוֹפֶה וּמַבִּיט עַד סוֹף כָּל הַדּוֹרוֹת
This seeing	וְהַבָּטָה זֹאת
is only with one (Divine) thought	בְּמַחֲשָׁבָה א' הִיא לְבַד
like it is written in Zohar and Midrash	כְּמוֹ שֶׁכָּתוּב בַּזֹּהַר וּבַמִּדְרָשׁ
that with one thought	דְּבְמַחֲשָׁבָה א'
the Holy One blessed be He created all the worlds.	בָּרָא הקב"ה כָּל הָעוֹלָמוֹת.

GADLUS MADE SIMPLE

Core Concepts	Key Terms
Creator	בּוֹרֵא
Goodness and kindness (without truly earning it)	חֶסֶד חִנָּם
All of history and creation is like one thought to Him	בְּמַחֲשָׁבָה א'

◣ KEY TERMS ◢

With one thought	בְּמַחֲשָׁבָה א'
Looks ahead	צוֹפֶה
Looks with concentration	מַבִּיט
Higher Gan Eden	גַּן עֵדֶן עֶלְיוֹן
Kingship, expression (Hashem speaking)	מַלְכוּת

WHAT IS MALCHUS (מַלְכוּת)?

Malchus refers to a number of concepts.

It refers to how Hashem:

- Makes the world with his speech;
- Supervises the world;
- Makes rules and laws.

Laws include the detailed laws of the Torah that involve every part of our daily life. It also includes the "laws" of nature, meaning how every object behaves and reacts. There are "laws" how feelings work and how they are triggered.

Every action of man has an outcome, even though you may not see it yet. If a melon is thrown out of a ten story building, perhaps for the moment it may seem that the melon has not been affected by the action. However, the melon will end up being affected unless another action is done to correct the situation, like setting up something to cushion the melon's fall.

If a person does an *aveira*, it may seem that the person did not change. However, the person has been affected with impurity (טוּמְאָה), as we will learn soon about *Ruach Shtus*.

Hashem created the world to be a king over it, a king can only rule on somebody separate from him, and a person can not be king over his sons. So if nothing is separate from Him, how can He rule as a king over us and the world? The answer is that Hashem dresses up in the "cloak" of Kingship and hides Himself so everything can seem like something separate. What motivates Hashem to keep on hiding Himself to make a world? It is us taking upon ourselves to keep His rules. It is you that keeps the rules of Hashem that causes the world to continue.

The above can be better understood with a metaphor of how a real king shows himself with royal clothes and the king does not put on these royal clothes alone.

The king's servants and personal attendants dress the king in the royal clothes. So too the royal clothes of Hashem is the Torah, Hashem reveals Himself through the Torah, and we through studying Torah and doing Mitzvos dress Hashem in His royal garments.

It's in the word מֶלֶךְ (King)

Mind מוֹחַ

Heart לֵב

Liver (Blood) כָּבֵד

When you use your parts in the correct order, i.e. the mind (מוֹחַ) rules over the feelings in your heart (לֵב) which then rules over your blood which enables you to do things, your blood is made in your liver (כָּבֵד), then you are a king (מֶלֶךְ) over yourself. If the order is reversed i.e. the body triggers your feelings and then your heart rules your mind, it spells כָּלֵם meaning shame.

MALCHUS
LIKKUTEI TORAH, SHELACH 48C

Hear and understand	שְׁמַע וְהָבֵן
how Hashem is One:	אֵיךְ שֵׁה' אֶחָד
Because everything before Him is as if it has no significance	דְּכוּלָּא קַמֵּיהּ כְּלָא חֲשִׁיב
and only "From His name and honor, His Kingship comes down to the world,"	וְרַק בָּרוּךְ שֵׁם כְּבוֹד מַלְכוּתוֹ לְעוֹלָם וָעֶד
meaning; only His blessed Kingship	שֶׁבְּחִינַת מַלְכוּתוֹ יִתְבָּרֵךְ לְבַד
gives life to the world.	מְחַיֶּה כָּל עוֹלָמוֹת

☞ QUESTIONS TO ASK

Find five places in *shacharis* ("morning prayers") that bring out גְּדוּלָה ("greatness") and מַלְכוּת ("kingship")?

How does thinking about מַלְכוּת and גְּדוּלָה lead to behaving with Yiras Shamayim?

MALCHUS MADE SIMPLE

Meditate on Each Idea	Core Concepts
The world is mades from His speech	מַלְכוּת דִּיבּוּר
He supervises the world in every detail	מַנְהִיג
He has rules and laws	דִּין דְּמַלְכוּת
My behavior maintains it	בִּשְׁבִילִי נִבְרָא הָעוֹלָם

THE PRINCIPLE OF TORAH

אמרי בינה הקדמה א, א

It says in Zohar Parhsas Teruma	ואמר בזהר תרומה
That this it the principal of the all the written and oral Torah	דדא כללא דכל אורייתא שבכתב ושבע"פ
The foundation of all the Mitzvos	יסוד כל המצות
This is the principal of uniting the Holy One Blessed be He and his Shechina	שהן רק יחוד **קוב"ה ושכינתיה**
This is the idea of two names of Hashem: Havaya and Elokim	שהוא ב' שמות ד**הוי' ואלקים**
As is known	כידוע
And this is what the Zohar calls	והוא הנקרא בזהר
surrounding and worlds and filling the worlds	**סוכ"ע וממכ"ע**
This is the idea of Shma Yisroel .. and the second line Baruch Shem.....	והיינו **שמע ישראל ובשכמל"ו**
These two ideas and the higher unity and lower unity as is known.	שנק' **יחו"ע ויח"ת** כידוע

☞ THESE DIFFERENT CONCEPTS ARE REALLY ONE

You may not have thought a lot about these concepts. However, the idea of how these things are really one, is the principle of all Torah and Mitzvos.

יחו"ע ויח"ת	שמע ישראל ובשכמל"ו	סוכ"ע וממכ"ע	הוי' ואלקים	קוב"ה ושכינתיה

In the following pages you will learn about

סוֹבֵב כָּל עָלְמִין and מְמַלֵּא כָּל עָלְמִין

And how to tell the difference between them.

WHAT IS מְמַלֵּא כָּל עָלְמִין ("HE FILLS ALL THE WORLDS")?

There are three general עָלְמִין (worlds)

- Beriah - בְּרִיאָה
- Yetzira - יְצִירָה
- Asiya - עֲשִׂיָּה

These three worlds are the;

- Thought - מַחֲשָׁבָה
- Speech - דִּיבּוּר
- Action - מַעֲשֶׂה

of Hashem.

Thought, speech and action are like garments. Just like a person changes and removes their garments, so too, they constantly switch their thoughts, speech and actions. You can't see Hashem, however, everything you can see are the "garments" of Hashem and Hashem is empowering them.

FROM THE SOURCE

הֲלֹא אֶת הַשָּׁמַיִם וְאֶת הָאָרֶץ אֲנִי מָלֵא
Do I not fill heaven and earth?

YIRMEYAHU 23:24

לֵית אֲתַר פָּנוּי מִנֵּיהּ
There is no place empty of Him

TIKKUNEI ZOHAR 123B:5

MAKING CONNECTIONS
קֶשֶׁר = דַעַת
MENTAL FOCUS = CONNECTION

Knowing or reflecting on details of the greatness of Hashem alone will not be enough to maintain your Yiras Shamayim. It is your דַעַת that maintains Yiras Shamayim.

How do you keep your דַעַת activated?

Below you will learn to make connections. They will help you maintain **דַעַת** and the key skill of "לְזִכָּרוֹן תָּמִיד" ("to always remember"), which is about constantly reminding yourself about ideas that bring you to have Yirah.

If you can only think about one thing at a time, how can you constantly be thinking about Yirah ("לְזִכָּרוֹן תָּמִיד"), and also get other things done?

The answer: Establish things that you will be exposed to throughout the day that will remind you about Hashem and Yiras Shamayim, e.g. a *Mezuzah*, *Tzitzis* etc.

Making a connection[1] between something in your environment to the ideas of Yirah can be called "making an anchor." Just like an anchor stops a ship from floating away, so too, "anchors" for your Yirah will protect it from leaving your consciousness.

---

1. שדעת הוא לשון התקשרות (תניא מ"ב)

There are multiple types of anchors:

Things that you **say**[2];

- Certain words in the *Siddur*
- *Brachos* that you say during the day

Things that you **do**;

- Wearing *Tzitzis*
- Stretching out your hand to touch a *Mezuzah*
- (They could be a Mitzvah, associated with a Mitzvah, or a *Hiddur* Mitzvah)

Things that you **see**;

- A *Sefer Torah*, *Mezuzah*, picture of a *Tzaddik*

There are also **advanced anchors**. These are things that on the outside don't look like they are associated with Yirah, however, once you have found a connection to Yirah, they become triggers that remind you of Yirah.

For example: Just like an artist and craftsman signs their artwork, so too, Hashem puts His name on everything He creates (e.g. underneath a human nose between the two nostrils and the sides of it, there is an upside-down ש from His holy name ש-ד-י). Once you have made the connection, then when you look at a nose, you will remember that you are actually looking at Hashem's signature. Then, every time you see a person's face, you will be reminded that the person is made by Hashem and it will trigger your Yiras Shamayim, helping you to treat the person with the proper respect they deserve as a creation of Hashem.

---

2. שתהא מחשבתו מקושרת בה' בקשר אמיץ וחזק כמו שהיא מקושרת בדבר גשמי שרואה בעיני בשר (תניא מ"ב)

Every time you learn Chassidus, try to find two anchors:

1. Look for a few words in the *siddur* that capture the concept. That way, every time you say those words in *Davening*, it will retrigger the idea in your mind.

2. Right after learning Chassidus, anchor the idea in action, in a Mitzvah, *Hiddur* Mitzvah, an act of kindness etc. That way, you connect the idea to the physical world.

"Anchoring" is about making and strengthening connections between ideas of Yirah and things that you will be exposed to during the day. "Triggering" is about making sure to expose yourself to multiple anchors that will remind you about Yirah.

Our World

We live in the world of *Asiya* (action), however, the other spiritual worlds are right here at the same time. How is this possible?

We can better understand this by using the example of the mathematical equation "one plus one equals two." There is no physical place you can point to where this equation exists. It exists everywhere, and at the same time, it is not in the physical domain.

Similarly, the higher worlds are right here and everywhere, although we can't see them with our physical eyes. Still, ideas from the higher worlds are hinted to, in physical changes in our world, and noticing these hints is part of advanced anchoring.

A few examples:

- Hashem put our nose right on top of our mouth. This way, if we mistakenly try to eat food that has spoiled, we will be able to smell it right before we put the poisonous food in our mouth. The physical design of the nose being attached right above the mouth reminds us of how much Hashem cares for our safety.

- The sun, moon and stars rise in the east and set in the west. As they move, they say *Shira* (praise) to Hashem and their movement is a bow to Hashem. When you look up at the sky, it becomes a trigger to remind you that just as they serve Hashem, it is also your duty to behave with Yiras Shamayim.

- A rose has thorns, which stop animals from eating the flowers, and allows the flowers to give off a good smell. In the higher worlds, this is the idea that being teased can make a person a stronger. Dovid HaMelech grew up with many people behaving very harshly towards him, yet those very experiences made him into a sweet smelling rose, shaping him into a great king. When you see the thorns of a rose, it triggers the idea that often unfortunate things make you stronger and that the experience comes from Hashem for your benefit.

It turns out, the more you learn, the more you can mature your Yirah by establishing anchors all around you to remind you of Yiras Hashem.

MAKING CONNECTIONS

TANYA CHAPTER 42

How to acquire Yirah and make a connection to what you see with your eyes.

The main point is to create a habit	הָעִיקָר הוּא הַהֶרְגֵּל
to constantly practice with your attention and thoughts	לְהַרְגִּיל דַּעְתּוֹ וּמַחֲשַׁבְתּוֹ תָּמִיד
that the following idea be constantly set in your heart and brain;	לִהְיוֹת קָבוּעַ בְּלִבּוֹ וּמוֹחוֹ תָּמִיד
All that you see with your eyes,	אֲשֶׁר כָּל מַה שֶׁרוֹאֶה בְּעֵינָיו
the skies, earth and everything that fills them,	הַשָּׁמַיִם וְהָאָרֶץ וּגְמלוֹאָהּ
are all the external clothes of the King	הַכֹּל הֵם לְבוּשִׁים הַחִיצוֹנִים שֶׁל הַמֶּלֶךְ
The Holy One, blessed be He.	הַקָּדוֹשׁ בָּרוּךְ הוּא
By doing so, you will always remember	וְעַל יְדֵי זֶה יִזְכּוֹר תָּמִיד
what is inside them and Who gives them life.	עַל פְּנִימִיּוּתָם וְחַיּוּתָם
This (thinking) practice is also hinted in the term	וְזֶה נִכְלָל גַּם כֵּן בִּלְשׁוֹן
Emunah (meaning training),	אֱמוּנָה
which implies doing something "regularly"	שֶׁהוּא לְשׁוֹן רְגִילוּת
training yourself	שֶׁמַּרְגִּיל הָאָדָם אֶת עַצְמוֹ
like a craftsman who trains his hands, etc.	כְּמוֹ אוּמָן הַמְאַמֵּן יָדָיו וְכוּ׳.

SEE THE WORDS

וּבְהַזְכִּירוֹ אֱ-לֹהִים, יְכַוֵּין שֶׁהוּא תַּקִּיף, בַּעַל הַיְכוֹלֶת, וּבַעַל הַכֹּחוֹת כֻּלָּם.

When you mention אֱ-לֹהִים *G-d A-lmighty (in a Bracha or Davening), focus on; that (1) He is strength, (2) He can do anything, and (3) rules over all powers.*

-SHULCHAN ARUCH MECHABER ORACH CHAIM 5:1

מְמַלֵּא כָּל עָלְמִין MADE SIMPLE

The Worlds	Hashem's Perspective	What you see[3]
World of בְּרִיאָה	Hashem's Thought	Includes: Torah (specifically Talmud), Laws of nature[4] etc..
World of יְצִירָה	Hashem's Speech	Includes: Feelings, Shape and appearance of everything etc..
World of עֲשִׂיָּה	Hashem's Action	Includes: The power of movement with the influence and contributions from the higher worlds.

---

3. שאו מרו' עניכ' בראי' גשמיי' וראו מי ברא אלה בגשמיו' התהוות' ליש גמור ממש בצמצו' היות' אחרון שבזה ממש שורה בבחי' א"ס דוקא (נר מצוה ותורה אור שער היחוד ז')

4. מיכאל שר של מים וגבריאל שר של אש (אגרת הקדש פרק י"ב)

👉 QUESTIONS TO ASK

Which word(s) in the Siddur hint to מְמַלֵּא כָּל עָלְמִין (He fills all the worlds)?

How does thinking about מְמַלֵּא כָּל עָלְמִין lead to behaving with Yiras Shamayim?

⤷ KEY TERMS ⤴

To make regular	לְהַרְגִּיל
Focus, concentration, deep knowing	דַּעַת
Connection, knot	קֶשֶׁר
His (your) eyes	עֵינָיו
Clothes	לְבוּשִׁים
Their inner part	פְּנִימִיּוּתָם
Language	לָשׁוֹן
Trained craftsman	אוּמָן
Belief / training	אֱמוּנָה
Master of all abilities, can do anything	בַּעַל הַיְכוֹלֶת
Master of all powers	בַּעַל הַכֹּחוֹת
Name of Hashem that focuses on His Divine ability to do anything	אֵ-ל

FIND OUT MORE

כי הנה המחשבה והדיבור שלמעלה הן בחינת 'ממלא כל עלמין'

לקוטי תורה דרושים ליוה"כ סט,א

עולם הבריאה עולם המחשבה בחי' עלמין סתימין.... ועולם היצירה עולם הדבור עלמין דאתגליין

נר מצוה ותורה אור שער היחוד קמה, ב

שבעולם הבריאה מאירות ומשפיעות שם חכמתו ובינתו ודעתו של א"ס ב"ה בבחי' צמצום עצום בכדי שיוכלו הנשמות והמלאכים שהם בעלי גבול ותכלית לקבל השפעה מבחי' חב"ד אלו ולכן נמשך משם התלמוד שהוא ג"כ בחי' חב"ד שהתלמוד הוא טעמי ההלכות על בוריין והטעמים הם בחי' חב"ד

ליקוטי אמרים פרק נב

הן הן הארת מדותיו של א"ס ב"ה בבחי' גילוי כמש"ל בשם התיקוני' דשית ספירן מקננין ביצירה

תניא שם

והצורה הוא כל ציור וכל תמונה במראה ושטח לכל דבר בדמותו בצלמו על איזה אופן נעשה כמו השמים והארץ הם כדורים ומן הארץ לרקיע כו' והשמש והירח הם גלגלים מאירים כו'.

תורה אור מקץ מא,ד

מעשה איז א שם התואר פון פועל. דער פועל פון וואס פאר א כח ער זאל ניט זיין צי פון מוחין חכמה בינה ודעת צי פון מדות אהבה און יראה חסד און גבורה, צי פון די כחות ראי' ושמיעה מחשבה און דיבור ווערט אנגערופען מעשה.

לקוטי דיבורים א' 206

כדור הארץ הלזו...דגלגל המזלות שנק' שמים משפיעים על הארץ שהיא כמו נקודת גרגיר חרדל באמצעית כו'...וזהו ומסדר את הכוכבים במשמרותיהם ברקיע כרצונו דווקא

דכל חלקי דצח"מ שבארץ מיוחדים ומובדלים זמ"ז כ"א לפי מקומו ושעתו שמקבל מהמזלות הסובבים עליו לפי הסדר הקבוע ומה שאנו רואים שינויי הטבעי' בכל פרט חלקי דצח"מ בכל אקלים מזמן לזמן הכל לפי אופן שינוי סדר מהלך הכוכבים ומזלות הסובבים שמה כי יש כוכבים ומזלות של חסד וטוב ויש של דין ורע בכלל... אין לך עשב שאין לו מזל המגדלו...וכן גם הדומם יש לו מזל מיוחד...וכן החלקי חי ומדבר מזל מחכים ומזל מעשיר ולהיפך כו'...וכן בשינוי טבעי המדות טוב ורע הכל תלוי במזל השופע...ומסדר את הכוכבים במשמרותיהם...שמקבלים שם הט' גלגלים מט' כלים חיצוני' והן שרשי הע"ש...והנה הארץ וכל אשר בה מחלקי דצח"מ נמשל לחומר בכלל ונעשה בה צורות שונות מטו"ר בחילופי' שונים תמיד מסבוב גלגל המזלות...ואמנם סיבת אופן שינוי סיבוב גלגל המזלות לפעמים כך ולפעמים כך זהו כרצון המאציל והבורא הכל וכמ"ש ומסדר כרצונו דוקא...וכמו גלגל היוצרים שהסיבוב שלו עושה הצורה בחומר כך סיבוב גלגל המזלות עושה אופן הצורה בחומר דצח"מ...ותלוי הכל במסבב וז"ש כחומר ביד היוצ' שממשיכים עליהם טוב או רע וכאנשי סדום שגרמו במעשיהם שיומשך עליהם הדין הקשה וכן כי לא שלם עון האמורי עד הנה וכך כל אקלים משתנה אופן קבלת שפעא מן השמים לפי אופן מעשיהם דוקא

כ"ק אדמו"ר האמצעי שערי תשובה שער הבחירה. ראה נתתי לפניך. יג"פ כ, א

WHAT IS סוֹבֵב כָּל עָלְמִין?
TANYA CHAPTER 48

The meaning (of *Sovev*) is not surrounding from the outside	אֵין הַפֵּירוּשׁ סוֹבֵב וּמַקִּיף מִלְמַעְלָה
in literal physical space, G-d forbid,	בִּבְחִינַת מָקוֹם חַס וְשָׁלוֹם
because you can't apply physical space to the domain of abstract spirituality.	כִּי לֹא שַׁיָּיךְ כְּלָל בְּחִינַת מָקוֹם בְּרוּחָנִיּוּת
Rather, the meaning of *Sovev* is that it is surrounding and higher	אֶלָּא רוֹצֶה לוֹמַר סוֹבֵב וּמַקִּיף מִלְמַעְלָה
regarding the way its sustenance is revealed.	לְעִנְיַן בְּחִינַת גִּילּוּי הַשְׁפָּעָה
Because sustenance that is revealed in the worlds	כִּי הַהַשְׁפָּעָה שֶׁהוּא בִּבְחִינַת גִּילּוּי בָּעוֹלָמוֹת
is called "enclothed,"	נִקְרֵאת בְּשֵׁם הַלְבָּשָׁה
for it clothes itself inside the worlds	שֶׁמִּתְלַבֶּשֶׁת בָּעוֹלָמוֹת
which clothe and grasp the sustenance	כִּי הֵם מַלְבִּישִׁים וּמַשִּׂיגִים הַהַשְׁפָּעָה
that they receive.	שֶׁמְּקַבְּלִים
In contrast to the sustenance that is not in a revealed state,	מַה שֶּׁאֵין כֵּן הַהַשְׁפָּעָה שֶׁאֵינָהּ בִּבְחִינַת גִּילּוּי
rather is concealed and hidden,	אֶלָּא בְּהֶסְתֵּר וְהֶעְלֵם
and the worlds don't grasp it.	וְאֵין הָעוֹלָמוֹת מַשִּׂיגִים אוֹתָהּ
This type of sustenance is not called "enclothed,"	אֵינָהּ נִקְרֵאת מִתְלַבֶּשֶׁת
rather it is called "hovering" and "surrounding"…	אֶלָּא מַקֶּפֶת וְסוֹבֶבֶת….
This can be brought closer to your intellect	וּלְקָרֵב אֶל הַשֵּׂכֶל יוֹתֵר
with a metaphor,	הוּא בְּדֶרֶךְ מָשָׁל.
like one who pictures in his mind	כְּמוֹ הָאָדָם שֶׁמְּצַיֵּיר בְּדַעְתּוֹ
something that he saw	אֵיזֶה דָּבָר שֶׁרָאָה
or that he sees.	אוֹ שֶׁרוֹאֶה
Even though the entire core body	הִנֵּה אַף שֶׁכָּל גּוּף עֶצֶם
of that object,	הַדָּבָר הַהוּא
outside, inside and deep inside,	וְגַבּוֹ וְתוֹכוֹ וְתוֹךְ תּוֹכוֹ
is all pictured in his mind and thoughts,	כּוּלּוֹ מְצוּיָּיר בְּדַעְתּוֹ וּמַחֲשַׁבְתּוֹ
because he saw the entire thing	מִפְּנֵי שֶׁרָאָהוּ כּוּלּוֹ

TANYA CHAPTER 48 (CONTINUED)

or he sees it now,	אוֹ שֶׁרוֹאֵהוּ
his mind is labeled as surrounding that entire object	הִנֵּה נִקְרֵאת דַּעְתּוֹ מַקֶּפֶת הַדָּבָר הַהוּא כֻּלּוֹ
and the object is enveloped by his mind and thoughts	וְהַדָּבָר הַהוּא מוּקָף בְּדַעְתּוֹ וּמַחֲשַׁבְתּוֹ
only that it is not enveloped in physical actuality	רַק שֶׁאֵינוֹ מוּקָף בְּפוֹעַל מַמָּשׁ
rather in the imagination of his mind and thoughts.	רַק בְּדִמְיוֹן מַחֲשֶׁבֶת הָאָדָם וְדַעְתּוֹ.
In contrast to the Holy One, Blessed be He, regarding whom it is written	אֲבָל הַקָּדוֹשׁ בָּרוּךְ הוּא דִּכְתִיב בֵּיהּ
"For My thoughts are not your thoughts etc."	כִּי לֹא מַחְשְׁבוֹתַי מַחְשְׁבוֹתֵיכֶם כו׳
His thoughts and knowledge	הֲרֵי מַחֲשַׁבְתּוֹ וְדַעְתּוֹ
with which He knows all the creations	שֶׁיּוֹדֵעַ כָּל הַנִּבְרָאִים
surround every single creation	מַקֶּפֶת כָּל נִבְרָא וְנִבְרָא
from its top to its bottom,	מֵרֹאשׁוֹ וְעַד תַּחְתִּיתוֹ
and its inside and deeper inside,	וְתוֹכוֹ וְתוֹךְ תּוֹכוֹ
everything is enveloped in real actuality.	הַכֹּל בְּפוֹעַל מַמָּשׁ.

👉 QUESTIONS TO ASK

Which word(s) in the Siddur hint to סוֹבֵב כָּל עָלְמִין?

Which things in nature that you can see with your eyes remind you of *Sovev*?

How does thinking about סוֹבֵב כָּל עָלְמִין lead to behaving with Yiras Shamayim?

◤ KEY TERMS ◢

Hashem speaking creating the world, to dwell .... שְׁכִינָה

Hashem how he is Holy – higher beyond the world and He is Blessed – down here. All at the same time .... הַקָּדוֹשׁ בָּרוּךְ הוּא

To reflect, to think over again .... הִתְבּוֹנְנוּת

SEFER MAAMARIM 5692-3 P. 41

Like the body of man	וּכְמוֹ בְּגוּף הָאָדָם
which weakens as time passes,	שֶׁבְּמֶשֶׁךְ הַזְּמַן נֶחְלָשׁ,
but regarding the hosts of the heavens (i.e., sun, moon & stars) it is not so,	וּבִצְבָא הַשָּׁמַיִם שֶׁאֵינוֹ כֵן,
from this is understood	הִנֵּה מִזֶּה מוּבָן
that an unlimited light and energy	דְּאוֹר וְחַיּוּת בִּלְתִּי בַּעַל גְּבוּל
is bringing them into existence from nothing.	מְחַיֶּה אוֹתָם מֵאַיִן לְיֵשׁ.
This is the meaning (of the verse) "The heavens tell over	וְזֶהוּ הַשָּׁמַיִם מְסַפְּרִים
the honor of G-d" (Tehillim 19:2),	כְּבוֹד אֵל (תהלים יט, ב),
And R' Yonasan's Aramaic translation explains this to mean	וּפֵירֵשׁ בְּתַרְגּוּם יוֹנָתָן
that when one looks at the sky,	דְּמִסְתַּכְּלִין בִּשְׁמַיָּא
they communicate the honor of Hashem.	מִשְׁתָּעִין יְקָרָא דַה',
The idea of looking at the sky	וּפֵירוּשׁ מִסְתַּכְּלִין בִּשְׁמַיָּא
means mentally reflecting on the hosts of the heaven.	הוּא עִנְיַן הַהִתְבּוֹנְנוּת בִּצְבָא הַשָּׁמַיִם,
They communicate the honor of Hashem,	מִשְׁתָּעִין יְקָרָא דַה'
which is "Kavod E-l" (mentioned in the above verse).	שֶׁהוּא בְּחִינַת כְּבוֹד אֵל,
Kavod is something that envelopes,	דְּכָבוֹד הוּא מַקִּיף*,
and it is the level of "Sovev" (Surrounding) all the worlds.	שֶׁהוּא בְּחִינַת סוֹבֵב כָּל עָלְמִין,
(Thus,) "The heavens tell over the honor of G-d" (means)	הַשָּׁמַיִם מְסַפְּרִים כְּבוֹד אֵל,
that by reflecting on the heavenly hosts,	דְּמֵהַהִתְבּוֹנְנוּת בִּצְבָא מַעְלָה,
we become aware of	הִנֵּה מִזֶּה אָנוּ יוֹדְעִים
"Kavod E-l,"	כְּבוֹד אֵל
the light that surrounds all the worlds.	שֶׁהוּא אוֹר הַסּוֹבֵב כָּל עָלְמִין.

KEY TERMS

Surround	סוֹבֵב
To envelope	מַקִּיף
Space (sometimes refers to Hashem who contains all space)	מָקוֹם

ON THE MEANING OF סוֹבֵב כָּל עָלְמִין
TANYA, IGERES HAKODESH, CH. 20

The existence and inner essence of the Infinite Light	מְצִיאוּתוֹ וּמַהוּתוֹ שֶׁל אוֹר הָאֵין סוֹף
is not in the realm of place at all,	אֵינוֹ בִּגְדֶר מָקוֹם כְּלָל
Rather it surrounds all the worlds equally.	וְסוֹבֵב כָּל עָלְמִין בְּשָׁוֶה
(It is written) "I fill the heavens and the earth"	וְאֶת הַשָּׁמַיִם וְאֶת הָאָרֶץ אֲנִי מָלֵא
equally everywhere.	בְּהַשְׁוָאָה אַחַת
There is no place that is void of Him,	וְלֵית אֲתַר פָּנוּי מִינֵיהּ
even in this physical world,	אַף בָּאָרֶץ הַלֵּזוּ הַגַּשְׁמִית
only that (this light) envelops and surrounds….	רַק שֶׁהוּא בִּבְחִינַת מַקִּיף וְסוֹבֵב….
To sprout greenery, trees and fruits	לְהַצְמִיחַ עֲשָׂבִים וְאִילָנוֹת וּפֵירוֹת
Constantly from non existence to existence, year by year,	מֵאַיִן לְיֵשׁ תָּמִיד מִדֵּי שָׁנָה בְּשָׁנָה
this occurrence is a taste of being limitless,	שֶׁהוּא מֵעֵין בְּחִינַת אֵין סוֹף
for if the world were to exist many tens of thousands of years,	שֶׁאִם יִתְקַיֵּים עוֹלָם הַזֶּה רִיבּוּי רְבָבוֹת שָׁנִים
they would sprout year by year…	יַצְמִיחוּ מִדֵּי שָׁנָה בְּשָׁנָה…
After these evident true words,	וְאַחֲרֵי הַדְּבָרִים וְהָאֱמֶת הָאֵלֶּה
it becomes easy to understand	דַּעַת לְנָבוֹן נָקֵל לְהָבִין
through everything mentioned above,	עַל יְדֵי כָּל הַנִּזְכָּר לְעֵיל
the great value of physical commandments	גּוֹדֶל מַעֲלַת הַמִּצְוֹת מַעֲשִׂיּוֹת
which are the purpose of the souls' descent this physical world,	אֲשֶׁר הֵן תַּכְלִית יְרִידַת הַנְּשָׁמוֹת לָעוֹלָם הַזֶּה הַגַּשְׁמִי
as it is written,	כְּמוֹ שֶׁכָּתוּב
"Today (in this world, the mission is to actually) do them (the Mitzvos)."	הַיּוֹם לַעֲשׂוֹתָם

KEY TERMS

Above	לְמַעְלָה
Revealed	גִּילּוּי
To hide, to "store" in hiding	הֶסְתֵּר
To grasp with the mind	מַשִּׂיג

👉 SUMMARY

Sovev

- It's like an object in your mind is surrounded by your mind and your mind has unlimited power to change the object in your mind.

- You can see a hint of it in the apparent limitless energy of the sun and stars as they rise and shine every day consistently.

- You can see a hint of it in the apparent limitless power of the physical earth to produce crops year after year.

- Just like some of Hashem's limitless power is hidden in the lowest elements of the physical world, Hashem's limitless power is inside physical Mitzvos.

↖ KEY TERMS ↘

Metaphor	מָשָׁל
Body	גּוּף
Creator	בּוֹרֵא
Manager, driver	מַנְהִיג
Core, essence	עֶצֶם
Inner part	תּוֹכוֹ
In actuality	בְּפוֹעַל מַמָּשׁ
Without any limits	בִּלְתִּי בַּעַל גְּבוּל
Honor (can refer to סוֹבֵב כָּל עָלְמִין)	כָּבוֹד, יְקָרָא
To gaze with concentration	מִסְתַּכְּלִין
There is no place empty of Him	לֵית אֲתַר פָּנוּי מִנֵּיהּ
This world	עוֹלָם הַזֶּה
Physical	גַּשְׁמִי

SOVEV MADE SIMPLE

Meditate on Each Idea	Core Concepts
Creation is like an idea surrounded in the mind, the mind can to anything to the idea	דִּמְיוֹן מַחֲשֶׁבֶת הָאָדָם וְדַעְתּוֹ
Limitless power of sun and stars	הַשָּׁמַיִם מְסַפְּרִים כְּבוֹד אֵ-ל
Limitless power of growth	יַצְמִיחוּ מִדֵּי שָׁנָה בְּשָׁנָה
Value of physical Mitzvos	גּוֹדֶל מַעֲלַת הַמִּצְוֹת מַעֲשִׂיּוֹת

REFLECTION FOR YIRAH MADE SIMPLE

Number	Name	Meditate on	Core ideas
ONE	גַּדְלוּת	The Creator	בּוֹרֵא
TWO	מַלְכוּת	Personally supervises	מַנְהִיג
THREE	מְמַלֵּא	Everywhere	כּוֹחֵנוּ וְחַיּוּתֵנוּ Actual Power Hashem is your power and life
FOUR	סוֹבֵב	His unlimited potential is here helping you!	הקב"ה Potential

LIKKUTEI TORAH, VAESCHANAN 8A

When you reflect	וְכַאֲשֶׁר יִתְבּוֹנֵן הָאָדָם
that Hashem, who surrounds all the worlds,	כִּי הוי' הַסּוֹבֵב כָּל עָלְמִין
is really standing with you,	נִצָּב עָלָיו מַמָּשׁ
for He is revealed below just as He is revealed above,	שֶׁהוּא לְמַטָּה כְּמוֹ לְמַעְלָה
this will lead you to	אֲזַי תִּפּוֹל עָלָיו
an awe and fear,	אֵימָה וָפַחַד
a feeling of embarrassment towards Him.	יִרְאָה בּוֹשֶׁת

☞ THE RESULTS

When you realize that Hashem Himself is with you, helping you keep His rules, it will inspire and motivate you to keep the rules.

EXERCISE

HOW TO DO HISBONENUS (הִתְבּוֹנְנוּת)

☞ **THERE ARE TWO QUESTIONS TO KEEP IN MIND WHEN DOING HISBONENUS:**

A. How are two ideas about the same concept different?

B. How are they the same (what is the common thread or connection)?

☞ **DISCUSS THE DIFFERENCE** between the quote from Tanya Shaar HaYichud VeHaEmuna (ch. 4 on pg. 75) and Likkutei Torah (Parshas Naso 20d on pg. 76) regarding גְּדוּלָה.

1. What is the connection and common denominator between them?

   _____

   _____

2. If *Gedulah* (גְּדוּלָה) means kindness, why doesn't the *Pasuk* use the term *Chessed* (חֶסֶד)?

   _____

   _____

☞ **THINK ABOUT GEDULAH**

3. How does thinking about גְּדוּלָה lead to acting with Yiras Shamayim?

   _____

   _____

4. Since יִרְאָה is connected with גְּבוּרָה (strength), wouldn't it be more appropriate to reflect on the גְּבוּרָה of Hashem? Why do we specifically reflect on גְּדוּלָה to reveal Yiras Shamayim?

   _____

   _____

👉 REFLECT ON MALCHUS

5. How does reflecting on the מַלְכוּת of Hashem lead to acting in a Yiras Shamayim way?

   _____
   _____

6. Why is keeping the rules of Hashem important to you?

   _____
   _____

7. Why is keeping the rules of Hashem important to the world?

   _____
   _____

8. What negative thing happens to a person when they don't keep the rules?

   _____
   _____

מְמַלֵּא כָּל עָלְמִין THINK ABOUT 👉

9. What does מְמַלֵּא כָּל עָלְמִין refer to?

   _____
   _____

10. How does thinking about this lead to behaviors of Yiras Shamayim?

    _____
    _____

HOW TO DO HISBONENUS (CONTINUED)

👉 ANCHORS & TRIGGERS FOR YIRAS SHAMAYIM

11. Explain the difference between how we explained anchoring and triggering.

   _____

   _____

12. Explain how advanced anchoring enhances Yiras Shamayim?

   _____

   _____

13. List as many Yiras Shamayim triggers, include many different types.

   _____

   _____

14. Explain how you made an advanced anchor for Yiras Shamayim.

   _____

   _____

👉 THINK ABOUT סוֹבֵב כָּל עָלְמִין

15. What are the three explanations for סוֹבֵב כָּל עָלְמִין in this unit?

   A. _____

   _____

   B. _____

   _____

   C. _____

   _____

16. What is the common thread in these three explanations?

_____

_____

17. How does thinking about סוֹבֵב כָּל עָלְמִין lead to behaving with Yiras Shamayim?

_____

_____

18. How does thinking about סוֹבֵב כָּל עָלְמִין lead to doing Mitzvos?

_____

_____

👉 WRAP IT UP

19. Look in **Reflection for Yirah Made Simple** (page 139) and list and describe ideas connected with:

גַּדְלוּת _____

_____

מַלְכוּת _____

_____

מְמַלֵּא _____

_____

סוֹבֵב _____

_____

STRATEGY PAGE - YOUR ONE-PAGE SUMMARY

Go to the beginning of this guide book and notice every time you put a dot in the margin.

In the left column below, record all the key ideas to marked. In the right column, explain the big ideas and how they affect your life.

List the key ideas:	Explain how they affect your life:
_____	_____
_____	_____
_____	_____
_____	_____
_____	_____
_____	_____
_____	_____
_____	_____

THREE EASY HABITS I CAN IMPLEMENT RIGHT AWAY:

1. _____

2. _____

3. _____

When will I do them? _____

_____

How can I track them on a score sheet? _____

_____

REFLECT ON THESE QUESTIONS BEFORE STARTING PART 2:

1. What is *Kabalas Ol* on a practical level?

2. How do you do *Kabalas Ol*?

3. When do you do *Kabalas Ol*?

4. What is *Kabalas Ol Malchus Shamayim*, and how does it enhance your life?

5. What is the opposite of *Kabalas Ol*?

6. What 6 actions constitute the opposite of *Kabalas Ol*?

👉 GETTING ANSWERED GUARANTEED

The deepest concepts in Chassidus are written in a *Sefer* called *Imrei Binah*. In fact, people would study each chapter five times to grasp the real meaning.

In the introduction to *Imrei Binah*, the author, the Mitteler Rebbe, son of the Baal HaTanya, hints to why he wrote the Sefer.

If people say *Shema* correctly, then their requests in *Shmoneh Esrei* are sure to be answered.

When a wife asks her husband for money and she says "I am really asking for **you** and for the needs of **your** children" - could the husband say no?

Similarly, when we properly give ourselves over and commit to Hashem during *Shema*, then our requests during *Shmoneh Esrei* are really for His needs because everything we do is for Him, and we will surely be answered.

The whole *Imrei Binah* was written to help you say *Shema* effectively and get your requests answered in *Shmoneh Esrei*. The following chapter in this guide book will give you a good start.

TAKING CHARGE OF RESPONSIBILITY (KABALAS OL)

Introduction

Hashem has created your mind with many abilities, amongst them the ability to;

A. Think about a concept;

B. Intention to do something;

C. Picture something in your imagination;

D. Awareness of your surroundings.

In the unit of Ahava, you learned about getting your

- thinking,
- speech, and
- ability to picture something

to work all together to reveal the AHAVA hidden in your heart.

In part 2 of unit 1, you learned how to use your power of intention to do something for Hashem. Animals can only intend to do something for their personal gain, while people can intend to do something for Hashem even without personal gain.

In part 2 of this unit, you will also learn about your

power of intention. Intention focuses your emotions and abilities towards reaching a goal. The Hebrew word for intention, *Kavana* (כַּוָּנָה), means to "aim," in contrast to *Hisbonenus* (הִתְבּוֹנְנוּת) which means to think something over again. You will learn how to use your power of כַּוָּנָה, and also how to align your words and actions to match your intention.

Making the Commitment

Before a public servant takes office, they take an oath. By doing so, they make a commitment to focus their abilities to fulfill their responsibilities. Their commitment also opens them up internally to receive new abilities and powers to fulfill their responsibility.

Even though intention is done with the mind, the process of taking responsibility is highly connected to emotion.

Part 1 of this unit was about הִתְבּוֹנְנוּת, and it leads to part 2, making the commitment (קַבָּלָה) to keep the rules of Hashem. A general commitment is made at the beginning of the day, and a more specific commitment is made before certain activities.

Due to the focus and new abilities being drawn into the person, a person can experience a major personal transformation through making the commitment (קַבָּלָה).

שִׂימַת לֵב - PERSONALIZATION

Between the הִתְבּוֹנְנוּת and the קַבָּלָה, there is an in-between stage called שִׂימַת לֵב (personalization), and this stage is the whole point of הִתְבּוֹנְנוּת!

Asking yourself certain questions can help you practice שִׂימַת לֵב:

- **What does this mean to me? (Or So what?)**
- **How does this idea affect me?**
- **When and how is it good for others?**
- **When and how is it good for me specifically?**
- **What am I going to do? (Or Now what?)**

FROM THE SOURCE

וְיָדַעְתָּ הַיּוֹם וַהֲשֵׁבֹתָ אֶל לְבָבֶךָ
Know this today and **place it on your heart**

DEVARIM 4:39

FIND OUT MORE

שהצווי הוא על ההתבוננות דעיקר ההתבוננות הוא השימת לב

סה"מ תש"א ע' 119

העיקר הוא מה שלו נוגע הדבר...שהדבר בעצמו הוא טוב ומועיל או הדבר בעצמו הוא רע ומזיק, הנה לבד זאת הנה לו לעצמו ביחוד הוא טוב ומועיל או לו לעצמו היחוד הוא רע ומזיק

סה"מ תש"א ע' 116

דהלא תכלית ועיקר הכל הוא העבודה בפועל שתהי' ע"פ דיני דרכי התורה, וכמאמר אין חכם כבעל נסיון דעיקר החכ' ותכליתה הוא כשבא בנסיון בפועל טוב בעשי' דוקא

ספר המאמרים תרפ"ט ע' 223

הלא מפורש אמרו אין חכם כבעל נסיון, נסיון הוא מעשה בפו"מ, והמעשה מאמת ומקיים את החכמה

אגרות קודש אדמו"ר מוהריי"צ חלק יד ה'קצד

> Quote from Tanya chapter 41

He (G-d) leaves aside (the creatures of) the higher (worlds) and (the creatures of) the lower (worlds)	וּמַנִּיחַ הָעֶלְיוֹנִים וְתַחְתּוֹנִים
and He uniquely bestows His Kingship upon His people Israel, in general,	וּמְיַחֵד מַלְכוּתוֹ עַל עַמּוֹ יִשְׂרָאֵל בִּכְלָל
and upon you in particular,	וְעָלָיו בִּפְרָט
for man is obligated to say	כִּי חַיָּב אָדָם לוֹמַר
"For my sake the world is created" (Sanhedrin 4:5).	בִּשְׁבִילִי נִבְרָא הָעוֹלָם
You, in turn, accept His Kingship upon yourself,	וְהוּא גַם הוּא מְקַבֵּל עָלָיו מַלְכוּתוֹ
that He will be King over you,	לִהְיוֹת מֶלֶךְ עָלָיו
to serve Him and do His Will in all kinds of work required of a servant.	וּלְעָבְדוֹ וְלַעֲשׂוֹת רְצוֹנוֹ בְּכָל מִינֵי עֲבוֹדַת עָבֶד.

חומש

And you shall serve the L-rd your G-d - וַעֲבַדְתֶּם, אֵת ה' אֱ-לֹהֵיכֶם

SHEMOS 23:25

Serve Him - וְאֹתוֹ תַעֲבֹדוּ

DEVARIM 13:5

משנה

לָמָּה קָדְמָה פָּרָשַׁת שְׁמַע לִוְהָיָה אִם שָׁמֹעַ, כְּדֵי שֶׁיְּקַבֵּל עָלָיו עֹל מַלְכוּת שָׁמַיִם תְּחִלָּה, וְאַחַר כָּךְ יְקַבֵּל עָלָיו עֹל מִצְווֹת

Why did the portion of "Shema" precede that of "Vehaya im Shamoa"? So that one will first accept upon himself the yoke of the kingdom of Heaven, and only then accept upon himself the yoke of the Mitzvos.

MISHNAH BERACHOS 2:2

שו״ע

בַּפָּסוּק רִאשׁוֹן שֶׁל קְרִיאַת שְׁמַע שֶׁהוּא שְׁמַע יִשְׂרָאֵל שֶׁהוּא עִיקַּר קַבָּלַת מַלְכוּת שָׁמַיִם

(It is imperative to think about the meaning of words) when saying the first Pasuk of Shema, for it is the main place we commit ourselves to the kingship of Heaven.

SHULCHAN ARUCH HARAV ORACH CHAIM 60:5

> **Quote from Tanya chapter 41**

Like it is written in Zohar [Parshas Behar]:	וּכְמוֹ שֶׁכָּתוּב בַּזֹהַר [פָּרָשַׁת בְּהַר]
"Like a bull	כְּהַאי תּוֹרָא
on which they place a yoke before (its work)	דְּיָהֲבִין עֲלֵיהּ עוֹל בְּקַדְמֵיתָא
so that it should bring good to the world (from the farming work it does)...	בְּגִין לְאַפָּקָא מִינֵּיהּ טַב לְעָלְמָא כוּ'
So too,	הָכֵי נַמֵי
a person must	אִצְטְרִיךְ לְבַר נָשׁ
accept on himself the yoke of the kingship of Heaven	לְקַבָּלָא עֲלֵיהּ עוֹל מַלְכוּת שָׁמַיִם
before (doing service),	בְּקַדְמֵיתָא כוּ'
and if this act is not found by him,	וְאִי הַאי לָא אִשְׁתְּכַח גַּבֵּיהּ
Kedusha will not dwell on him...	לָא שַׁרְיָא בֵּיהּ קְדוּשָׁה כוּ'

☞ TAKE NOTE

A yoke is a farming device that focuses the power of the bull to move a plowing tool that prepares a field for planting. Similarly, when we commit to use our abilities for the service of Hashem, it is as if we put a special yoke device upon ourselves that will help us.

AUTOMATIC UNITY
FROM TANYA CHAPTER 47

The moment you want	מִיָּד שֶׁרוֹצֶה
and accept	וּמְקַבֵּל
and bring G-dliness upon yourself	וּמַמְשִׁיךְ עָלָיו אֱ-לֹהוּתוֹ יִתְבָּרֵךְ
and say, the L-rd is our A-mighty the L-rd is one,	וְאוֹמֵר ה' אֱ-לֹהֵינוּ ה' אֶחָד
automatically,	הֲרֵי מִמֵּילָא
your soul becomes united with His blessed Oneness,	נִכְלֶלֶת נַפְשׁוֹ בְּיִחוּדוֹ יִתְבָּרֵךְ
because a spirit (below) evokes and draws a spirit (from Above)	דְּרוּחַ אַיְיתִי רוּחַ וְאַמְשִׁיךְ רוּחַ

👉 TAKE NOTE

From this quote from Tanya ch. 47, you see that when you commit and open yourself to receive Hashem's kingship, you actually bring down abilities and power from Hashem. You may find it hard to keep *Dinim*, however the *Eibershter* gives you the abilities together with the fortitude to do complex and difficult tasks.

Imagine someone who is not Jewish who has no training about Shabbos trying to keep the laws of Shabbos. He would certainly stumble on one of the many details of the Shabbos prohibitions. The fact that a Jew is able to keep Shabbos is only becomes Hashem helps him and gives him the ability to do so.

RECOGNIZING THE OPPOSITE OF קַבָּלַת עוֹל

As we have already explained, the main place for קַבָּלַת עוֹל is during the first line of the Shema.

The third paragraph of the Shema mentions some Mitzvos that will help us have an effective קַבָּלַת עוֹל.

Before we learn how to do some of these Mitzvos, let us learn about the three basic steps of *Teshuvah*.

1. Stop doing bad;

2. Regretting in your heart and verbally stating that you sinned;

3. Taking protective steps not to become overwhelmed with a desire for the sin.

The third step helps us not to sin again, it protects your *Teshuvah* and protects your קַבָּלַת עוֹל.

This is the idea behind "do not follow your heart and eyes (Devarim 15:39)."

Why does the Torah state "heart" before "eyes"?

Is it not the other way around? A person first looks with *Kavana* at something then the heart desires. The answer is that the Mitzvah not to follow the heart means: Not to open oneself to being a **receiver** from all sorts of influences. It is about deciding not to be a **receiver** and stay **focused**, this decision is made in the heart.

וְלֹא־תָתֻרוּ אַחֲרֵי לְבַבְכֶם וְאַחֲרֵי עֵינֵיכֶם אֲשֶׁר־אַתֶּם זֹנִים אַחֲרֵיהֶם:
And do not follow your heart and eyes in your lustful urge.

DEVARIM 15:39

וִהְיִיתֶם קְדֹשִׁים לֵא־לֹהֵיכֶם:
And be holy to your G-d

DEVARIM 15:40

If a person decides in their heart to be a receiver, which is פְּרִיקַת עוֹל (throwing off the yoke), this will lead them to look with their eyes.

If the main Mitzvah is a decision in the heart, why did the Torah mention "eyes"? The Torah does not mention extra words without teaching us something.

The answer is that sometimes it happens that a person sees something they desire and they did not intend to.

In such a case, the Mitzvah of "do not follow… your eyes" is: Do not add *Kavana* (concentration) on what you see; focus your *Kavana* on something more important, until you can look away.

Firstly, do not put yourself in a position to be tested, do not go to a place where you will be tested if you can avoid it. If you can not avoid it, decide with your heart not to be a receiver. If it happened that you see something inappropriate then do not add *Kavana*, and instead focus on something else. For sure don't turn your head to look a second time because it means you just decided with your heart to be a receiver.

Keeping this Mitzvah and being vigilant will protect you from drawing טוּמְאָה into yourself. You will avoid drawing down desires that are very hard to deal with.

If your mind starts to think of something inappropriate, as soon as you remember that willingly thinking about this is פְּרִיקַת עוֹל and you are going to become a **receiver**; **immediately** get busy with some activity to help you think of something else and the frequency and intensity of such thoughts falling into your mind will become less and weaker.

As long as you focus on something else immediately when you realize your thought is making you into a receiver of טוּמְאָה, then your קַבָּלַת עוֹל will still protect you, and the intensity of the bad thought will not be so strong that it is overwhelmingly difficult to push away.

There is another behavior that is part of this Mitzvah and it is avoiding wasting time. If a person sits around wasting time, they automatically become a **receiver** which is פְּרִיקַת עוֹל.

FIVE ACTIONS THAT AVOID פְּרִיקַת עוֹל

1. **Avoid** situations you will be tested.
   - 👉 **PLACE**

2. **Decide** with your heart not to be a receiver. Beware when turning your head with intention to see something inappropriate.
   - 👉 **HEART**

3. **Take care** of *Kavana*; if you see something inappropriate, put your *Kavana* (concentration) somewhere else, e.g. helping, caring, serving, understanding someone.
   - 👉 **EYES**

4. **Focus elsewhere**; when your mind wanders to the inappropriate (e.g. thinking bad wishes on someone), focus elsewhere as soon as you realize. You will do a big Mitzvah and be protected.
   - 👉 **MIND**

5. **Be Busy**; do not waste time and you will not be open to be a receiver.
   - 👉 **TIME**

Exercise

👉 **POINT TO THE GROUND, HEART, EYES, FOREHEAD AND YOUR WATCH WHILE REPEATING THESE FIVE.**

If you did פְּרִיקַת עוֹל or you are not sure if you did, immediately ask Hashem for help. If your boat gets a hole in the base, do you close it immediately or do you wait until it fills up with swamp water?

Note that avoiding putting yourself in a place of test includes a virtual place.

↖ KEY TERMS ↘

Compassion	רַחֲמִים
Behaving beyond what the rational mind dictates for Kedusha	שְׁטוּת דִּקְדֻשָּׁה
Behaving lower than is rational	שְׁטוּת דִּקְלִיפָּה
Spirit that leads to bad behavior	רוּחַ שְׁטוּת

There is a Mitzvah that will help you become better in avoiding the five types of פְּרִיקַת עוֹל.

This is the Mitzvah of וִהְיִיתֶם קְדֹשִׁים (**being holy**). You can fulfill this Mitzvah by delaying gratification. For example, when you see something you want to eat, stop and wait a minute or two and then eat it. Just leave it on your plate for a minute until your initial urge becomes weaker. You could also make a short speaking fast, not speaking (or texting) for 15 minutes.[1]

☛ RIGHT BEFORE YOU EAT, ADD A GOOD KAVANA, E.G.

- How lucky I am to have the opportunity to make a בְּרָכָה before I eat.[2]

- This will give me energy to learn Torah and do Mitzvos.[3]

- This will open my mind so I can understand Hashem's Torah better.[4]

- How lucky I am to experience Hashem in the taste He created in this food.[5]

Fulfilling this Mitzvah of וִהְיִיתֶם קְדֹשִׁים by delaying gratification results with אִתְכַּפְיָא - unholy energy becomes subdugated to the holy. It also helps maintain your empathy[6] for others.

The Mitzvah of avoiding פְּרִיקַת עוֹל is mainly done with your *Kavana*, i.e intent and focus.

The good way to protect your Kavana is by keeping it busy with doing Mitzvos in an extravagant and beautiful way. This is called שְׁטוּת דִּקְדוּשָּׁה.

---

1. כל מה שהאדם זובח יצרו אפי' שעה קלה ומתכוין לאכפיא ל ט"א שבחלל השמאלי כגון שחפץ לאכול ומאחר סעודתו עד לאחר שעה או פחות ועוסק בתורה באותה שעה. כדאיתא בגמ' שעה רביעית מאכל כל אדם ששית מאכל ת"ח. והיו מרעיבים עצמם שתי שעות לכוונה זו אף שגם אחר הסעודה היו לומדים כל היום. וכן אם בולם פיו מלדבר דברים שלבו מתאוה מאד לדברם מעניני העולם וכן בהרהורי מחשבתו אפי' במעט מזעיר דאתכפיא ס"א לתתא אסתלק יקרא דקב"ה וקדושתו לעילא הרבה ומקדושה זו נמשכת קדושה עליונה על האדם למטה לחייטו סיוע רב ועצום לעבודתו ית'. וז"ש רז"ל אדם מקדש עצמו מעט למטה מקדשין אותו הרבה מלמעלה לבד מה שמקיים מצות עשה של תורה והתקדשתם וכו' (תניא פרק כ"ז).

2. מאה ברכות שהן ליראה את ה' ולאהבה אותו ולזכרו תמיד על ידי הברכות שמברך תמיד (שולחן ערוך הרב אורח חיים ס' מו סעי' א)

3. כוונת אכילתו לש"ש שיהיה לו כח אח"כ לעבודת הש"י (כתר שם טוב חלק ראשון קיג-ב)

4. דאמר רבא חמרא וריחני פקחין (יומא עו,ב)

5. בכל דרכיך דעהו (משלי ג:ו)

6. מענשליכע געפיהלען צום צווייטען מענש (לקוטי דיבורים ב' ע' 640)

It turns out that קַבָּלַת עוֹל is best done with enthusiastic energy and it becomes much easier to avoid פְּרִיקַת עוֹל.

In general, there are two types of inappropriate emotions a person can have: inappropriate love towards something and inappropriate fear from something.

To deal with an inappropriate fear of something, e.g. being afraid of a insect that is not dangerous and the fear affects you way too much. The approach to respond to such an emotion seems counterintuitive. **The strategy is "exposure."**

Step one: Gradually expose yourself to the fear and specifically intend to "feel" the fear, abandonment, betrayal, anxiety, confusion, sorrow, despair, rejection, overwhelm, panic, shame etc.

Step two: Name the negative emotion.

Step three: Ask yourself what lesson this emotion might be coming to teach you about yourself.

E.g. Am I hungry, am I tired, am I thirsty, do I need to apologize for something, what did I just do that triggered this feeling, what do I need to avoid?

Your animal soul is programed by Hashem to protect you, and the emotion probably comes to warn you of some perceived problem. If you use your intellect to recognize the negative emotion and to learn a lesson from it, your animal soul is usually willing to let the intellect take over and deal with the perceived possible threat.

On the other hand, if your intellect deals with the situation by avoiding the feeling, the animal may decide to make the feeling more intense and the intellect may not be aware of the negative ways this feeling is affecting you.

Once you have allowed yourself to "feel" the feeling, you can focus your mind on different positive thoughts.

Notice the paradox: when you want to weaken a feeling, specifically intend to feel it, and let yourself be uncomfortable for a while. When you want to have a good feeling, like love and fear of Hashem, reflect on the concepts and let the feelings happen naturally by themselves. When it comes to Ahava and Yirah, focus on thinking the concepts and focus on doing Mitzvos.

FIND OUT MORE

דרך חיים אות ו-ז

MADE SIMPLE קַבָּלַת מַלְכוּת שָׁמַיִם
TOOLS THAT PROTECT

וְלֹא תָתוּרוּ אַחֲרֵי לְבַבְכֶם וְאַחֲרֵי עֵינֵיכֶם אֲשֶׁר אַתֶּם זֹנִים אַחֲרֵיהֶם:

Step	Action	Ideas
	Delay gratification (this box is a separate Mitzvah so it deserves differentiation from the 5 below.)	וִהְיִיתֶם קְדֹשִׁים
ONE	**Avoid** situations you will be tested.	וְלֹא תָתוּרוּ
TWO	**Decide** with your heart not to be a receiver.	אַחֲרֵי לְבַבְכֶם
THREE	**Take care** of Kavana; if you see something inappropriate.	וְאַחֲרֵי עֵינֵיכֶם
FOUR	**Focus elsewhere** when your mind wanders to the inappropriate.	מַחֲשָׁבָה
FIVE	**Be Busy**; do not waste time.	וּבְמוֹשַׁב לֵצִים לֹא יָשָׁב

◤KEY TERMS◢

Accepting the yoke .... קַבָּלַת עוֹל

Throwing off the yoke .... פְּרִיקַת עוֹל

> Quote from Tanya chapter 42

וְגַם לִהְיוֹת לְזִכָּרוֹן תָּמִיד	Also constantly remind yourself
לְשׁוֹן חֲכָמֵינוּ זִכְרוֹנָם לִבְרָכָה	the phrase used by our sages:
קַבָּלַת עוֹל מַלְכוּת שָׁמַיִם	"accepting the yoke of Hashem's kingship,"
שֶׁהוּא כְּעִנְיָן	which is similar to (the Mitzvah of)
שׂוֹם תָּשִׂים עָלֶיךָ מֶלֶךְ	placing a king upon yourself
כְּמוֹ שֶׁנִּתְבָּאֵר בְּמָקוֹם אַחֵר וְכוּ׳	as explained elsewhere etc.
כִּי הַקָּדוֹשׁ בָּרוּךְ הוּא מַנִּיחַ אֶת הָעֶלְיוֹנִים וְהַתַּחְתּוֹנִים	Because Hashem left aside (the beings of) the higher and lower worlds
וּמְיַיחֵד מַלְכוּתוֹ עָלֵינוּ וְכוּ׳	and focused His kingship on us, etc.
וַאֲנַחְנוּ מְקַבְּלִים וְכוּ׳	And we accept, etc.
וְזֶהוּ עִנְיַן הַהִשְׁתַּחֲוָואוֹת שֶׁבִּתְפִלַּת י״ח	This is the idea of bowing in Shmoneh Esrei
אַחַר קַבָּלַת עוֹל מַלְכוּת שָׁמַיִם	after accepting the yoke of Hashem's kingship
בְּדִבּוּר בִּקְרִיאַת שְׁמַע	verbally when reading the Shema,
לַחֲזוֹר וּלְקַבֵּל בְּפוֹעַל מַמָּשׁ	in order to accept it again in a practical way
בְּמַעֲשֶׂה וְכוּ׳	by doing an action
כְּמוֹ שֶׁנִּתְבָּאֵר בְּמָקוֹם אַחֵר:	as explained elsewhere.

FROM THE SOURCE

שׂוֹם תָּשִׂים עָלֶיךָ מֶלֶךְ
Place a king over yourself

DEVARIM 17:15

וְאֹתוֹ תִירָאוּ וְאֶת־מִצְוֹתָיו תִּשְׁמֹרוּ וּבְקֹלוֹ תִשְׁמָעוּ וְאֹתוֹ תַעֲבֹדוּ וּבוֹ תִדְבָּקוּן
...revere none but Him; observe His commandments alone, and heed only His orders; serve none but Him, and hold fast to Him.

DEVARIM 13:5

TANYA (END OF) CHAPTER 25

To read the Shema	לִקְרוֹת קְרִיאַת שְׁמַע
twice every day (morning and night)	פַּעֲמַיִם בְּכָל יוֹם
to accept on yourself the kingship of Heaven	לְקַבֵּל עָלָיו מַלְכוּת שָׁמַיִם
with self sacrifice (giving yourself over).	בִּמְסִירַת נֶפֶשׁ

☞ QUESTION TO ASK

What is the difference between מְסִירָה and קַבָּלָה?

HOW TO DO קַבָּלַת עוֹל WHEN SAYING שְׁמַע יִשְׂרָאֵל....אֶחָד

Reflection (הִתְבּוֹנְנוּת) with the intention to recognize goodness which will reveal love for Hashem (אַהֲבָה) leads a person to מְסִירָה, which means to give oneself over and rise above towards one's Divine source. In contrast, הִתְבּוֹנְנוּת with the intention to recognize your responsibility which will reveal fear of Hashem (יִרְאָה) leads a person to קַבָּלָה, which means to stay in your position and accept from above. This commitment leads to הַמְשָׁכָה, to bring אֱלֹקוּת (meaning more ability from the Divine) into yourself to do your mission.

Both קַבָּלָה and מְסִירָה[1] are done when saying Shema Yisroel...Echad. Yisroel hints to the Divine source of a Yid, and Echad hints to the soul coming down from the seven heavens to earth in order to keep Hashem's rules in all the four directions of this world.

---

1. בק"ש למסור נפשו באחד. ועניין מס"נ אינו כמו שסוברים העולם שהוא הצעקה בהתלהבות ברעש אלא הוא כמ"ש אליך ה' נפשי אשא שאינו רוצה להיות יש ודבר נפרד אלא להיות בחי' ביטול לשאת נפשו ורוחו אליו ית' שהוא מקור החיים דכולא קמי' כלא חשיבי לך ה' הגדולה כו'. (ליקוטי תורה האזינו עד, א)

The word אֶחָד ("one") has three letters, each representing a different concept connected with its numerical value:

א = **One, representing One Hashem** to whom you give yourself over (מְסִירָה).

ח = **Eight, hinting to your soul's great journey down the seven heavens to this one earth.** When thinking about the ח, you make an emotional שִׂימַת לֵב, asking yourself, "Why did my soul come down all the seven heavens to this world?"

To keep the rules of Hashem, and set aside time for Torah wherever I may be in the **four directions of the world, hinted in the ד.**

There is a minhag to say the ח for longer while moving one's head, right, left, forward, back and then up, down. According to this minhag, one does מְסִירָה when saying the Alef (א); one does קַבָּלָה while reciting the ח when moving the head in the four directions; and when moving the head up and down, one does the שִׂימַת לֵב, which will enthuse the קַבָּלָה with feelings of personalization so that you actually behave with Yiras Shamayim.

WHEN YOU SAY:

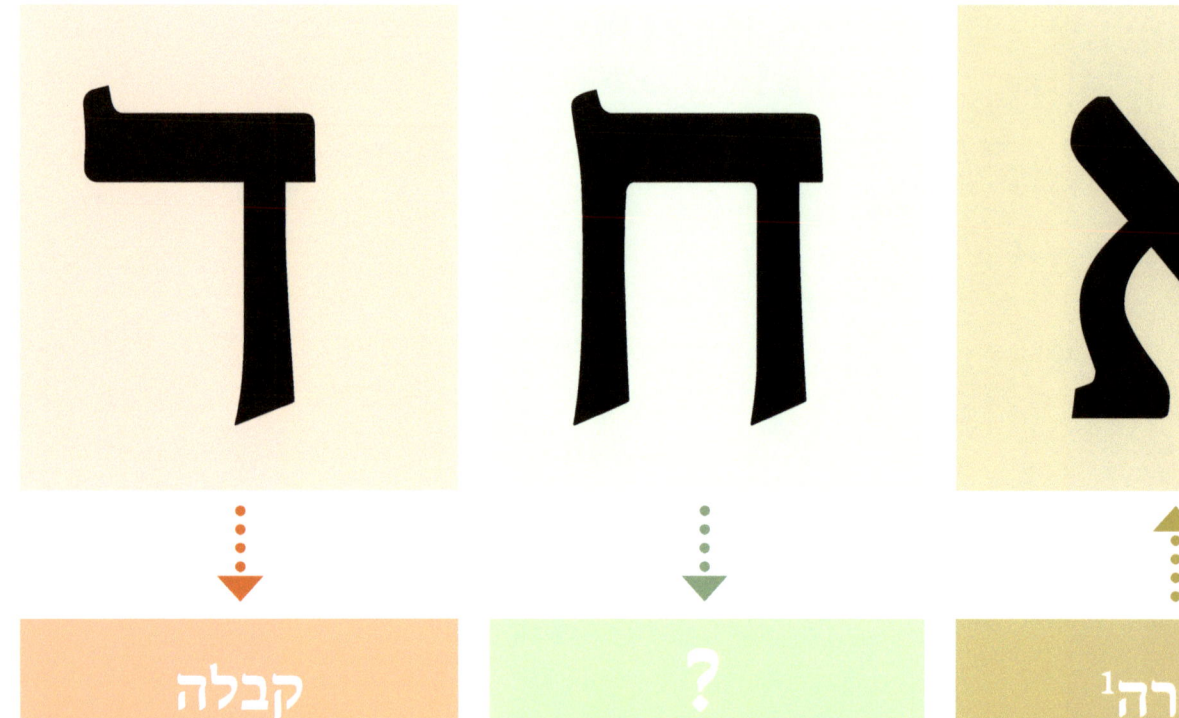

קבלה	?	מסירה¹
Commit to do Torah and Mitzvos wherever you are!	**Why** did my soul come down the seven heavens to this earth?	**Give** yourself to Hashem.

☞ TAKE NOTE
You align your intention to make the קַבָּלָה commitment with your words when you say Shema Yisroel…Echad, and when you bow in Shmoneh Esrei, you align your קַבָּלָה with the physical bowing of your body, thus bringing the קַבָּלַת מַלְכוּת שָׁמַיִם into your entire body.

---

1. דקריאת שמע הוא בחינת העלאה והתכללות ביחוד עליון דעשר ספירות איך שהם נכללים ובטלים ממש שמזה נעשה ביטול הנפש והתכללותה לעצמות ומהות, דזהו עיקר מצות קריאת שמע וכוונתה בהביטול דו״ק והוא למס״נ באחד (אמרי בינה קיצורים ט״ז)

KAVANA - INTENTION MADE SIMPLE

Your Part	Fear, Responsibility יִרְאָה	Love, Enthusiasm אַהֲבָה
Intellectual חב"ד **Reflect** התבוננות **Show up!**	Reflection on גַּדְלוּת הַבּוֹרֵא With intention to **take responsibility**	Reflection on גַּדְלוּת הַבּוֹרֵא With intention to **recognize goodness**
LEADS TO ↓↓↓	**LEADS TO** ↓↓↓	**LEADS TO** ↓↓↓
Emotional חג"ת **Prepare** הכנה **Step up!**	Commitment קַבָּלָה[1] **Taking upon yourself to get it done**	Commitment מְסִירָה[2] **Giving yourself to higher, transcend**
LEADS TO ↓↓↓	**LEADS TO** ↓↓↓	**LEADS TO** ↓↓↓
Practical **Do** עשיה **Give back!**	**Power coming down** - הַמְשָׁכָה[3] Bringing new abilities down into yourself	**Strong Connection** - דְּבֵיקוּת[4] Filling your faculties (thought, speech and action) only with things that connect to him

SHOW UP become aware, become present and awake.
STEP UP give yourself over and commit.
GIVE BACK make a difference.

---

1. שמקבל עליו מלכות שמים וממשיך עליו יראתו ית' בהתגלות מחשבתו ורצונו שבמוחו (תניא מ"א)

2. מעתה אני מוסרה ומחזירה לך לייחדה באחדותך וכמ"ש אליך ה' נפשי אשא והיינו על ידי התקשרות מחשבתי ודיבורי בדיבורך באותיות התורה והתפלה (תניא מ"א)

3. ובקריאתו או בלבישתו הוא ממשיך אורו ית' עליו דהיינו על חלק אלוה ממעל שבתוך גופו ליכלל וליבטל באורו יתברך (תניא מ"א)

4. עיקר האהבה היא אתדבקות רוחא ברוחא כמ"ש ישקני מנשיקות פיהו וכו' כנודע. וע"ז נאמר ובכל נפשך שהם הם כל חלקי הנפש שכל ומדות ולבושיהם מחשבה דיבור ומעשה לדבקה כולן בו ית' דהיינו המדות במדותיו ית' מה הוא רחום וכו'. (תניא אגרת התשובה ט')

KAVANA WORKSHEET

1. What are four abilities of the mind?

A _____

B _____

C _____

D _____

2. Write down the in-between stage that comes after הִתְבּוֹנְנוּת and is the main point of הִתְבּוֹנְנוּת?

_____

3. Identify the שִׂימַת לֵב in the words of the first page of Tanya 41 (pgs 72-73).

_____

4. What are three names for the commitment?

A _____

B _____

C _____

5. Discuss the difference between הִתְבּוֹנְנוּת and כַּוָּנָה.

Exercise
☞ TRAIN YOUR MIND
Practice moving from one ability of your mind to another in a circle. First use the thinking part of your brain, then quickly use the intention part of your mind, then picture something in

your imagination for 30 seconds, then focus your attention on your surroundings (e.g. where you are? and what time is it?). Afterwards, go back and use your thinking ability for one minute, then intention etc., and go through all four stages 3 times in a row.

Experience

6. Write down something small that you find difficult to do.

_____

☞ **USE YOUR POWER OF INTENT TO COMMIT TO DO IT AND INTEND TO RECEIVE POWER FROM HASHEM TO DO IT.**
With this in mind, say the Pasuk Shema Yisrael, and immediately do something small towards your commitment. Do this exercise together with a friend under the guidance of your teacher. Make sure your commitment is small, just as a farmer does not train a young bull with a yoke for an entire day, rather the farmer starts small and slowly increases the challenges in the yoke training process.

7. What are five types of פְּרִיקַת עוֹל?

1 _____

2 _____

3 _____

4 _____

5 _____

8. What is the main common idea behind these five?

_____

9. Explain the difference between מְסִירָה and קַבָּלָה?

_____

10. Explain how to say Shema together with how and when to do קַבָּלָה and מְסִירָה?

___

11. Explain a practical way to fulfill the Mitzvah of being holy?

___

12. After delaying gratification what are the four intentions (in order) you can have before you eat something?

1. ___
2. ___
3. ___
4. ___

13. Explain the difference between three and four?

___

14. Explain what you do differently with intention to make your הִתְבּוֹנְנוּת lead to קַבָּלָה or מְסִירָה?

___

15. Explain what does דְּבֵיקוּת mean?

___

16. Explain practically what do you do to be in a state of דְּבֵיקוּת?

___

17. Explain a practical difference between דְּבֵיקוּת and הַמְשָׁכָה? How is your behavior different with each?

___

18. When you want to weaken the intensity of an emotion that is counterproductive do you:

A. Pretend you do not have this feeling.

B. Allow yourself to feel uncomfortable for a little while until the emotion loses intensity naturally.

19. If the way to weaken a counterproductive feeling is to intend to feel it, when it comes to productive feeling, do you want you;

A. Intend to feel love for Hashem

B. Focus on ideas that show Hashem's goodness and let the emotion come by itself

EFFECTIVE IMPLEMENTATION

Have you ever studied something and when it came to action you just did not do it?

Have you ever made a commitment and you did not live up to it?

The following strategies will help you implement more effectively.

The suggestions below are organized in order of the *Sefiros* they correspond with to make it easier to understand, organize and remember.

The leading *Sefira* is called *Kesser* (crown). Your behavior in this world causes a mirror effect in the corresponding *Sefiros* above. When you do behaviors that trigger *Kesser*, you will find it easier and faster to implement.

How can you access *Kesser*?

Kesser is divided into two parts,

1. *Taanug* - pleasure

2. *Ratzon* - want, desire

TRIGGERING TAANUG

In the Chabad system, the flagship strategy to access *Kesser (Taanug)* is through *Binah*.

Binah, the detailed thinking ability of your mind that mainly dwells in the left side of your brain, has three parts.

1. **Orech Binah**

When you communicate to others well, you are using *Orech Binah*. This is your ability to deliver information that is understood correctly by others.

In the Chabad system, this is when you can explain a concept in Chassidus to a child. This shows you have mastery of the metaphor taught in Chassidus.

2. **Rochev Binah**

When you compare and contrast the details of a topic, you are in the process of content mastery.

In the Chabad system, this is when you compare the multiple metaphors in Chassidus in search of the nuances of the core concept. By doing so, you are activating *Rochev Binah*. This is the main activity of *Hisbonenus*.

3. Omek Binah

When you put effort in *Rochev Binah*, you reach the undistorted core concept with its nuances, and *Omek Binah* has a direct connection to *Kesser*.

It turns out that the practice of mental effort is core to the Chabad system.

First you understand the metaphor well enough to explain to a child. Then you compare the different metaphors to find out what unique lesson each one contributes. You put mental effort to reach *Kesser* and you immediately anchor by doing a Mitzvah / *Hiddur Mitzvah*, give some money to *Tzedakah* etc. The best time you can reach *Omek Binah* correctly is when you are saying words from the Siddur.

What if you want faster results? Is there a shortcut?

Make the implementation fun!

This is why summer camps can help children implement good behaviors that would otherwise take a long time because they make the activities fun.

Students of the Baal Shem Tov would say jokes at the beginning of their lessons, because a good joke will reveal *Kesser* of the soul.

Best practice for great implementation is to use multiple strategies: short techniques, like jokes, together with long lasting, effort-based techniques from the Chabad system.

A master is an expert that has reached *Kesser* through the subject they put effort in over a number of years.

The fundamentals you are learning in this specific guide book are taught in the Tanya, Chabad system. However, they do not take a long time since you are only required to reveal what you already have in your soul.

The Chabad system first uses fundamental short strategies which give you a good internal environment to have the clarity to be able to work on the enduring effort-based strategies.

TRIGGERING RATZON - WILL POWER

There is a saying אֵין דָּבָר הָעוֹמֵד בִּפְנֵי הָרָצוֹן - there nothing that stands in the way of want (will).

How can you rapidly access Ratzon?

Experience has shown that loss aversion triggers *Ratzon*. Loss aversion means that when you realize that you have something substantial to lose, this reveals a deep want.

When a person really understands that any *Aveira* against the Torah makes them lose their Judaism, Jewishness and their connection to Hashem for that moment, the person will want to to protect it and nothing will stand in their way. (Tanya 18-25)

When you want to motivate yourself with *Ratzon*, think about the reality of the substantial loss that will happen when you do and don't do something. This will help you to implement rapidly.

When you tell your friend about a commitment you made, you won't want to weaken your connection to that person. The relationship loss aversion will help you reveal the solid *Ratzon* to keep your commitment.

TRIGGERING CHOCHMA

We explained previously that the flash of insight from *Chochma* comes after mental effort. Is there a shortcut method to access *Chochma* and rapidly implement correctly?

Chassidus explains that the two eyes correspond to *Netzach* and *Hod* of *Chochma*, and they have access to *Taanug*. (To illustrate, many people will pay more money for a home with a good view.) Both *Binah* and *Chochma* can access *Taanug*, however *Chochma* will be more rapid.

Considering the importance and effect of what we see, if one looks at things that are contrary to their studies, what do you think that will do to their implementation?

Imagine on the positive, when the images that you look at are holy (e.g. Alef Beis, Tzaddikim) and these images match your studies (*Hisbonenus*), then you will be accessing *Kesser* through multiple strategies.

First responders, like police and firefighters may find themselves in chaotic confusing situations. At these times, their heart beat may rise and blood flow may decrease in the extremities thereby affecting rational thinking. However, visualization has the power to guide their action when they mentally rehearsed their response behavior during training.

Athletes as well use visualization during mental rehearsal as part of their training.

When you mentally rehearse how you will wake up in the morning, you will find that you will be more effective in implementation.

Visualization is part of the Chabad system. This is especially emphasized in the practice of storytelling.

USING BINAH TO IMPLEMENT QUICKLY

Is there a way to use *Binah* to rapidly implement a behavior?

There is a concept called *Chashmal*, meaning "quietly speak," which metaphorically surrounds *Binah*. *Chashmal* guides and protects rational thought that directs good behavior.

How does it work?

When a mother trains a child, she will often use easy-to-remember "one liners" that guide implementation of good behavior. For example, "work hard and succeed," "look both ways before crossing the street," "stop drop and roll," "nothing stands in the way of your will," the 12 pesukim.

Firemen may lose their ability to think rationally in an overwhelming situation. Therefore, some memorize the *Chashmal* of "Put the white stuff on the red stuff" so they still remember what to do, even when they have temporarily lost their ability to think clearly due to great rise in their heartbeat.

Next time you feel overwhelmed, countdown from 10. This will help you activate *Binah*, think rationally and make the right choice.

The fundamentals of practical implementation from Tanya mainly use the tactics of visualization and verbalization.

STRATEGY PAGE - YOUR ONE-PAGE SUMMARY

Go to the beginning of this guide book and notice every time you put a dot in the margin.

In the left column below, record all the key ideas to marked. In the right column, explain the big ideas and how they affect your life.

List the key ideas:	Explain how they affect your life:
_____	_____
_____	_____
_____	_____
_____	_____
_____	_____
_____	_____
_____	_____

THREE EASY HABITS I CAN IMPLEMENT RIGHT AWAY:

1. _____
2. _____
3. _____

When will I do them? _____
_____

How can I track them on a score sheet? _____
_____

STRATEGY PAGE - PERSONAL EVALUATION
חשבון הנפש

Go back and read your previous personal summary sheets, and then fill in the questions below:

What worked?

_____
_____
_____
_____
_____
_____
_____
_____

What did not work?

_____
_____
_____
_____
_____

What are my barriers?

_____
_____
_____

How can I do things to make things better? _____
_____
_____

What small change can I make in the things around me to remind and inspire me? _____
_____
_____

How can I expose myself to people who will inspire me? _____
_____
_____

THE POWER OF IMAGINATION

Your ability to picture something is a very useful tool.

You could picture something from the past to trigger useful emotions that could help you with a challenge now. You can also connect two visions at the same time, meaning that you can do an activity now and picture how it looked when you did a similar thing before. This helps you trigger useful emotions and helps you unlock skills in doing the task at hand.

Soldiers, athletes, firefighters, police and medical first responders all train using some visualization techniques.

Yidden use visualization every day. Shulchan Aruch starts with a number of visualizations to help you start your day with enthusiasm. Shulchan Aruch uses the visualization of a king. In present times, when we can't relate to the concept of a physical king, we should try to create a visualization that is similar to standing before king. Interaction with a boss is a very common interaction where there is a lot to lose.

Imagine you trained for a specific job for a few years and you finally you get a job. You realize that you need experience to be good at what you do, so even though you are not that competent yet, it's important to keep your job to gain experience. You are not used to the workload and you get tired, but then your boss comes in. If you do not look awake and focused, your boss might get the impression that you are not really worth the money he is paying you. He just fired two people that were not producing yesterday. This is a high-stakes interaction, meaning you have a lot to lose and you are going to give it your best.

Now apply the understanding and feeling you just created to the way you behave to Hashem. Hashem is here watching how you are serving Him.

Commitment is made **before** commencing a service, and visualization can be used **during** an actual service, helping you **unlock** the correct feelings and skills you will need on the spot.

> **Quote from Tanya chapter 41**

"And, behold, G-d is standing over him (you),"	וְהִנֵּה ה׳ נִצָּב עָלָיו
and "The whole world is filled with His Glory,"	וּמְלֹא כָל הָאָרֶץ כְּבוֹדוֹ
and He is watching you,	וּמַבִּיט עָלָיו
and is checking (your) innermost thoughts and feelings	וּבוֹחֵן כְּלָיוֹת וָלֵב
[to see] if you are serving Him properly.	אִם עוֹבְדוֹ כָּרָאוּי.
Therefore, you must	וְעַל כֵּן צָרִיךְ
serve in His Presence with awe and fear	לַעֲבוֹד לְפָנָיו בְּאֵימָה וּבְיִרְאָה
as if you were standing before the King.	כְּעוֹמֵד לִפְנֵי הַמֶּלֶךְ

☞ TAKE NOTE

If you have never seen a real king, imagine being in any high-stakes interaction with someone in a position of power.

KEEP IN MIND
SHULCHAN ARUCH HARAV ORACH CHAIM 1:5

When a person places on their heart	כְּשֶׁיָּשִׂים הָאָדָם אֶל לִבּוֹ
that the great King, the King of kings	שֶׁהַמֶּלֶךְ הַגָּדוֹל מֶלֶךְ מַלְכֵי הַמְּלָכִים
the Holy one, blessed be He, is standing by him	הקב"ה עוֹמֵד עָלָיו
and sees his actions,	וְרוֹאֶה בְּמַעֲשָׂיו
as it is written,	כְּמוֹ שֶׁכָּתוּב
"'If a person hides in hidden places	אִם יִסָּתֵר אִישׁ בַּמִּסְתָּרִים
will I not see him?' says Hashem.	וַאֲנִי לֹא אֶרְאֶנּוּ נְאֻם ה'
'For I fill the heavens and the earth!'"	הֲלֹא אֶת הַשָּׁמַיִם וְאֶת הָאָרֶץ אֲנִי מָלֵא
Then straight away, "Fear" will come upon him	מִיָּד יַגִּיעַ אֵלָיו הַיִּרְאָה
and he will be humbled in the awe of Hashem	וְהַהַכְנָעָה בְּפַחַד ה'
and embarrassed (to do something wrong) from him constantly.	וּבוֹשְׁתּוֹ מִמֶּנּוּ תָּמִיד
And if the "Awe" does not come upon him (from Hashem),	וְאִם לֹא יַגִּיעַ אֵלָיו מִיָּד
he must think more deeply about this idea	יַעֲמִיק הַרְבֵּה בְּעִנְיָן זֶה
until it comes upon him.	עַד שֶׁיַּגִּיעַ אֵלָיו
He must also completely return (to Hashem and your real self)	וְגַם יָשׁוּב בִּתְשׁוּבָה שְׁלֵימָה
from all his transgressions	עַל כָּל עֲוֹנוֹתָיו

☞ TAKE NOTE

The Shulchan Aruch is instructing us to use the power of **Personalization** and **Visualization** to trigger the gift of Yiras Shamayim. Even after using these two tools, there may be a blockage to receiving the gift of Yiras Shamayim. It is therefore imperative to do Teshuvah to remove any blockages.

In Unit 3, you will learn the skills of רַחֲמִים to assist you in doing effective Teshuvah and removing any blockages.

> Quote from Tanya chapter 42

Hashem sees and looks	ה' הַצּוֹפֶה וּמַבִּיט
and hears and listens	וּמַאֲזִין וּמַקְשִׁיב
and understands all your deeds.	וּמֵבִין אֶל כָּל מַעֲשֵׂהוּ
He checks your kidneys and heart (your inner feelings and emotions)	וּבוֹחֵן כְּלִיוֹתָיו וְלִבּוֹ
Like the sages said,	וּכְמַאֲמַר רַבּוֹתֵינוּ זִכְרוֹנָם לִבְרָכָה
"Look carefully at three things (and you will not come to sin):	הִסְתַּכֵּל בִּשְׁלֹשָׁה דְבָרִים כוּ'
The eye that sees,	עַיִן רוֹאָה
the ear that hears (and everything you do is recorded in a book)."	וְאֹזֶן שׁוֹמַעַת כוּ'
Although He (G-d) does not have any concept of body,	וְגַם כִּי אֵין לוֹ דְמוּת הַגּוּף
this actually strengthens the point that	הֲרֵי אַדְּרַבָּה
everything is revealed and known before Him	הַכֹּל גָּלוּי וְיָדוּעַ לְפָנָיו
in a very clear way and infinitely greater	בְּיֶתֶר שְׂאֵת לְאֵין קֵץ
than the seeing of an eye	מֵרְאִיַּת הָעַיִן
or the hearing of the ear	וּשְׁמִיעַת הָאֹזֶן
by way of metaphor.	עַל דֶּרֶךְ מָשָׁל
Rather, a closer metaphor is	רַק הוּא עַל דֶּרֶךְ מָשָׁל

> **Quote from Tanya chapter 42**

like a person who is aware and feels in himself	כְּמוֹ אָדָם הַיּוֹדֵעַ וּמַרְגִּישׁ בְּעַצְמוֹ
all that happens and is done to	כָּל מַה שֶׁנַּעֲשֶׂה וְנִפְעָל
any one of his 248 limbs,	בְּאֶחָד מִכָּל רַמַ"ח אֵיבָרָיו
like cold or heat,	כְּמוֹ קוֹר אוֹ חוֹם
and even the heat in one of his toenails,	וַאֲפִילוּ חוֹם שֶׁבְּצִפָּרְנֵי רַגְלָיו
for example, if it was burned with fire.	עַל דֶּרֶךְ מָשָׁל אִם נִכְוָה בָּאוּר
Also the essence and core (of the limbs)	וְכֵן מַהוּתָם וְעַצְמוּתָם
and all that is affected in them,	וְכָל מַה שֶׁמִּתְפָּעֵל בָּהֶם
he feels in his brain.	יוֹדֵעַ וּמַרְגִּישׁ בְּמוֹחוֹ
Similar to this way of knowing, by way of metaphor,	וּכְעֵין יְדִיעָה זוֹ עַל דֶּרֶךְ מָשָׁל
G-d knows all that is done	יוֹדֵעַ הַקָּדוֹשׁ בָּרוּךְ הוּא כָּל הַנִּפְעָל
in all the higher and lower creations,	בְּכָל הַנִּבְרָאִים עֶלְיוֹנִים וְתַחְתּוֹנִים
since they all come from His blessed self,	לִהְיוֹת כּוּלָּם מוּשְׁפָּעִים מִמֶּנּוּ יִתְבָּרֵךְ
as it is written	כְּמוֹ שֶׁכָּתוּב
"Everything is from You."	כִּי מִמְּךָ הַכֹּל

VISUALIZATION EXERCISE
כְּעוֹמֵד לִפְנֵי הַמֶּלֶךְ

Visualization can rapidly affect how you do something. Did you ever find it difficult to do a certain task and as soon as you saw with your eyes somebody else doing it, it became much easier for you to do it? This is the power of visualization.

Did you ever see an image on a screen, like a car driving fast and it caused you to have an emotional response even though you knew it's not really happening and only on a screen?

Just like seeing an image on a screen will cause an emotional response, visualization with your imagination has the power to change how you do something.

Mental reflection (הִתְבּוֹנְנוּת) and emotional preparation (like קַבָּלָה/מְסִירָה) may not be so effective in the middle of a situation. Visualization is the tool of choice to prepare for a situation because it is so easy to recall even under stress.

Did you ever play a role in a school or camp play and as soon as you imagined the character you were going to play you were able to behave appropriately like that character? Your power of imagination becomes more effective with practice, the more practice the better you become.

Some people unlock their power of visualization by jumping straight into role play, others like to practice visualization only in the mind first. The following exercise will help you recognize some components of this tool in your mind.

☞ **ASK A FRIEND TO READ THE FOLLOWING PARAGRAPH AND THEN RAPIDLY ASK YOU THE LIST OF QUESTIONS.**

Don't pause until the questions are complete. The rapid speed will help access the part of your mind that is in charge of visualization, and avoid discussion, as it uses a different part of the mind.

Can you remember a time that you had a high stakes interaction? Can you remember a specific time when your meeting a specific person was important?

When the answer is yes, ask the following questions.

Where is the vision - in the center, right or left of your eyes? Is it black and white or color? Clear or blurry? Big or small?

Can you make some changes to make it more vivid?

**Can you center it? Make it bigger?
Add color? Make it very clear and in focus?
Make it even bigger?**

Now can you picture yourself waking up tomorrow morning? Add the vivid picture of the high-stakes interaction on top and picture yourself getting up with enthusiasm. The next morning, use this visualization to wake up with enthusiasm.

☞ **REPORT BACK TO YOUR PARTNER ON HOW YOU GOT UP DIFFERENTLY AND THEN WRITE ABOUT YOUR EXPERIENCE BELOW.**

_____

_____

Exercise 1

Step 1: As part of an exercise, ask someone to do a simple task.

Step 2: Video record them doing the same task and let them know others will see the video.

☞ **DESCRIBE HOW THEIR BEHAVIOR IMPROVED WHEN THEY KNEW THEY WERE BEING RECORDED.**

Exercise 2

When you are looking after children and they misbehave, record them and show them a video of themselves misbehaving.

How did this activity affect their behavior?

_____

_____

Exercise 3

☞ **EXPLAIN THE THREE PARTS OF YIRAS SHAMAYIM TO ANOTHER PERSON.**

YIRAS HASHEM MADE SIMPLE
EXPLAIN IT FROM THE HEART....

Your 3 Parts	Reflect on Core Concepts	Results
Intellectual Understanding **Think**	The Creator and Supervisor of the world, He is your power and life.	יִרְאַת אֱ-לֹהִים
Emotional Commitment **Prepare**	He has rules, like do not murder, do not steal etc..	קַבָּלַת עוֹל
Practical Action (guided by visualization) **Do**	There is an eye that sees and ear that hears; you are being held accountable.	יִרְאַת חֵטְא

Take a "Moment of silence" every day to reflect on this.

BONUS ACTIVITY
וּבוֹחֵן כְּלָיוֹת וָלֵב

Learn the following with a teacher or chavrusa and discuss the questions on the following page.

וכמ"ש לגבי נפש הבהמית בעץ חיים שער נון פרק יוד שאין כוונתה אלא לתועלת הגוף לבד... להכין צרכי הגוף... לשמירת הגוף ובהזנתו ולרחק רעותיו ונזקיו... ולהתעורר לבחור מדות הטובות שיש בהם תועלת לגוף ולרחק מדות הרעות מן הגוף... אלא שע"י נמשך נזק לנפש המדברת בכונת היצה"ר עכ"ל דהיינו שהנזוק הוא מהכוונה לשם הגוף לבד וכשמכוון לשם שמים כתוב גומל נפשו איש חסד וגו' משלי יא יז וכמ"ש אפס לא יהיה בך אביון וגו' דברים טו ד וכדי לברר הכוונה שיהיה נקי מפניות של הנפש הבהמית ולשם שמים צריך עבודת התפילה כל יום מחדש וגם כשעסק בתורה ומצוות כל יום מתערבים פניות של הנפש הבהמית וכדי לברר דרוש תפילה כל יום וכמ"ש בלקוטי תורה במדבר ג, ג שמצד הנפש הבהמית הרי הוא מעורב טוב ורע יחדיו. והגם שהוא עושה מצות ואינו עושה עבירות מ"מ בהעלם יש בו הרע שהרי יוכל להתאוות תאוה ועוד זאת שיוכל למצוא בנפשו איך התורה ומצות שמקיים אינם זכים ומיוחדים בתכלית לקיים רצון הבורא ית' לבד בלי שום פניה אחרת כי מתערב בזה איזו פניה וכוונה אחרת בפנימיותו. נמצא יש תערובות טו"ר אפילו בקיום התורה ומצות שהם בחי' לבושים דתורה ומצות שהוא מקיים.

ואצ"ל בפנימית המדות דנה"ב שלא נתהפכו עדיין מטבעם ותולדתם והרי בטבעם הם מעורבים טו"ר לפי שנלקחה מקליפת נוגה המעורבת טו"ר כנודע. וכשמתפלל בכוונה הנה ע"י שלהבת האהבה של הנפש אלקית הבאה מהתבוננות בגדולת ה' אזי מתברר הטוב מן הרע....נמצא ע"י התפלה נתגלה הרע מה שהיה תחלה מעורב בטוב ולא היה ידוע כלל שהוא רע שהיה נדמה לו שדרכו זכה וישרה עכשיו ע"י הבירור נתגלה הרע. וע"י יופרד מן הטוב וישאר הטוב לבדו בלי תערובות רע. וכמו שהוא הבירור בנפשות האדם שהנפש אלקית מבררת את הנפש הבהמית בשעת התפלה.

BONUS ACTIVITY QUESTIONS

☞ **DISCUSS OR WRITE DOWN THE ANSWERS**

1. What is Hashem checking for?

_____

_____

2. What two things together help purify your intentions?

A_____

B_____

3. When is looking after the body considered bad?

_____

_____

4. What tools do you use to purify the intentions of your heart and kidneys?

_____

_____

5. What is the tool of choice to reveal and maintain your Yiras Shamayim for a dynamic situation?

_____

_____

6. What is the tool of choice to reveal your Yiras Shamayim in a deep, internal and mature way?

_____

_____

7. Discuss how this is so and explain.

_____

_____

8. Which tool will help your Ahava be stable and consistent? (from Unit 1)

_____

_____

9. Which tool will bring out your best before you are faced with doing a Mitzvah?

_____

_____

10. Discuss how this is so and explain.

_____

_____

EVALUATE YOUR PERSONAL PROGRESS

1. How do you reveal *Yiras Elokim* and *Yiras Cheit*?
2. What things do you think about to reveal *Yiras Elokim*?
3. How do you do *Kabalas Ol Malchus Shamayim* and how does it enhance your life?
4. How do you use visualization and verbalization?
5. List 6 actions that constitute *Prikas Ol*?
6. Explain the benefit of delaying gratification?
7. How can you reveal *Yiras Shamayim* in others?

☞ **COMPARE YOUR ANSWERS TO HOW YOU ANSWERED SIMILAR QUESTIONS EARLIER IN THIS GUIDE BOOK.**

8. What are the three fundamentals in the path of *Yiras Shamayim*?
9. What do you do in *Shema* to guarantee that your prayers be answered in *Shmoneh Esrei*?
10. How has Unit 2 contributed to your life?

☞ **HOW DO YOU KNOW YOUR YIRAH ALSO HAS AHAVA?**

When any pressure is taken off you, how do you behave? If you have Ahava, you will still keep a Torah schedule because that is who you are! It's not a burden and you love it.

MAKE FUNDAMENTALS PRACTICE YOUR HABIT
Pause 3x Daily

You are now a warrior that has completed most of the basic training. Soon you will be effective and you have already learned a method of study that will help you continue your training with everything you learn in the future.

Even when you learn something and do not understand, you will find certainty in the fact that you know how to figure out how to behave (e.g. looking in *Shulchan Aruch*, consulting a *Rov*, asking 3 experts), and you know this fundamental method to motivate yourself to implement.

The practice of fundamentals will help you motivate others, especially in the living example you show.

FUNDAMENTALS PRACTICE:

INSTRUCTIONS:

1. **Start with anchoring in action, give some money to *Tzedaka*.**

2. **Read from Tanya 41 (on the next page) quietly in your mind.**

Notice when the intellectual reflection leads into emotional commitment and when this becomes a visualization.

3. **Mentally list the four concepts in the intellectual part of this thinking strategy.**

Think about what these four concepts mean and how they contribute to *Yiras Shamayim*.

4. **Say the first line of the Shema when you are *Mekabel Ol Malchus Shamayim* (indicated on the Tanya page).**

5. **When you get to the end of the Tanya 41 page,**

A) Visualize yourself in front of an important person, and then visualize yourself doing something different later today with the spirit of how you would behave in front of an important person. Envision doing something good or avoiding something or doing something better.

Imagine the feeling you are going to feel when you do this.

B) Visualize yourself spending time with people who will encourage you and limiting your exposure to people who discourage you.

Visualize yourself being a positive inspiration to someone else.

C) Visualize yourself changing something in your surroundings that will make it easier to do the good behavior or make it harder to do the bad behavior.

MAKE FUNDAMENTALS PRACTICE YOUR HABIT
Pause 3x Daily

PAUSE #1: YIRAH - TAKE RESPONSIBILITY
FROM TANYA, CHAPTER 41

Instructions on previous page.

It is important to remind myself constantly

what actually is the beginning of service

and its core and (living) root.

Even though fear (of G-d) is the root of turning from evil

and love (is the root) of doing good,

nevertheless, it is not sufficient to awaken love alone

to do good

and it is important to first awaken

at least the natural fear

which is hidden in the heart of all of Israel

which leads one to refrain from rebelling

against the King of kings

the Holy One, blessed be He, as mentioned above,

that this awe be revealed in my heart

or at least in my mind.

This means to at least reflect in my thoughts,

the greatness of G-d A-lmighty

and His Kingship (rules)

which extend to all the words,

both higher and lower.

He fills all worlds

and is also in a higher dimesion in all worlds

as it is written

"Do I not fill heaven and earth?" (Yirmeyahu 23:24)

Yet, He leaves aside (the creatures of) the higher (worlds)

and (the creatures of) the lower (worlds)

and he uniquely bestows His Kingship

upon His people Israel, in general,

and upon me in particular,

for man is obligated to say

"For my sake the world is created" (Sanhedrin 4:5).

I, in turn,

accept His Kingship upon myself,

that He will be King over me,

to serve Him and do His Will

in all kinds of work required of a servant. **Say שְׁמַע**

And, behold, G-d is standing over him (me),"

and "The whole world is filled with His Glory,"

and He is watching you,

and is checking (my) innermost thoughts and feelings

that I serve Him properly.

Therefore, I serve in His Presence

with awe and fear

as I would, when standing before a King.

REVEAL AHAVA (PAUSE #2)
FROM TANYA, CHAPTER 44

Read from "And this is what…" until "Do we not have One Father" out loud.

And this is what's written in the Zohar (Vol. 3, pg. 68a)

on the Pasuk (Yeshayahu 26:9)

"My soul, I desire You (Hashem) at night…"

(the Zohar says) "Love Hashem,

with the love for the soul and spirit

when they are attached to the body,

the body loves them (the soul and spirit)…"

(In other words,) this is what the verse,

"My soul, I desire You," is saying.

"Since You, G-d, are my true energy and life,

therefore I desire You."

That is to say, "I long for and yearn for You (Hashem)

like a man who craves the life of his soul."

And when I am weak and exhausted,

I long and yearn for my soul to revive me.

Likewise, when I go to sleep,

I long and yearn for my soul to return to me

when I wake up from my sleep.

The same way, I long and yearn

for the light of the Infinite One,

blessed is He,

the true Life of life,

to be drawn into me

through my occupation in Torah (study),

when I awaken from my sleep during the night.

For the Torah and the Holy One, blessed be He,

are one and the same.

Like the Zohar says (ibid.)

"A man is required,

out of love for the Holy One, blessed be He,

to rise each night

and exert himself in His service until the morning…"

UPGRADED AHAVA
FROM TANYA, CHAPTER 44

"Like a son who exerts himself

for his father and mother,

whom he loves

more than self,

his Nefesh, Ruach etc.

for "Do we not have One Father"?

Immediately make an anchor by learning Torah; read the following short paragraph from Tehillim:

TEHILLIM, CHAPTER 117

א: הַלְלוּ אֶת ה' כָּל גּוֹיִם שַׁבְּחוּהוּ כָּל הָאֻמִּים:
1: Praise the L-RD, all you nations; give tribute to Him, all you peoples.

ב: כִּי גָבַר עָלֵינוּ חַסְדּוֹ וֶאֱמֶת ה' לְעוֹלָם הַלְלוּיָ-הּ:
2: for great is His steadfast love toward us; the faithfulness of the L-RD endures forever. Praise the L-rd.

Continue on next page. »

MAKE FUNDAMENTALS PRACTICE YOUR HABIT
— Pause 3x Daily —

PAUSE #3: RACHAMIM - HAVE COMPASSION

Make the evaluation below. Give yourself a score of 1-10, 1 represents very little and 10 represents a lot. Notice that even if you score highly, since your *Giluy Elokus* (experience of Hashem in your life) is not in the entire world, then even what you have is not a revelation of the real essence of Hashem.

SCORE

- [ ] You feel warm and refreshed
- [ ] Mitzvos feel easy to do even when challenged
- [ ] You feel tranquil when you do things
- [ ] You feel pleasure in Torah study
- [ ] The atmosphere around you is refined
- [ ] You are a positive influence on others

Make an anchor by reading the following request to Hashem

וְתֶחֱזֶינָה עֵינֵינוּ בְּשׁוּבְךָ לְצִיּוֹן בְּרַחֲמִים

May our eyes see Your return to Zion with compassion.

☞ FROM TANYA CHAPTER 36

עת קץ הימין שאז יזדכך גשמיות הגוף והעולם ויוכלו לקבל גילוי אור ה' שיאיר לישראל ע"י התורה שנקרא עוז ומיתרון ההארה לישראל יגיה חשך האומות גם כן.

In the time of the redemption, the physical body will become refined, enabling it to receive a revelation of the light of G-d that will shine to the Jews through the Torah that is called strength, and from the extra light to the Jews, the darkness of the nations will also be lit up.

- The soul gets Divine revelation from Torah study
- The body is refined by using it to do Mitzvos, the refinement of the body enables the light of the Torah to be revealed in it
- The Torah lights up the soul through the preparation of prayer

STRATEGY PAGE - YOUR ONE-PAGE SUMMARY

Go to the beginning of this guide book and notice every time you put a dot in the margin.

In the left column below, record all the key ideas to marked. In the right column, explain the big ideas and how they affect your life.

List the key ideas:

_____

_____

_____

_____

_____

_____

_____

Explain how they affect your life:

_____

_____

_____

_____

_____

_____

_____

THREE EASY HABITS I CAN IMPLEMENT RIGHT AWAY:

1. _____
2. _____
3. _____

When will I do them? _____

How can I track them on a score sheet? _____

REFLECT ON THESE QUESTIONS BEFORE STARTING UNIT 3:

1. What is *Rachamim*?

2. How is *Rachamim* core to Judaism?

3. Explain the thinking strategy that reveals *Rachamim*?

4. How does *Rachamim* help in achieving your goals?

5. How does *Rachamim* help bring Moshiach?

UNIT 3

THE THIRD FIGHTING FORCE
AN ARMY AGAINST THE YETZER HARA

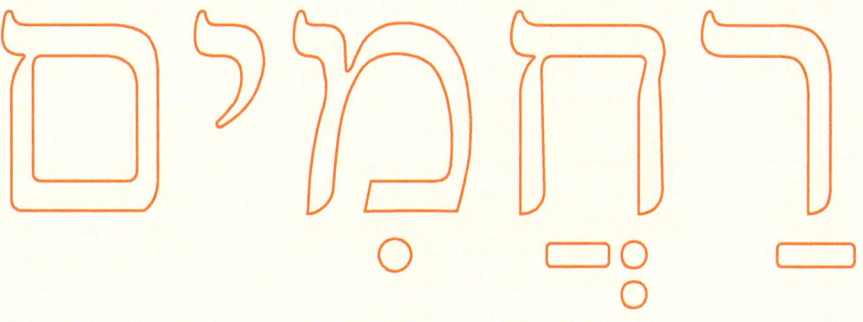

GOAL

A thinking strategy that evokes the emotion of compassion charging the request for Rachamim.

TANYA – CHAPTER 45
INTRODUCTION

Asking for Rachamim

(RAMBAM) MITZVAH 77

לְהִתְפַּלֵּל בְּכָל יוֹם

DAVENING TO HASHEM

וַעֲבַדְתֶּם אֵת ה' אֱ-לֹהֵיכֶם
(שמות כג, כה)

And you should serve the L-rd your G-d

Ask Hashem for all your needs everyday.

Why Daven to Hashem each day?

Doesn't He already know what you need?

The Torah answers this question by explaining that the Mitzvah to Daven to Hashem is to ask for Hashem's compassion. When you think about your true situation in the ways you will learn in this unit, you are able to make real changes in your life.

In the words of the Alter Rebbe:

FROM THE SOURCE

שֶׁהַתְּפִלָּה בַּקָּשַׁת רַחֲמִים הִיא וְצָרִיךְ כָּל אֶחָד לְבַקֵּשׁ רַחֲמִים עַל עַצְמוֹ

Prayer is the request for Divine **compassion**, and everyone needs to ask for compassion on themselves.

SHULCHAN ARUCH HARAV ORACH CHAIM 59:4

☞ SUMMARY

The Mitzvah to Daven to Hashem is a Mitzvah which helps you to focus on the areas of your life that need Hashem's compassion.

What is Rachamim?

The emotion of compassion which is a mix between Chessed-kindness and Gevura-strictness.

How is the emotion of Rachamim triggered?

Rachamim is triggered when a person widens their mental **perspective** to see the bigger picture and sees the **contrast** between the extremes of a situation.

The Effect of Rachamim

Rachamim charges your connection to Hashem which then facilitates bringing Elokus into the world when you learn Torah and do Mitzvos with Ahava and Yirah together with Kabalas Ol.

☞ RACHAMIM AS A TOOL

Rachamim;

- Helps you attain Ahavas and Yiras Hashem.
- Helps in Chinuch.
- Helps in Ahavas Yisrael.
- Is part of doing Teshuvah.
- Brings the Geula.

Rachamim comes from Tiferes, the attribute of truth. When you contrast the extremes of a situation, you channel into the truth. Yaakov Avinu used this attribute to educate his children and was successful; at every stage, Yaakov would recognize what his children are and what they could be at the same time.

Tanya at a Glance

To be able to make everything you have learned up until now effective, you will add the skill of Rachamim.

Rachamim is an emotion that comes from a mental process that you will learn in this unit.

You are here

THE 53 CHAPTERS OF TANYA AT A GLANCE

Intro	**1-5** Spiritual Anatomy

6-8 Spiritual Anatomy	**9-11** Conquering Ourselves

12-17 Conquering Ourselves

18-23 Revealing Hidden Love

24-25 Revealing Hidden Love	**26-29** Reaching Happiness

30-31 Reaching Happiness	**32** Ahavas Yisroel	**33-34** Reaching Happiness	**35** Implementation

36-40 Implementation	**41** Skill: Fearing Hashem

42 Skill: Fearing Hashem	**43** Skill: Loving & fearing Hashem	**44** Skill: Loving Hashem	**45** Awakening Compassion	**46-47** Becoming Effective

48-50 Becoming Effective	**51-53** Implementation

TANYA CHAPTER 45
RACHAMIM

SEE THE CONTRAST

Just like Rachamim is a mix of opposite emotions, kindness and strictness, so too the "mental process" that gives birth to Rachamim requires you to focus on (at least) 2 extremes.

For example:

a) Where you are now vs. where you could be;

b) Your limitations vs. Hashem's power;

c) Your level of knowledge and how your knowledge is very little.

What is Divine Compassion?

When you see a person's current situation along with where they could be, you will have compassion on the person.

In Tanya ch. 45, you will learn that to reveal Divine compassion on your soul, you reflect on two extremes of;

   A. The pure Divine source of your soul;

   B. The situation of your soul now in a body.

Even if you do not intellectually understand these extremes, your Divine soul does understand and will be aroused when you follow this process.

על הכסף וכו' כמ"ש לקמן וגם כי זה כל האדם ותכליתו למען דעת את כבוד ה' ויקר תפארת גדולתו איש איש כפי אשר יוכל שאת כמ"ש בר"מ פ' בא בגין דישתמודעון ליה וכו' וכנודע:

פרק מה עוד יש דרך ישר לפני איש לעסוק בתורה ומצות לשמן ע"י מדתו של יעקב אע"ה שהיא מדת הרחמי' לעורר במחשבתו תחלה רחמים רבים לפני ה' על ניצוץ אלהות המחיה נפשו

128 ליקוטי אמרים

נפשו אשר ירד ממקורו חיי החיים א"ס ב"ה הממלא כל עלמין וסובב כל עלמין וכולא קמיה כלא חשיב ונתלבש במשכא דחויא הרחוק מאור פני המלך בתכלית ההרחק כי העה"ז הוא תכלית הקליפ' הגסות כו' ובפרט כשיזכור על כל מעשיו ודבוריו ומחשבותיו מיום היותו אשר לא טובים המה ומלך אסור ברהטים ברהיטי מוחא כי יעקב חבל נחלתו. וכמשל המושך בחבל וכו' והוא סוד גלות השכינה. וע"ז נאמר וישב אל ה' וירחמהו לעורר רחמים רבים על שם ה' השוכן אתנו כדכתיב השוכן אתם בתוך טומאתם · וזש"ה וישק יעקב לרחל וישא את קולו ויבך. כי רחל היא כנסת ישראל מקור כל הנשמות · ויעקב במדתו העליונה שהיא מדת הרחמים שבאצילות הוא המעורר רחמים רבים עליה · וישא את קולו למעלה למקור הרחמים העליונים הנק' אב הרחמים ומקורם · ויבך לעורר ולהמשיך משם רחמים רבים על כל הנשמות ועל מקור כנסת ישראל להעלותן מגלותן וליחדן ביחוד העליון אור א"ס ב"ה בבחי' נשיקין שהיא אתדבקות רוחא ברוחא כמ"ש ישקני מנשיקות פיהו דהיינו התקשרות דבור האדם בדבר ה' זו הלכה וכן

> **Quote from Tanya chapter 45**

There is an additional direct path	עוֹד יֵשׁ דֶּרֶךְ יָשָׁר
before man (you)	לִפְנֵי אִישׁ
(empowering you) to fulfill Torah and Mitzvos with the proper intention,	לַעֲסוֹק בַּתּוֹרָה וּמִצְוֹת לִשְׁמָן
by using the attribute of Yaakov our father,	עַל יְדֵי מִדָּתוֹ שֶׁל יַעֲקֹב אָבִינוּ עָלָיו הַשָּׁלוֹם
the attribute of compassion.	שֶׁהִיא מִדַּת הָרַחֲמִים
(How?) Firstly, arouse in your mind	לְעוֹרֵר בְּמַחֲשַׁבְתּוֹ תְּחִלָּה
great compassion before G-d	רַחֲמִים רַבִּים לִפְנֵי ה'
on the Divine spark	עַל נִיצוֹץ אֱ-לֹהוּת
which gives life to your soul,	הַמְחַיֶּה נַפְשׁוֹ
which came down from its source,	אֲשֶׁר יָרַד מִמְּקוֹרוֹ
the Life of life,	חַיֵּי הַחַיִּים
the infinite One, blessed be He,	אֵין סוֹף בָּרוּךְ הוּא
who fills all the worlds,	הַמְמַלֵּא כָּל עָלְמִין
and encompasses all the worlds,	וְסוֹבֵב כָּל עָלְמִין
and all that is before of Him is like naught,	וְכוּלָּא קַמֵּיהּ כְּלָא חֲשִׁיב
and this (Divine spark) became enclothed in the skin of the snake,	וְנִתְלַבֵּשׁ בְּמַשְׁכָּא דְחִוְיָא
which is far from the light of the face of the king	הָרָחוֹק מֵאוֹר פְּנֵי הַמֶּלֶךְ
in the greatest degree of distance.	בְּתַכְלִית הַהֶרְחֵק

👉 TAKE NOTE

All that is before Him is like naught - כּוּלָּא קַמֵּיהּ כְּלָא חֲשִׁיב

Picture something in your mind, like a table or chair. You have the potential to make many pictures in your mind. Compared to you, this picture is insignificant, as you can make an unlimited number of pictures. So too, the world is made from the words of Hashem, and everything in the world is like one thought in the mind and compared to Hashem is insignificant, besides thoughts that Hashem chooses to give significance to.

Note that we start by reflecting on concepts easier for the mind to relate to, like how Hashem is מְמַלֵּא כָּל עָלְמִין, and then we reflect on more exalted concepts like כּוּלָּא קַמֵּיהּ כְּלָא חֲשִׁיב and then סוֹבֵב כָּל עָלְמִין.

> Quote from Tanya chapter 45

Because this world is the epitome of the most coarse of klipos (peels).	כִּי הָעוֹלָם הַזֶּה הוּא תַּכְלִית הַקְּלִיפוֹת הַגַּסּוֹת כוּ'
Specifically	וּבִפְרָט
when he remembers all his deeds,	כְּשֶׁיִּזְכּוֹר עַל כָּל מַעֲשָׂיו
words and thoughts	וְדִבּוּרָיו וּמַחְשְׁבוֹתָיו
from the day he became (alive)	מִיּוֹם הֱיוֹתוֹ
that were not good (self-centered and not holy),	אֲשֶׁר לֹא טוֹבִים הֵמָּה
and the King is jailed with chains,	וּמֶלֶךְ אָסוּר בָּרְהָטִים
the chains (that come from thoughts) of the mind,	בִּרְהִיטֵי מוֹחָא
because Yaakov is the rope of G-d's inheritance,	כִּי יַעֲקֹב חֶבֶל נַחֲלָתוֹ.
and like the metaphor of a rope that when you pull one side, the other side is pulled as well.	וְכִמְשַׁל הַמּוֹשֵׁךְ בְּחֶבֶל וְכוּ'

👉 TAKE NOTE

הַמָּקוֹם וְהַזְּמַן הֵם רְחוֹקִים מֵאוֹר פָּנָיו יִתְבָּרֵךְ

"Space and time are far from His blessed light"

Likkutei Torah, Behaaloscha 30:3

One need not focus on one's own lowliness in detail, as this may lead to negative results. Instead, focus on the fact that even "time and space" themselves compared to Hashem Himself are a great contrast.

▸ KEY TERMS ◂

Compassion	רַחֲמִים
Divine spark	נִיצוֹץ אֱ-לֹהוּת
All that is before of Him is like naught	כּוּלָּא קַמֵּיהּ כְּלָא חֲשִׁיב
skin of the snake*	מַשְׁכָא דְחִוְיָא
chains (that come from thoughts) of the mind	רְהִיטֵי מוֹחָא

---

*The body is called a skin, since it is a garment for the soul and it is called skin of a "snake", since the body is in its unrefined state.

UNIT 3 / THE THIRD FIGHTING FORCE - RACHAMIM TANYA – CHAPTER 45

> Quote from Tanya chapter 45

This is the secret behind the exile of the Shechina,	וְהוּא סוֹד גָּלוּת הַשְּׁכִינָה.
and on this (the solution) is stated	וְעַל זֶה נֶאֱמַר
"And he will return to G-d	וְיָשׁוֹב אֶל ה'
and he will have compassion on Him,"	וְיִרַחֲמֵהוּ
Meaning, to arouse great compassion	לְעוֹרֵר רַחֲמִים רַבִּים
on the name of G-d which dwells inside of us,	עַל שֵׁם ה' הַשּׁוֹכֵן אִתָּנוּ
as it is written, "The One who dwells with them	כְּדִכְתִיב הַשּׁוֹכֵן אִתָּם
within their impurities."	בְּתוֹךְ טוּמְאֹתָם.

FROM THE SOURCE

וְיַחְשׁוֹב קוֹדֶם הַתְּפִלָּה מֵרוֹמְמוּת הָאֵ-ל יִתְעַלֶּה וּבְשִׁפְלוּת הָאָדָם

Before prayer, one should think about the exalted loftiness of Hashem and the lowliness of humankind.

SHULCHAN ARUCH ORACH CHAIM 98:1

👉 TAKE NOTE

The Torah's requirement is to first think about the exalted loftiness of Hashem which will automatically lead to recognizing the contrast to man; there is no need to dwell on the lowliness of man.

Note that the Shulchan Aruch does not use the term גַּדְלוּת (greatness of Hashem) rather רוֹמְמוּת (exalted loftiness), which emphasizes greater contrast. Specifically contrast leads to awakening רַחֲמִים (Divine mercy and compassion).

אֵין עוֹמְדִין לְהִתְפַּלֵּל אֶלָּא מִתּוֹךְ כֹּבֶד רֹאשׁ.

[One] should not stand up to pray unless he is in a serious frame of mind.

MISHNA BRACHOS 5:1

רֹאשׁ = Shechina • כֹּבֶד = Heavy (in Galus)

כּוֹבֶד רֹאשׁ זֶהוּ כְּמוֹ שֶׁכָּתוּב עֲוֹנוֹתַי עָבְרוּ רֹאשִׁי כְּמַשָּׂא כָבֵד יִכְבְּדוּ מִמֶּנִּי (תהלים ל״ח ה׳)... בְּחִינַת גָּלוּת שֶׁהַשְּׁכִינָה...מְקוֹר כָּל נִשְׁמוֹת יִשְׂרָאֵל נִקְרָא רֹאשׁ...

A head (Rosh) that is heavy means like it is written "For my iniquities have overwhelmed me; they are like a heavy burden, more than I can bear (Tehillim 38:5)."...this is the concept of the exile of the Shechina...the source of the souls of Yisroel is called "Rosh".

LIKKUTEI TORAH 35A

👉 TAKE NOTE

There is an intrinsic contrast in the words כֹּבֶד רֹאשׁ, which refers to the Divine source of the soul and the heavy descent the source of the Divine soul has made into Galus, called the Galus of the Shechina.

RACHAMIM EXERCISE (I)

1. On each line in the chart below, write each of the points mentioned in Tanya ch. 45:

☞ CONTRAST THE ORIGINAL (HIGHER) POSTION OF THE NESHAMA WITH ITS CURRENT (LOWER) POSITION.

Higher Extreme	Lower Extreme

2. What does this mean to you? So what? Explain:
   _____
   _____

3. Ask for Rachamim in your mind.
4. Verbally ask for something specific.
5. How many times is רַחֲמִים written in Shmoneh Esrei?
   _____
6. What is the connecting theme between כֹּבֶד רֹאשׁ and the bonus section in Unit 1?
   _____
   _____

RACHAMIM IS PART OF TESHUVAH
TANYA IGERES HATESHUVAH CHAPTER 7

Part of the process of Teshuvah is asking Hashem to change the very feelings inside you that brought you to the problem in the first place.

In the following quote from Tanya Igeres HaTeshuvah, you will read how asking for Rachamim is part of doing Teshuvah.

However, the real and direct path	וְאוּלָם דֶּרֶךְ הָאֱמֶת וְהַיָּשָׁר
to lower Teshuvah (return to Hashem and self)	לִבְחִינַת תְּשׁוּבָה תַּתָּאָה
(which results in the) second ה (to be returned to its place in the name of G-d)	הֵ"א תַּתָּאָה
as mentioned above	הַנִּזְכֶּרֶת לְעֵיל
is through two things in general:	הֵם ב' דְּבָרִים דֶּרֶךְ כְּלָל.
The first is to arouse compassion from above	הָא' הוּא לְעוֹרֵר רַחֲמִים הָעֶלְיוֹנִים
from the source of compassion on his soul and Divine spirit	מִמְּקוֹר הָרַחֲמִים עַל נִשְׁמָתוֹ וְנַפְשׁוֹ הָאֱלֹקִית
that fell from a high tower, the Life of life, Blessed be He,	שֶׁנָּפְלָה מֵאִיגְרָא רָמָה חַיֵּי הַחַיִּים בָּרוּךְ הוּא
to a low pit,	לְבִירָא עֲמִיקְתָּא
namely, the chambers of impurity and the other side which is not Holy,	הֵן הֵיכְלוֹת הַטּוּמְאָה וְהַסִּטְרָא אָחֳרָא.
and (arouse compassion) on its source in the Source of Life,	וְעַל מְקוֹרָהּ בִּמְקוֹר הַחַיִּים
which is the name of G-d, Blessed be He,	הוּא שֵׁם הוי' בָּרוּךְ הוּא
as it is written, "And he will return to G-d and he will have compassion on Him,"	וּכְמוֹ שֶׁכָּתוּב וְיָשֹׁב אֶל הוי' וִירַחֲמֵהוּ.
meaning, to arouse compassion	פֵּירוּשׁ לְעוֹרֵר רַחֲמִים
on the channel of life from the name of G-d, Blessed be He,	עַל הַשְׁפָּעַת שֵׁם הוי' בָּרוּךְ הוּא
which came down and descended	שֶׁנִּשְׁתַּלְשְׁלָה וְיָרְדָה
into the impure chambers of the other side,	תּוֹךְ הֵיכְלוֹת הַסִּטְרָא אָחֳרָא הַטְּמֵאִים
to give them life.	לְהַחֲיוֹתָם
This (descent) results from the actions of man and his schemes	עַל יְדֵי מַעֲשֵׂה אֱנוֹשׁ וְתַחְבּוּלוֹתָיו
and his bad thoughts,	וּמַחְשְׁבוֹתָיו הָרָעוֹת
as it is written, "The king is jailed in chains,"	וּכְמוֹ שֶׁכָּתוּב מֶלֶךְ אָסוּר בָּרְהָטִים
the chains made from the thoughts of the mind,	בִּרְהִיטֵי מוֹחָא וְכוּ'
And this situation is called the exile of the Shechina as mentioned earlier.	הִיא בְּחִינַת גָּלוּת הַשְּׁכִינָה כַּנִּזְכָּר לְעֵיל.

RACHAMIM EXERCISE (II)

1. On each line, explain each of the points mentioned in Tanya Igeres HaTeshuvah Chapter 7:

Higher Extreme	Lower Extreme

2. What does this mean to you? So what?

_____

_____

3. Ask for Rachamim in your mind.

4. Ask for something specific and write it here.

_____

_____

5. How is asking for Rachamim part of Teshuvah?

_____

_____

RACHAMIM BRINGS SPECIAL SPIRIT
TANYA IGERES HATESHUVAH CHAPTER 8

When a person does a sin G-d forbid, then the sin causes a blockage that makes the person unresponsive to things that would normally inspire them. After a person asks for Rachamim, Hashem sends a spirit to spiritually clean the person.

For then it will be really instilled in his (your) heart	כִּי אֲזַי תִּקָּבַע בְּלִבּוֹ בֶּאֱמֶת
the immense (reason to feel) compassion on the Divine (spark) in your soul	גּוֹדֶל הָרַחֲמָנוּת עַל בְּחִינַת אֱלֹקוּת שֶׁבְּנַפְשׁוֹ
and the (Divine that is) above as mentioned before.	וְשֶׁלְּמַעְלָה כַּנִּזְכָּר לְעֵיל.
And this will arouse supernal compassion	וּבָזֶה יְעוֹרֵר רַחֲמִים הָעֶלְיוֹנִים
from the 13 attributes of compassion…	מִי"ג מִדּוֹת הָרַחֲמִים…
The 13 attributes of compassion	הַי"ג מִדּוֹת הָרַחֲמִים
clean all the blemishes…	מְנַקִּים כָּל הַפְּגָמִים…
From then on, your sins cease to separate (you from G-d)…	שׁוּב אֵין עֲוֹנוֹתֵיכֶם מַבְדִּילִים…
Because this spirit passed over and cleaned them,	וּמֵאַחַר שֶׁרוּחַ עָבְרָה וַתְּטַהֲרֵם
then your soul can	אֲזַי תּוּכַל נַפְשָׁם
really return to G-d Blessed be He	לָשׁוּב עַד הוי' בָּרוּךְ הוּא מַמָּשׁ
and go up higher and higher	וְלַעֲלוֹת מַעְלָה מַעְלָה
to its source	לִמְקוֹרָהּ
and strongly connect to Him	וּלְדָבְקָה בּוֹ יִתְבָּרֵךְ
in a super Oneness.	בְּיִחוּד נִפְלָא.

👉 TAKE NOTE

Positive Contrast

Boys under 13 and girls under 12 can understand the concept of empathy however they will not experience the full emotion of compassion yet, therefore it is extra important to focus on the positive of the contrast, the gift.

לֵב טָהוֹר בְּרָא לִי אֱ-לֹהִים וְרוּחַ נָכוֹן חַדֵּשׁ בְּקִרְבִּי:

Fashion a pure heart for me, O God; create in me a steadfast **spirit**.

אַל תַּשְׁלִיכֵנִי מִלְּפָנֶיךָ וְרוּחַ קָדְשְׁךָ אַל־תִּקַּח מִמֶּנִּי:

Do not cast me out of Your presence, or take Your holy **spirit** away from me.

הָשִׁיבָה לִּי שְׂשׂוֹן יִשְׁעֶךָ וְרוּחַ נְדִיבָה תִסְמְכֵנִי:

Let me again rejoice in Your help; let a vigorous **spirit** sustain me.

TEHILLIM 51:12-14

☞ TAKE NOTE

Study Chassidus

When a person studies a concept in Chassidus, investing time and effort, then they recognize that they really understand less than a drop in an ocean. This creates a contrast which leads to the feeling of רַחֲמִים which prepares a person to effectively ask Hashem for Divine mercy and compassion.

RACHAMIM MADE SIMPLE

Step	Action	Detail
Pre-Step Anchor	Give Tzedaka	Behave with compassion to trigger compassion from Above
One	Establish Contrast	Contrast the… Higher Extreme Lower Extreme
Two	Ask for רַחֲמִים in your mind	Think of the situation of your soul now
Three	Verbally ask for something specific	(e.g. Please help me to…..)

Follow these steps each day during davening.

SEE IT IN THE WORDS OF PRAYER
TANYA IGERES HAKODESH SECTION 6

The best way to maintain a skill is by connecting it with something you do every day. The following quote from Tanya Igeres HaKodesh explains how to ask for Rachamim every day in a specific place before Shema.

It's known that Yaakov's prime emotion	אַךְ הִנֵּה מוּדַעַת זֹאת דְּמִדַּת יַעֲקֹב
Is the emotion of compassion	הִיא מִדַּת רַחֲמָנוּת
And serving Hashem using compassion	וַעֲבוֹדַת ה' בְּמִדַּת רַחֲמָנוּת הִיא
Is done by arousing great compassion in your heart	הַבָּאָה מֵהִתְעוֹרְרוּת רַחֲמִים רַבִּים בְּלֵב הָאָדָם
On the Divine spark inside you	עַל נִיצוֹץ אֱלֹקוּת שֶׁבְּנַפְשׁוֹ
Which at present is far from the light of Hashem's countenance	הָרְחוֹקָה מֵאוֹר פְּנֵי ה'
As it walks in the darkness of empty worldly pursuits	כַּאֲשֶׁר הוֹלֵךְ בְּחֹשֶׁךְ הַבְלֵי עוֹלָם
Awakening this compassion	וְהִתְעוֹרְרוּת רַחֲמָנוּת זוֹ
Comes from focusing and thinking practically about the greatness of Hashem	הִיא בָּאָה מֵהִתְבּוֹנְנוּת וְהַדַּעַת בִּגְדוּלַּת ה'
How even the higher worlds, that go higher and higher	אֵיךְ שֶׁאֲפִילוּ הָעוֹלָמוֹת הָעֶלְיוֹנִים לְמַעְלָה מַעְלָה
till no end	עַד אֵין קֵץ
compared to Him are all considered like nought ….	כֻּלָּא מַמָּשׁ חֲשִׁיבֵי קַמֵּיהּ….
And this is (the meaning of) what we say (in the daily prayers)	וְזֶהוּ שֶׁאוֹמְרִים
"The King that is alone exalted from way back"	הַמֶּלֶךְ הַמְרוֹמָם לְבַדּוֹ מֵאָז
This means	פֵּירוּשׁ
Just like way back before the creation	כְּמוֹ שֶׁמֵּאָז קוֹדֶם הַבְּרִיאָה
He was the only One	הָיָה הוּא לְבַדּוֹ הוּא
So too now	כָּךְ עַתָּה
"He is exalted (and only)" etc	הוּא מְרוֹמָם כו'
"He is higher than the days of the world"	וּמִתְנַשֵּׂא מִימוֹת עוֹלָם
This means He is exalted higher	פֵּירוּשׁ שֶׁהוּא רָם וְנִשָּׂא
Way beyond	לְמַעְלָה מַעְלָה
The idea of time	מִבְּחִינַת זְמַן
Which is called the days of the world	הַנִּקְרָא בְּשֵׁם יְמוֹת עוֹלָם

And this is because the life force of the days of the world	וְהַיְנוּ לְפִי שֶׁחַיּוּת כָּל יְמוֹת עוֹלָם
Comes only from the level of "the King - Malchus" etc	הוּא רַק מִבְּחִינַת הַמֶּלֶךְ כוּ'
And like it is written in another place	וּכְמוֹ שֶׁכָּתוּב בְּמָקוֹם אַחֵר.
And because the reason to have compassion is very very great	וְאֵי לָזֹאת הָרַחֲמָנוּת גְּדוֹלָה מְאֹד מְאֹד
On the spark that dwells inside the body	עַל הַנִּיצוֹץ הַשּׁוֹכֵן בַּגּוּף
Which is extremely dark and the skin of a snake	הֶחָשׁוּךְ וְהָאָפֵל מַשְׁכָּא דְחִוְיָא
And it is very susceptible to take in impurity	הֶעָלוּל לְקַבֵּל טוּמְאָה
And to dirty itself in all the pleasures may the merciful one protect us	וּלְהִתְגָּאֵל בְּכָל הַתַּאֲווֹת רַחֲמָנָא לִצְּלָן
Where it not that the Holy One, blessed be He, protects him (you)	לוּלֵי שֶׁהַקָּדוֹשׁ בָּרוּךְ הוּא מָגֵן לוֹ
And gives you strength and power	וְנוֹתֵן לוֹ עוֹז וְתַעֲצוּמוֹת
To wage war with the body and its pleasures	לִלְחוֹם עִם הַגּוּף וְתַאֲוֹתָיו
And to win over them	וּלְנַצְּחָן
And this is (the meaning of) what it is written (in the same prayer)	וְזֶהוּ שֶׁאוֹמְרִים
"You are the master of our strength etc, the protector of our salvation etc"	אֲדוֹן עוּזֵּנוּ כוּ' מָגֵן יִשְׁעֵנוּ כוּ'.

FROM THE SOURCE

הַמֶּלֶךְ הַמְרוֹמָם לְבַדּוֹ מֵאָז. הַמְשֻׁבָּח וְהַמְפֹאָר וְהַמִּתְנַשֵּׂא מִימוֹת עוֹלָם. אֱ-לֹהֵי עוֹלָם. בְּרַחֲמֶיךָ הָרַבִּים רַחֵם עָלֵינוּ. אֲדוֹן עֻזֵּנוּ. צוּר מִשְׂגַּבֵּנוּ. מָגֵן יִשְׁעֵנוּ. מִשְׂגָּב בַּעֲדֵנוּ.

The King Who alone is exalted from then. Who is praised and glorified and uplifted, from the beginning of time. Eternal G-d, in Your abundant mercy, have compassion on us. Master, Who is our strength, Rock, Who is our stronghold Shield, of our deliverance, [Be] a stronghold for us.

SIDDUR · SHACHARIS

FIND OUT MORE

מקיף דיחידה ...והו"ע רחם עלינו כו',...והמדרי' הב' בחי' מקיף דחי' והוא אדון עוזינו...ואח"כ ג' מקיפים צור משגבינו מגן ישענו משגב בעדינו בחי' דנר"ן מקיפים שהן מקיפים בעדינו בי"ע הכללים

המשך תער"ב חלק ראשון ע' קלו

UNIT 3 / THE THIRD FIGHTING FORCE - RACHAMIM   TANYA – CHAPTER 45

MAKE FUNDAMENTALS PRACTICE YOUR HABIT
Pause 3x Daily

PAUSE AND CONTRAST וְצָרִיךְ כָּל אֶחָד לְבַקֵּשׁ רַחֲמִים עַל עַצְמוֹ

SEE THE WORDS

BIRCHOS KRIAS SHEMA
IN TEFILAS SHACHRIS

TANYA IGERES HAKODESH
SECTION 6

PAUSE

1. MENTALLY CONTRAST
2. ASK FOR COMPASSION
3. ASK FOR SPECIFIC DIVINE ASSISTANCE
   1. GIVE STRENGTH AND EMUNA
   2. FORTIFY OUR MIND
   3. SHIELD OUR FEELINGS
   4. GUARD OUR ACTIONS

☞ **TAKE NOTE**

If after doing the skill you still do not feel רַחֲמִים, ask for רַחֲמִים anyways! Hashem will help!

216

RACHAMIM EXERCISE (III)

1. On each line, explain each of the points mentioned in Tanya Igeres HaKodesh Section 6:

Higher Extreme	Lower Extreme

2. What does it mean to you? So what?

_____

_____

3. What are we asking for in the siddur?

_____

_____

_____

RACHAMIM EXERCISE (IV)

☞ **FIND THE FOLLOWING QUOTE IN THE ENGLISH TRANSLATION OF THE SIDDUR.**

> רִבּוֹן כָּל הָעוֹלָמִים. לֹא עַל צִדְקוֹתֵינוּ אֲנַחְנוּ מַפִּילִים תַּחֲנוּנֵינוּ לְפָנֶיךָ כִּי עַל רַחֲמֶיךָ הָרַבִּים. מָה אָנוּ מֶה חַיֵּינוּ מֶה חַסְדֵּנוּ מַה צִּדְקֵנוּ מַה כֹּחֵנוּ מַה גְּבוּרָתֵנוּ. מַה נֹּאמַר לְפָנֶיךָ יְיָ אֱ-לֹהֵינוּ וֵא-לֹהֵי אֲבוֹתֵינוּ, הֲלֹא כָּל הַגִּבּוֹרִים כְּאַיִן לְפָנֶיךָ, וְאַנְשֵׁי הַשֵּׁם כְּלֹא הָיוּ, וַחֲכָמִים כִּבְלִי מַדָּע, וּנְבוֹנִים כִּבְלִי הַשְׂכֵּל, כִּי רוֹב מַעֲשֵׂיהֶם תֹּהוּ, וִימֵי חַיֵּיהֶם הֶבֶל לְפָנֶיךָ, וּמוֹתַר הָאָדָם מִן הַבְּהֵמָה אָיִן, כִּי הַכֹּל הָבֶל: לְבַד הַנְּשָׁמָה הַטְּהוֹרָה שֶׁהִיא עֲתִידָה לִתֵּן דִּין וְחֶשְׁבּוֹן לִפְנֵי כִסֵּא כְבוֹדֶךָ. וְכָל הַגּוֹיִם כְּאַיִן נֶגְדֶּךָ. שֶׁנֶּאֱמַר הֵן גּוֹיִם כְּמַר מִדְּלִי וּכְשַׁחַק מֹאזְנַיִם נֶחְשָׁבוּ הֵן אִיִּים כַּדַּק יִטּוֹל:

1. Underline the mention of רַחֲמִים in this Tefilla.

2. Find the extremes:

Higher Extreme	Lower Extreme

3. What does it mean to you? So what?

_____

_____

4. In the siddur, what are we commiting to do as a result?

_____

_____

5. Look into Tanya Chapter 45 and find the visualization that is the outcome that Rachamim leads to?

_____

_____

6. What are the practical behaviors associated with this visualization?

_____

_____

7. Find the same visualization explained in chapter 46 of Tanya and write down the words that begin the visualization section.

_____

_____

8. Discuss with a friend and explain more details about this visualization that you learned in Chapter 46.

_____

_____

9. Write down the three visualizations associated with Ahava, Yirah and Rachamim.

Ahava_____

Yirah_____

Rachamim_____

RACHAMIM EXERCISE (IV) CONTINUED

10. What is the difference between the actions of the three visualizations explained in Tanya associated each with Ahava, Yirah and Rachamim?

Ahava_____

Yirah_____

Rachamim_____

11. Look into Igeres HaTeshuvah Chapter 9. What behaviors are associated with the higher level of Teshuvah?

_____

_____

12. What behavior is associated with the lower level of Teshuvah?

_____

_____

13. Explain what to do with your mind, mouth and arms when you do the higher level of Teshuvah.

Mind_____

Mouth_____

Arms_____

☞ **YIRAH AND AHAVA**

Now that you have practiced the skill of awakening Rachamim, go back and reveal Yirah and then Ahava.

HOW TO ASK FOR RACHAMIM

LIKUTEI DIBURIM א-ב שמג

What should we ask for?

When you have compassion on yourself…	…דער וואס וועט אויף זיך רחמנות האבין
And understand	און ער וועט פארשטיין
That you stand by a fork in the path	אז ער שטייש אויף דעם פרשת דרכים
Of being connected to the Divine	פון זיין א דבוק פון געטליכקייט
Or G-d forbid	אדער חלילה וחס זיין
Distanced from the Divine…	…א מרוחק פון געטליכקייט
You will ask G-d, Blessed be He	וועט בעטין בא דעם אויבערשטין ב"ה
That He have compassion on you	אז ער זאל אויף איהם רחמנות האבין
And set up a situation for you	און מזמין זיין סיבות
Where you will learn how	אז ער זאל וויסין דעם דרך ווי אזוי
To be	ער זאהל ווערן
Brought close to the Divine…	…א מקורב צו געטליכקייט
That you will start to study Chassidus	אז ער זאהל אנהויבין לערנען חסידות
And get a trainer and coach	און האבין א מחנך און מדריך
Who will direct you	וואס זאהל איהם ארויף פיהרין
On the path of service of Chassidus	אויף דעם דרך העבודה פון חסידות

STRATEGIES AND TACTICS FOR YOU TODAY

ואתה תצוה, קונטרס פורים-קטן תשנ"ב

The reason why Yidden feel broken from the fact that they are in Galus	דזה שישראל שבורים מזה שהם בגלות
(Even when they have physical and spiritual abundance)	(גם כשיש להם הרחבה בגשמיות וברוחניות),
Is because, the true desire of every Yid	הוא, כי רצונו האמיתי של כל אחד מישראל
Is that there be a revelation of Divine,	הוא שיהי' גילוי אלקות,
To the point that this (Divine revelation) touches the core of their being...	ועד שזה (גילוי אלקות) נוגע לעצם מציאותו...
The luminary of the soul that is revealed	המאור דהנשמה המתגלית ע"י
Through being crushed that we are in Galus...	הענין דכתית מזה שנמצאים בגלות.....
This is achieved through	דענין זה הוא ע"י
The internal work of Yidden	עבודתם של ישראל
That also their revealed soul powers (thought, speech, action etc.)	שגם כחות הגלויים שלהם
Should align with the core of their soul	יהיו מתאימים לעצם הנשמה,
And the luminary of the soul that is revealed through this is	ובחי' המאור דהנשמה שמתגלית עי"ז היא
The core of the soul the way it is rooted in the core of G-d A-lmighty	עצם הנשמה כמו שהיא משרשת בהעצמות

GOAL: GEULA SHLEIMA

Grand Strategy: Reveal the core of the soul

Strategy: Feel crushed that there is lacking Divine revelation, like it was in the *Beis Hamikdash*

Grand Tactic: Ask for the *Geula*, from a feeling of being crushed

Tactic: Match our thought, speech and action to our soul core. Stop and pause to make this evaluation.

Preparation tactic: Learn about Divine revelation and Moshiach, so that we understand.

What reminders can you set to do the tactics?

How our tactics work:

When we attempt to match our revealed abilities with the core of our soul, we may see that we don't act fully in line with our real core. This will bother us and motivate us to ask for *Rachamim* and Divine assistance to reveal the core of the Divine in our revealed abilities of thought, speech, action, mind and heart.

Since this lack bothers us, our request for *Rachamim* will be authentic and thus be effective in revealing the core of our soul. This will lead to a personal redemption, a component of the grand collective redemption.

HOW TO JOURNAL
TO REVEAL THE CORE OF YOUR SOUL AND BRING MOSHIACH

כחות הגלויים = עצם הנשמה

Core of your soul = revealed abilities

Get a 3x5 inch journal to make a habit of the following alignment work:

The following exercise has four parts:

1. Describing your soul core potential.
2. Describing how much time you invest into your potential now.
3. Creating habits that will help align your potential with your schedule.
4. Keeping a scorecard journal of how you implemented the new habits.

STEP 1. Your Core Potential - עצם הנשמה

In the boxes below, briefly write out what's really important to you in that area. How would you be if the unlimited power of your soul core was revealed?

Personal Energy בריאות גופו

```
┌─────────────────────────────────────┐
│                                     │
│                                     │
└─────────────────────────────────────┘
```

Friends and Other People בין אדם לחברו

```
┌─────────────────────────────────────┐
│                                     │
│                                     │
└─────────────────────────────────────┘
```

Working on Self עבודה עם עצמו

```
┌─────────────────────────────────────┐
│                                     │
│                                     │
└─────────────────────────────────────┘
```

Connecting to Hashem בין אדם למקום

```
┌─────────────────────────────────────┐
│                                     │
│                                     │
└─────────────────────────────────────┘
```

Continue on next page. »

STEP 2. Revealed Abilities - כחות הגלויים

In the boxes below, write what you do for each goal. How long does it take? How often do you do it?

Personal Energy בריאות גופו

┌───┐
│   │
│   │
└───┘

Friends and Other People בין אדם לחברו

┌───┐
│   │
│   │
└───┘

Working on Self עבודה עם עצמו

┌───┐
│   │
│   │
└───┘

Connecting to Hashem בין אדם למקום

┌───┐
│   │
│   │
└───┘

STEP 3. Alignment - להתאים

In the boxes below, write down a few small habits you can do to get what you deeply want in your schedule. When will you do the habit? Include small changes you will do to the objects around you that will create an environment to do the habits.

Personal Energy בריאות גופו

┌───┐
│   │
│   │
└───┘

Friends and Other People בין אדם לחברו

Working on Self עבודה עם עצמו

Connecting to Hashem בין אדם למקום

STEP 4. Score Board - חשבון הנפש

Fill out a simple easy-to-read scoreboard that will record the times you did your habit. Design a score board based on your goals.

☞ SAMPLE SCORE BOARD

Sample	__2__ times per __week__
Personal Energy	_____ times per _____
Dealing with Others	_____ times per _____
Working on Self	_____ times per _____
Connecting to Hashem	_____ times per _____

What worked?

What did not work?

How could my habits be made more effective?

היום יום יד מנחם אב

מנ"א תש"א - נמלאו חמשים שנה מיום שאמר לי אאמו"ר שאתחיל לרשום הסיפורים שמספר לי. כאשר התחיל הצ"צ לכתוב בעניני נגלה וחסידות, אמר לו אדמו"ר הזקן: וקנה לך חבר, וקנה (קוף בקמץ, נון בסגל) - ל' קולמוס - לך חבר. פעם אמר אאמו"ר בשם אדמו"ר הזקן וקנה - ל' קולמוס - לד חבר, ופירש אאמו"ר קולמוס הלב, אז יעדער זאך וואס מ'לערענט זאל מען איבערלעבען.

The 14th of Menachem Av 5701 (1941) marked fifty years since my father told me to begin recording the stories he told me. When the Tzemach Tzedek began writing on Talmudic and chassidic subjects, the Alter Rebbe said to him: Uknei l'cha chaver (lit. "acquire a friend for yourself"); read v'kaneh l'cha chaver (a slight change in vowels) - "the quill (pen) shall be your friend."

My father once quoted the Alter Rebbe, "v'kaneh etc..., the quill shall be your friend" - and elaborated: This refers to the quill of the heart, meaning that whatever one learns one must experience emotionally.

How do you experience something emotionally?

Write it down with a pen.

DURING PRAYER
TANYA IGERES HAKODESH 7

Those who occupy themselves in Torah and Mitzvos	העוסקים בתורה ובמצות
Then the limitless light of Hashem shines	מאיר אור ה' א"ס ב"ה
in an open way in their soul	בבחינת גילוי בנשמתם
and the time for this revelation	וזמן גילוי זה
in quality and power	ביתר שאת ויתר עז
shines in their mind and heart	ההארה במוח ולבם
during the time of prayer	הוא בשעת התפלה

☞ GRAND TACTIC: ASKING FOR THE GEULA

אז ניט קוקנדיק אויף די תפלות ובקשות וואס זיינען געוווען ביז איצטער, דארף מען נאכאמאל און וויעדעראמאל מתפלל זיין בעטן בא דעם אויבערשטן "עד מתי"... (ספר השיחות ה'תשנ"א ש"פ דברים, שבת חזון ת"ב) נדחה) ע' 730)

Not looking at all the prayers and requests that have been done until now, we need to ask over and over again and request by Hashem, "Until when (will we be in Galus).."

די איינציקע זאך אויף וואס מ'ווארט איז - אז א איד זאל געבן נאך א געשריי, מיט נאך א בקשה ותביעה און נאך א דערמאנונג:"עד מתי?!"... (שם ע' 735)

The only thing that we are waiting for is that a Yid will cry out another time, with a request and demand, another mention, "Until when (will we be in Galus)?"

ומבקש ג' פעמים בכל יום (או יותר) ותחזינה עינינו בשובך לציון ברחמים, שאז יהי' גילוי אלקות ועד לגילוי העצמות (ואתה תצוה קונטרס פורים-קטן תשנ"ב)

And you ask three times a day (or more), "May our eyes see your return," that then the Divine will be revealed and even the essence will be revealed.

WHEN TO ASK FOR COMPASSION

In turns out that the *Giluy Elokus*, revelation of Divine, comes from your Torah and Mitzvos. However, the main time to experience it is at the time of your prayer.

The time of prayer is the best time to ask that in addition to your personal revelation of Divine, the entire world should experience it.

If you lack the revelation of the Divine during prayer, it is fundamental to ask for compassion that you experience it.

HOW TO ASK WITH COMPASSION

After you feel compassion, you then ask Hashem to have compassion on you. The way you ask is similar to how you ask for a free gift.

Even though you have put effort to do the thinking strategy of Rachamim, you are asking that Hashem respond in an incomparably greater way than the effort you invested.

Below you will see this concept from Pesukim and Halacha, including anchoring the concepts in practical behavior.

חַנּוּן וְרַחוּם ה׳

The LORD is gracious and compassionate

TEHILLIM 145:8

אֵין חַנּוּן בְּכָל מָקוֹם אֶלָּא לְשׁוֹן מַתְּנַת חִנָּם

Gracious (Chanun) does not mean anything else other than an undeserved free gift

RASHI DEVARIM 3:23

אל יעשה תפלתו קבע אלא רחמים ותחנונים...

Do not make your prayers automated rather ask for compassion and for a free gift....

וגם יאמרנה בלשון תחנונים כרש המבקש בפתח:

Say your prayer using words that mean that you are asking for a free gift like a very poor person by the door.

SHULCHAN ARUCH HARAV ORACH CHAIM 98:3

👉 PRACTICALLY FREE

Our request for a free gift, is that Hashem gives us incomparably more than our efforts.

ספר השיחות ה'תשנ"א ש"פ דברים, שבת חזון ת"ב (נדחה) ע' 730

👉 ANCHORING COMPASSION

מצות עשה מן התורה לילך בדרכי ה' שנאמר והלכת בדרכיו (בפ' תבא כח ט) וכך למדו בפירוש מצוה זו מה הוא נקרא חנון אף אתה היה חנון ועושה מתנת חנם מה הוא נקרא רחום אף אתה היה רחום...

It is a positive Mitzvah from the Torah to walk in the path of Hashem, as it is written, "And walk in His ways (Parshas Ki Savo 28:9)." And the wise men learned that the meaning of this Mitzvah is that just as Hashem gives free gifts, so should you do favors for others without anticipating anything in return. And just as Hashem is called compassionate so should you be compassionate to others...

שולחן ערוך הרב אורח חיים סי' קנו סעי' ג

STRATEGY PAGE - YOUR ONE-PAGE SUMMARY

Go to the beginning of this guide book and notice every time you put a dot in the margin.

In the left column below, record all the key ideas to marked. In the right column, explain the big ideas and how they affect your life.

List the key ideas:	Explain how they affect your life:
_____	_____
_____	_____
_____	_____
_____	_____
_____	_____
_____	_____
_____	_____

THREE EASY HABITS I CAN IMPLEMENT RIGHT AWAY:

1. _____
2. _____
3. _____

When will I do them? _____
_____

How can I track them on a score sheet? _____
_____

STRATEGY PAGE - PERSONAL EVALUATION
חשבון הנפש

Go back and read your previous personal summary sheets, and then fill in the questions below:

What worked?	What did not work?
_____	_____
_____	_____
_____	_____
_____	_____
_____	**What are my barriers?**
_____	_____
_____	_____

How can I do things to make things better? _____
_____
_____

What small change can I make in the things around me to remind and inspire me? _____
_____
_____

How can I expose myself to people who will inspire me? _____
_____
_____

EVALUATE YOUR PERSONAL PROGRESS

1. What is *Rachamim*?

2. How is *Rachamim* core to Judaism?

3. Explain the thinking strategy that reveals *Rachamim*?

4. How does *Rachamim* help in achieving your goals?

5. How does *Rachamim* help bring Moshiach?

☞ **COMPARE YOUR ANSWERS TO HOW YOU ANSWERED BEFORE STARTING UNIT 3.**

UNIT 4

THE FUNDAMENTALS
AN ARMY AGAINST THE YETZER HARA

אַהֲבָה
יִרְאָה
רַחֲמִים

GOAL

Implementation;
Actually fulfill the Mitzvos of Ahava, Yirah and Rachamim

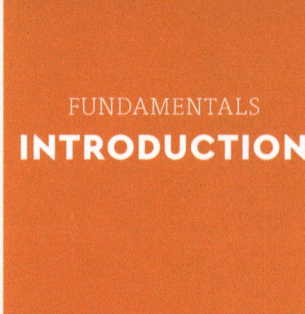

FUNDAMENTALS
INTRODUCTION

PUTTING THE FUNDAMENTALS TOGETHER

You have trained yourself how to use the three fighting forces against the Yetzer Hara.

In this guide, we have focused on 6 out of 12 fundamentals of *Ahava* and *Yirah* (*Mesuteres*) that is hidden in your heart.

REMEMBER	TOOL	AHAVA	YIRAH	RACHAMIM	CHOSSID
SHOW UP[1]	Mental **THINK**	1.	4. יְרְאַת אֱלֹקִים	7. הִתְעוֹרְרוּת רַחֲמִים	10.
STEP UP	Emotional **PREPARE**	2.	5. קַבָּלַת עוֹל	8.	11.
GIVE BACK	Practical **DO**	3. כִּי הוּא חַיֶּיךָ\ נַפְשִׁי אִוִּיתִיךָ נחת רוח	6. יְרְאַת חֵטְא והנה ה' נצב	9.	12. כִּבְרָא דְּאִשְׁתַּדֵּל

A **mental** tool is a thinking strategy mainly done with your mind.

Real-life dynamic situations are complicated with many nuances. It takes time to understand the possible nuances and there is no such time in the middle of the dynamic situation. Mental reflection in the morning, when your mental faculties are at their best, is the best time to use the tool of

---

1. You are where your thoughts are.

reflection and commit to make the right decisions using an emotional tool.

An **emotional** tool is a preparation (הכנה) before actually doing something. It can focus your powers and bring out your very best!

The **practical** tools give you visualizations to be used before and during real-life dynamic situations. They illustrate the spirit of how to do Torah and Mitzvos. The visualizations show you what type of energy and enthusiasm is most appropriate.

The reason why visualization is so effective in changing our behavior is because it allows us to actually experience a new behavior and our new upgraded identity before we did anything yet, so when it comes to actually doing something, it's like we did it already and it's much easier to implement.

Visualizations help us make better decisions. In the middle of an ever-changing situation, decisions need to be made quickly. Therefore, the thinking strategy to help you make these decisions is simple, easy for the mind to do, and therefore rapid. Visualization helps you to manage the large amount of mental processing needed to make good decisions on the spot in a real-life situation.

The maturity of these small decisions depends on the reflection you did earlier in the day at length.

Each tool has its own mini tools which consist of mental, emotional and practical components. However, a tool is categorized as primarily mental, emotional or practical depending on the main focus of the tool and when this specific tool is most useful.

UNIT 4 / THE FUNDAMENTALS   TANYA – CHAPTERS 41-45

FUNDAMENTAL SKILLS EXERCISE

Six out of twelve skills of Ahava and Yirah Mesuteres you have learned so far:
(B'ezras Hashem, you will learn the other six fundamental skills in the next training manual.)

#	Tool	Skill	Soulwaze
3.	Practical	כִּי הוּא חַיֶּיךָ\נַפְשִׁי אִוִּיתִיךָ - נחת רוח	UNIT 1 PART 1-3
4.	Mental	יִרְאַת אֱלֹקִים	UNIT 2 PART 1
5.	Emotional	קַבָּלַת עוֹל	UNIT 2 PART 2
6.	Practical	יִרְאַת חֵטְא - וְהִנֵּה ה' נִצָּב	UNIT 2 PART 3
7.	Mental	הִתְעוֹרְרוּת רַחֲמִים	UNIT 3
12.	Practical	כִּבְרָא דְּאִשְׁתַּדֵּל	UNIT 1 BONUS PART

☞ **DISCUSS THE UPSIDE AND DOWNSIDE OF EACH FUNDAMENTAL.**

1. **Mental Tools**

    Upside: _____   Downside: _____
    _____   _____
    _____   _____

2. **Emotional Tool**

    Upside: _____   Downside: _____
    _____   _____
    _____   _____

3. **Practical Tools**

    Upside: _____   Downside: _____
    _____   _____
    _____   _____

Explain the following:

👉 **SKILL NUMBERS REFRENCED FROM OPPOSITE PAGE:**

1. How does each tool belong in its category?

#3 _____

#4 _____

#5 _____

#6 _____

#7 _____

#12 _____

2. When is it used?

#3 _____

#4 _____

#5 _____

#6 _____

#7 _____

#12 _____

3. What is it used for?

#3 _____

#4 _____

#5 _____

#6 _____

#7 _____

#12 _____

4. What do you actually do to use it?

#3 _____

#4 _____

#5 _____

#6 _____

#7 _____

#12 _____

5. Why would your reflection be ineffective if you visualize sights that contradict the התבוננות (reflection)?

_____

6. In the Yiras Shamayim thinking strategy, how does proper reflection (התבוננות) contribute to the visualization of כעומד לפני המלך, acting like you would when standing in front of a king (or any person in power) and how does it make the visualization more mature? _____

_____

7. Explain how the king looks in your visualization after proper reflection? Is the king smiling, strict, or in between? Explain how? _____

_____

8. Explain how this mature visualization affects your action? _____

_____

9. Explain how the visualization of giving Nachas affects your action? _____

_____

10. How would you act when you want to give nachas compared to when you are in front of an important person? _____

11. Could you act with both visualizations at the same time? How? _____

12. In the visualization of כְּבְרָא דְּאִשְׁתַּדֵּל, does the son act with both enthusiasm and responsibility? Or is there only a sense of enthusiasm and urgency? Explain. _____

13. What could happen if you only use the tool of התבוננות without the tool of visualization? Explain. _____

14. What could happen if you only use the tool of visualization without proper התבוננות? Explain. _____

15. How did the tool of רחמים enhance both אהבה and יראה? Explain your experience? _____

16. How did the tool of רחמים enhance כְּבְרָא דְּאִשְׁתַּדֵּל? How did the combination affect your behavior? _____

MAKE FUNDAMENTALS PRACTICE YOUR HABIT
Pause 3x Daily

YOU have completed the first part (of two) of basic training. You can be effective and implement a high level of personal conduct and good balance.

- Pause 3x makes you a special warrior.
- Pause 3x helps to keep you safe.
- Pause 3x gives you a base of certainty in situations of uncertainty.
- Pause 3x connects you with a growing global community.
- Pause 3x is a basis for your growth.

1. How will you continue to make Pause 3x a habit you do?

2. What small, easy, simple steps can you take to set reminders?

3. How will you know it's a habit (e.g. when you stop and pause naturally 3 times a day)?

4. How can you spend time with influencers, people who encourage you to pause, people who do it themselves?

5. How can you stay away from people who discourage you?

6. How can you improve your diet and sleep so you will have high energy and be productive?

7. How can you set things up around you so it's easy to Pause 3x Daily? (e.g. keep a Tanya, or Tanya pages, near you when you pause.)

8. How can you set reminders in your physical surroundings?

FUNDAMENTALS PRACTICE:

INSTRUCTIONS:

1. Start with anchoring in action, give some money to *Tzedaka*.

2. Read from Tanya 41 (on the next page) quietly in your mind.

3. Mentally contemplate on everything you know about this thinking strategy.

    Learn some Chassidus before you reflect because reflection is best done when you have something new to think about.

4. Say the first line of the Shema when you are *Mekabel Ol Malchus Shamayim* (indicated on the Tanya page).

5. When you get to the end of the Tanya 41 page,

A) Visualize yourself in front of an important person, and then visualize yourself doing something different later today with the spirit of how you would behave in front of an important person. Envision doing something good or avoiding something or doing something better.

   Imagine the feeling you are going to feel when you do this.

B) Visualize yourself spending time with people who will encourage you and limiting your exposure to people who discourage you.

   Visualize yourself being a positive inspiration to someone else.

C) Visualize yourself changing something in your surroundings that will make it easier to do the good behavior or make it harder to do the bad behavior.

THE FUNDAMENTALS IN PRACTICE

MAKE FUNDAMENTALS PRACTICE YOUR HABIT
Pause 3x Daily

PAUSE #1: YIRAH - TAKE RESPONSIBILITY
FROM TANYA, CHAPTER 41

Instructions on previous page.

It is important to remind myself constantly

what actually is the beginning of service

and its core and (living) root.

Even though fear (of G-d) is the root of turning from evil

and love (is the root) of doing good,

nevertheless, it is not sufficient to awaken love alone

to do good

and it is important to first awaken

at least the natural fear

which is hidden in the heart of all of Israel

which leads one to refrain from rebelling

against the King of kings

the Holy One, blessed be He, as mentioned above,

that this awe be revealed in my heart

or at least in my mind.

This means to at least reflect in my thoughts,

the greatness of G-d A-lmighty

and His Kingship (rules)

which extend to all the words,

both higher and lower.

He fills all worlds

and is also in a higher dimesion in all worlds

as it is written

"Do I not fill heaven and earth?" (Yirmeyahu 23:24)

Yet, He leaves aside (the creatures of) the higher (worlds)

and (the creatures of) the lower (worlds)

and he uniquely bestows His Kingship

upon His people Israel, in general,

and upon me in particular,

for man is obligated to say

"For my sake the world is created" (Sanhedrin 4:5).

I, in turn,

accept His Kingship upon myself,

that He will be King over me,

to serve Him and do His Will

in all kinds of work required of a servant. **Say שְׁמַע**

And, behold, G-d is standing over him (me),"

and "The whole world is filled with His Glory,"

and He is watching you,

and is checking (my) innermost thoughts and feelings

that I serve Him properly.

Therefore, I serve in His Presence

with awe and fear

as I would, when standing before a King.

REVEAL AHAVA (PAUSE #2)
FROM TANYA, CHAPTER 44

Read from "And this is what…" until "Do we not have One Father" out loud.

And this is what's written in the Zohar (Vol. 3, pg. 68a)

on the Pasuk (Yeshayahu 26:9)

"My soul, I desire You (Hashem) at night…"

(the Zohar says) "Love Hashem,

with the love for the soul and spirit

when they are attached to the body,

the body loves them (the soul and spirit)…"

(In other words,) this is what the verse,

"My soul, I desire You," is saying.

"Since You, G-d, are my true energy and life,

therefore I desire You."

That is to say, "I long for and yearn for You (Hashem)

like a man who craves the life of his soul."

And when I am weak and exhausted,

I long and yearn for my soul to revive me.

Likewise, when I go to sleep,

I long and yearn for my soul to return to me

when I wake up from my sleep.

The same way, I long and yearn

for the light of the Infinite One,

blessed is He,

the true Life of life,

to be drawn into me

through my occupation in Torah (study),

when I awaken from my sleep during the night.

For the Torah and the Holy One, blessed be He,

are one and the same.

Like the Zohar says (ibid.)

"A man is required,

out of love for the Holy One, blessed be He,

to rise each night

and exert himself in His service until the morning…"

UPGRADED AHAVA
FROM TANYA, CHAPTER 44

"Like a son who exerts himself

for his father and mother,

whom he loves

more than self,

his Nefesh, Ruach etc.

for "Do we not have One Father"?

Immediately make an anchor by learning Torah; read the following short paragraph from Tehillim:

TEHILLIM, CHAPTER 117

א: הַלְלוּ אֶת ה' כָּל גּוֹיִם שַׁבְּחוּהוּ כָּל הָאֻמִּים:
1: Praise the L-RD, all you nations; give tribute to Him, all you peoples.

ב: כִּי גָבַר עָלֵינוּ חַסְדּוֹ וֶאֱמֶת ה' לְעוֹלָם הַלְלוּיָ-הּ:
2: for great is His steadfast love toward us; the faithfulness of the L-RD endures forever. Praise the L-rd.

Continue on next page. »

THE FUNDAMENTALS   IN PRACTICE

MAKE FUNDAMENTALS PRACTICE YOUR HABIT
Pause 3x Daily

PAUSE #3: RACHAMIM - HAVE COMPASSION

Make the evaluation below. Give yourself a score of 1-10, 1 represents very little and 10 represents a lot. Notice that even if you score highly, since your *Giluy Elokus* (experience of Hashem in your life) is not in the entire world, then even what you have is not a revelation of the real essence of Hashem.

SCORE

- [ ] You feel warm and refreshed
- [ ] Mitzvos feel easy to do even when challenged
- [ ] You feel tranquil when you do things
- [ ] You feel pleasure in Torah study
- [ ] The atmosphere around you is refined
- [ ] You are a positive influence on others

Make an anchor by reading the following request to Hashem

וְתֶחֱזֶינָה עֵינֵינוּ בְּשׁוּבְךָ לְצִיּוֹן בְּרַחֲמִים

May our eyes see Your return to Zion with compassion.

☞ PAUSE 3X DAILY

קודם שיתפלל צריך לשהות

Pause before you pray

Shulchan Aruch Orach Chaim 93

YOUR FUNDAMENTALS SCORE BOARD

Put a check by the days you completed all the steps of the fundamentals

Fundamentals	Day 1	Day 2	Day 3	Day 4	Day 5	Day 6	Day 7
Rachamim							
Yirah							
Ahava							
Upgraded Ahava							

MAKE FUNDAMENTALS PRACTICE YOUR HABIT

Describe the changes these fundamentals made to your day.

	How did it change you?	What did you do differently?
Day 1		
Day 2		
Day 3		
Day 4		
Day 5		
Day 6		
Day 7		

YOUR SOULWAZE EXPERIENCE

1. What do you like about Soulwaze? _____
_____

2. How has it changed you? _____
_____

3. What would you like to see more of? _____
_____

4. What would you like to be done differently? _____
_____

5. How do you see it affecting other people and schools? _____
_____

6. What is the greatest change you have experienced? _____
_____

7. How do you measure this change? _____
_____

8. What do you want to achieve in your life? _____
_____

9. What steps are you taking to achieve this goal in the future? _____

_____

_____

10. How will you know that you have achieved your goal? _____

_____

11. How will you measure the benchmarks? _____

_____

12. How have you made fundamentals practice, pause x3 daily your habit?

_____

_____

13. How do you define a habit? _____

_____

14. What are the next steps you will take to make it a stronger habit?

_____

_____

👉 **READ THE ANSWERS YOU WROTE AT THE BEGINNING OF THE BOOK AND EXPLAIN HOW YOUR ANSWERS HAVE CHANGED.**

GLOSSARY OF TERMS
Compiled by Chaya Chyrek and Sarah Chyrek

A

Ahava / Ahavas Hashem - Love of G-d.

Ahava and Yirah Mesuteres - The natural love and fear of G-d that are in a hidden state.

Ahava Kamayim - Love like water

Ahava Rabba - Great and complete love of a complete Tzadik to G-d.

Alter Rebbe - Rabbi Shneur Zalman of Liadi (18 Elul 5505 – 24 Tevet 5573 / September 4, 1745 – December 15, 1812) was an Orthodox rabbi and the founder and first Rebbe of Chabad, a branch of Chassidic Judaism. He authored many works, and is best known for *Shulchan Aruch HaRav*, *Tanya* and his *Siddur* compiled according to the *Nusach Ari*.

Alter Rebbe's Shulchan Aruch (Shulchan Aruch HaRav) - Code of Jewish law that includes contributions from the revealed and hidden Torah written by Rabbi Shneur Zalman of Liadi upon the request of his teacher the Maggid of Mezritch student of the Baal Shem Tov.

Amalek - A nation that was a recurrent enemy of the Jews, descendants of Eisav.

Asiya - The world of action.

Asur - Forbidden.

Atzilus - The highest of four worlds which exists here on a deeper dimension.

Aveira - Sin.

Avoda / Avodas Hashem - Religious devotion and service to G-d.

Avos / Avraham Yitzchak and Yaakov - Forefathers of the Jewish nation.

Avraham Avinu - The first of the forefathers, the founding father of the covenant.

B

Baal Peh - To learn something by heart and thus be able to say it without looking inside the text.

Bamidbar - Book of Numbers.

Beficha Uvilvavecha - In your mouth and heart.

Beis Hamikdash - The Holy Temple in Jerusalem.

BEZ"H / B'ezras Hashem - With the help of G-d.

Bitul - Humility.

Brachos - Blessings.

C

ChaGaS - Acronym for Chessed (kindness), Gevurah (strictness/focus) and Tiferes (beauty/synthesis).

Chabad - Acronym for Chochma (insight),

Binah (detailed comprehension) and Daas (focus), this acronym refers to the Chabad movement as these abilities are the prime tools in the study of Chassidus.

Chassidishkeit - A chossid is one who is kind to his Creator and goes beyond the letter of the law, chassidishkeit is the Yiddish term for the practice of a chossid.

Chassidus - The study of the inner aspect of Torah.

Chazal - Acronym for "Our Sages, may their memory be blessed"); refers to all Jewish sages of the Mishna, Tosefta and Talmud eras, spanning from the times of the final 300 years of the Second Temple of Jerusalem until the 6th century CE.

Chitas Study - Hebrew acronym for Chumash (the five books of Moses), Tehillim (Psalms), and Tanya (The seminal work of Chassidus by Rabbi Schneur Zalman of Liadi, the Alter Rebbe). Chitas is studied in a yearly cyclical study cycle. Visit Chayenu.org for more information.

Chossid - A person who is kind to his Creator and goes beyond the letter of the law.

Chovos HaLevavos - A treatise on the core principles of Judaism written by Rabbi Bachya ibn Paquda in the eleventh century.

Chumash Study - The study of the five books of Moses; a Torah in printed form as opposed to a *sefer* Torah, which is a scroll.

Ch"V / Chas Veshalom - Acronym for chas v'shalom, Heaven forbid.

D

Daas - Knowledge, focus of the mind.

Daily Rambam Study - Daily study of Maimonides' 14 volumes of Mishneh Torah that include all the laws of the Torah, in an annual or three year study cycle.

Davening - The Yiddish term for Tefilah (prayer).

Devarim - Book of Deuteronomy

Dibbur within Machshava - Words of speech within thought; thinking what you are going to speak before you speak.

Dinim - Laws of the Torah.

Dira BeTachtonim - Making a home for G-d A-lmighty in this lower world.

Divrei Hayamim - Chronicles, a book of the Bible that lists the events from creation until the return from Babylon to Israel.

Dovid HaMelech - The second king of the United Kingdom of Israel and Judah.

E

Eishel Avraham - A halachic work by Rabbi Avraham of Butchatch (1770-1840).

Emunah - Belief in Hashem.

Erev Shabbos - Friday, the eve of Shabbos.

Galus - The time of the Jewish exile.

Gedulah - Greatness [of G-d].

Gemara - The Talmud, comprising rabbinical analysis of and commentary on the Mishnah.

Geulah Shleima - The complete redemption.

Gevurah - Strength [of G-d].

Giluy Elokus - Revelation of the Divine.

H

Halacha - Jewish law.

Hashem - Refers to the Creator of the heaven and earth, G-d.

Hayom Yom - An anthology of Chassidic aphorisms and customs arranged according to the calendar for the Hebrew year of 5703 (1942–43). The work was compiled and arranged by Rabbi Menachem Mendel Schneerson.

Hiddurim / Hiddur Mitzvah - Beautification, doing Mitzvos in a beautiful way.

Higher Gan Eden - The garden of Eden, where souls get rewarded. There are higher and lower levels depending on the level of a person's Divine service.

Hisbonenus - Contemplation / reflection on a Chassidic teaching.

I

Imrei Binah - A book written by the Mitteler Rebbe describing the Mitzvah of Krias Shema. It is known to contain many difficult concepts in Chassidus.

Iskafya - Holding back or delaying fulfilling the impulses and drives of one's animal soul.

Iyov - Job, a prophet.

K

Kabolas Ol Malchus Shamayim - Acceptance of the yoke of Heaven.

Kapital Tehilim - A chapter in the Psalms written by King David.

Kavana - Intention.

Kedusha - holiness.

Kessef - Silver.

Kesser - Crown, the head of the Sefiros.

Ki Hu Chayecha - G-d is your life.

Kosher - Jewish religious dietary laws; food that may be consumed according to Jewish law.

Behaving according to the Din.

Kosher media exposure - To listen and look only at things that are permitted according to Torah.

Krias Shema - A prayer that serves as a centerpiece of the morning and evening Jewish prayer services proclaiming G-d as One.

Krias Shema She'al Hamitah - Shema recited before bed.

Kudsha Brich Hu - Hashem (The Holy One, blessed be He).

L

Lashon Kodesh - the Holy Tongue (Hebrew) in which the Torah, Jewish religious texts and prayers were written.

Likutei Sichos - An anthology of talks by the Lubavitcher Rebbe, Rabbi Menachem Mendel Schneerson.

Likutei Torah - A compilation of Chassidic treatises, *maamarim*, by the first Chabad Rebbe, Rabbi Shneur Zalman of Liadi.

Lishma - The service of Hashem and the study of the Torah with the intention to unite one's thoughts and speech with G-d.

M

Maamar - Chassidic discourse given over by a Rebbe (Chassidic leader)

Maaseh - Action.

Maaseh BePoel - Practical action.

Machshava - Thought.

Malchus - Kingship [of G-d].

Mashpia - Spiritual coach

Memalei Kol Almin - Refers to how G-d fills the entire world.

Mesiras Nefesh - Self sacrifice for the observance of Torah and Mitzvos. Giving self over.

Mesuteres - Hidden

Mezuzah - Parchment on the doorpost with the Shema written inside.

Midos - Character traits.

Midrash - Early interpretations and commentaries on the Written Torah and Oral Torah.

Mikvah - A specific body of water in which one immerses the entire body that triggers a transformation in state, e.g. from impurity to purity.

Mitzrayim - The land of Egypt.

Mitzvah (plural: Mitzvos) - The Torah's 613 commandments commanded by G-d; a good deed or religious action.

Mitzvahs Asei - Positive commandment

Mivtzoyim - A mission of outreach to merit people with fundamental mitzvot.

Moshe Rabeinu - Moses, the leader who led the Jews out of Egypt to Mount Sinai.

N

Nachas / Nachas Ruach - Deep satisfaction and pleasure.

Nafshi Ivisicha - "My soul, I desire You" Refers to a love of Hashem, in which you recognize Hashem is your soul and life.

Nefesh Habehamis - The animal soul, subconscious mind.

NeHiY - Acronym for Netzach Hod Yesod: victory, recognition and connection.

Neshama - The essence of a Jew, the soul.

Nevuah - Prophecy.

O

Orach Chayim - The first volume of Shulchan Aruch, the Code of Jewish Law, which deals with day-to-day life.

P

Paradigm shift - Complete change in the way one views a situation.

Pasuk - A verse in the Bible.

Prikas Ol - Removing from oneself the yoke of Heaven.

R

Raaya Mehemna / Faithful Shepherd - Book of the Zohar written about Moshe Rabbeinu.

Rabbi Akiva - A Tannaic sage during the first century and the beginning of the second century. Rabbi Akiva was a leading contributor to the *Mishnah* and to Midrash and Halacha.

Rabbi Avraham of Butchatch - Rabbi Avraham of Butchatch (1770-1840) was a Torah scholar and Halachic authority, the author of the Eishel Avraham printed in many prints of the Shulchan Aruch.

Rabbi Shimon Bar Yochai - Author of the Zohar, work of Kabbalah, after the destruction of the Second Temple in 70 CE.

Rachamim - Mercy [of G-d], compassion.

Rambam - Maimonides; Rabbi Moses ben Maimon. A leading sage in Jewish Law during the middle ages.

Rasha - A person who does a sin; a wicked person.

Rashi - Rabbi Shlomo Yitzchaki (1040 – 1105), author of a comprehensive commentary on the Bible and Talmud.

Ratzon - Divine Will.

Rebbe - Acronym for Rosh Bnei Yisroel, the head of the Jewish people, who sees the world from G-d's perspective.

Ritva - One of the Rishonim, Torah commentator from the middle ages.

Rov - Rabbi with training and experience in Jewish law that is in a position to make a Torah ruling.

R' Avraham Hamalach - Son of the Mezritcher Magid, who was the leader of the Chassidic movement after the Baal Shem Tov. He was a study partner of the Alter Rebbe, the founder of Chabad.

S

Sanhedrin - An assembly of twenty-three or seventy-one rabbis appointed to sit as a tribunal in every city in the ancient Land of Israel and in the Temple in Jerusalem.

Sefer Devarim - Book of Deuteronomy, the fifth book of the Torah.

Sefer HaMitzvos - Maimonides' work which lists all the commandments of the Torah, with a brief description for each.

Sefer shel Beinonim - Guide for the regular person. A part of the Tanya written by the Alter Rebbe.

Sefer Torah - A Hebrew hand written scroll, containing the five books of Moses.

Sefiros - Divine character traits; building blocks of creation.

Shaar HaYichud Ve'Haemunah - A section of the Tanya, by Rabbi Shneur Zalman of Liadi, which discusses G-d's unity.

Shabbos - A day of rest on the seventh day of each week; the day that testifies that G-d A-lmighty created the world in six days and rested on the seventh. Hence, 39 specific acts of creative labor are prohibited.

Shacharis - Morning prayer.

Shechina - The Divine presence, G-d's speech that creates the world.

Shema - Most essential Jewish prayer in the siddur that proclaims that G-d is one and only.

Shemos - Book of Exodus.

Shliach Tzibbur - Emissary of the congregation to lead the communal prayer service in the synagogue.

Shmoneh Esrei - The climax of the three daily prayers, which contains eighteen blessings.

Siddur - Jewish prayer book.

Simas Lev - Place on the heart; pay attention.

Simcha - Happiness.

Six Mitzvos Temidios - Six mitzvot which are perpetual and constant, applicable at all times, all the days of our lives.

T

Taanis - One of the 60 tractates of Mishna and Talmud.

Taanug - Divine Pleasure.

Talmud - A collection of discussions on the oral laws taught by G-d to Moses and applications to life, it is a central text of Judaism and the primary source of Jewish religious law and theology.

Tanya - An early work of Chassidic philosophy by Rabbi Shneur Zalman of Liadi; mystical psychology and theology as a handbook for daily spiritual life in Jewish observance.

Tefilah (plural: Tefilos) - Prayer (Connecting), with "service of the heart," a fundamental practice in Jewish observance.

Tehillim - Psalms, by King David.

Teshuvah - Return to Hashem; remorse and regret over a sin; creating a situation in which one does not sin again. Becoming one's real self.

Tetzaveh - One of the Torah portions in the Book of Exodus.

Teves - The fourth month on the Jewish calendar, which falls out in the winter in the northern hemisphere. It follows Kislev and precedes Shevat.

The Oral Torah - The Oral Torah was passed down orally in an unbroken chain from generation to generation from Moses until it was finally written down following the destruction of the Second Temple in 70 CE.

Tiferes - Beauty, synthesis, balance.

Tikunei Zohar - A text of the Kabbalah

Torah - The bible; the Five Books of Moses, prophets, the holy writings and the general body of Jewish religious teachings received on Mt. Sinai including the Jewish law, practice and tradition.

Tumah - Ritual impurity.

Tzaddik - One who does everything just to serve G-d.

Tzedaka - Charity, doing the just and correct action.

Tzemach Tzedek - Rabbi Menachem Mendel Schneersohn (29 Elul 5549 - 13 Nissan 5626 / September 9, 1789 – March 17, 1866) was a great Orthodox rabbi, the third Rebbe (spiritual leader) of the Chabad Lubavitch Chassidic movement.

Tzitzis - Garment with strings on its four corners, reminding of one's constant mission to Hashem.

Vayikra - Book of Leviticus.

Yahadus - Judaism, the code of behavior given to Moses on Mount Sinai over 3000 years ago.

Yeshayahu - The Jewish prophet for whom the Book of Isaiah is named.

Yeshiva - Jewish school

Yetzer Hara - An inclination or impulse to do evil.

Yetzer Tov - An inclination or impulse to do good.

Yid (plural: Yidden) - The Yiddish term for a Jew; a person born to a Jewish mother or converted according to the Din.

Yiddishkeit - The Yiddish term for Judaism.

Yirah - Fear/awe of G-d.

Yiras Cheit - Fear of sin.

Yiras Elokim - Fear of the A-lmighty.

Yiras Shamayim - Fear of the One in heaven.

Yirah-tata - Lover level of fear

Yirah-ila - Higher fear/awe.

Yirmeyahu - The prophet Jeremiah.

Yitzchak Avinu - The third of the forefathers.

Zeir Anpin - A Kabbalistic term that refers to the personality of G-d.

Zohar - The central text of Jewish mystical thought known as Kabbalah, passed down from Moshe.

WEEKLY EVALUATION

The following chart has six markers that can be used to measure your personal mini *Giluy Elokus*. Fill in the chart daily for seven days after you practice the other basic fundamentals.

It does not matter what number you score yourself, the very fact that your attention is on *Giluy Elokus* and the lack of it, will help you to ask for Divine compassion for it, during Tefilla.

Score yourself with 1-10 on each of the following 6 points »

1. **You feel warm and refreshed**
2. **Mitzvos feel easy to do even when challenged**
3. **You feel tranquil when you do things**
4. **You feel pleasure in Torah study**
5. **The atmosphere around you is refined**
6. **You are a positive influence on others**

	Day 1	Day 2	Day 3	Day 4	Day 5	Day 6	Day 7
1							
2							
3							
4							
5							
6							

www.ingramcontent.com/pod-product-compliance
Lightning Source LLC
Chambersburg PA
CBHW042129010526
44111CB00031B/39